THE DORR WAR

THE DORR WAR

REPUBLICANISM ON TRIAL, 1831-1861

George M. Dennison

The University Press of Kentucky

ISBN: 0-8131-1330-X

Library of Congress Catalog Card Number: 75-3543

Copyright © 1976 by The University Press of Kentucky

A statewide cooperative scholarly publishing agency
serving Berea College, Centre College of Kentucky,
Eastern Kentucky University, Georgetown College,
Kentucky Historical Society, Kentucky State University,
Morehead State University, Murray State University,
Northern Kentucky State College, Transylvania University,
University of Kentucky, University of Louisville, and
Western Kentucky University.

Editorial and Sales Offices: Lexington, Kentucky 40506

For Jane, Rob, and Rick

        well, there's the *New*—
Ah, joyless and ironic too!
. . . .
They vouch that virgin sphere's assigned
Seat for man's re-created kind:
Last hope and proffer, they protest.
Brave things! sun rising in the west;
And bearded centuries but gone
For ushers to the beardless one.
Nay, nay; your future's too sublime:
The Past, the Past is half of time,
The proven half.
. . . .
Our New World bold
Had fain improved upon the Old;
But the hemispheres are counterparts.
. . . .
The vast reserves—the untried fields;
These long shall keep off and delay
The class-war, rich-and-poor-man fray
Of history. From that alone
Can serious trouble spring.
. . . .
Columbus ended earth's romance:
No New World to mankind remains!

Melville, *Clarel* (1876)

"Do these buttons that we wear attest that
our allegiance is to Nature? No, to the King."

Melville, *Billy Budd* (1924)

CONTENTS

PREFACE

Sloganeers of the 1960s took up the cry of "power to the people" as if it represented something new and different in American history. Black nationalists, Chicano militants, Indian rights spokesmen, Poor People's marchers, and radical Weathermen chanted it in unison with great numbers of plain Americans. Undoubtedly the new "populism" bespoke a pervasive consciousness of malaise in American life. A general yearning for the transfer of power to the hands of those most affected by its exercise stimulated diverse political movements broadly inclusive of discrete groups within the society. Most who sympathized with or joined the movements accepted the claims of originality and acted with conviction. Few realized how traditional their demands sounded when placed in perspective.

Far from being novel, the demands for "power to the people" had characterized American constitutional and political history during the first three-quarters of a century after independence. For Americans of the early national period, as for the new "populists" of the 1960s, these demands symbolized a deep-seated attitude toward relationships between government and people, institutions and individuals, practice and theory. The ideal forms of these relationships were subsumed under the rubrics of popular government, self-government, or republicanism. But the concept of popular government—or self-government or republicanism—was not monolithic. Many variants of it appeared during the years between the adoption of the Constitution and the outbreak of the Civil War. To explore the historical career of one of those ideas is my major purpose here.

I began the work nearly a decade ago. The most difficult problem, one that caused many delays and necessitated multiple revisions, was that of a strategy. I proceeded on the basis of trial and error, but after the final revision a book came to hand that outlined the theory and method I had sought but still could not articulate. As I read Gene Wise's *American Historical Explanations: A Strategy for Grounded Inquiry* (Homewood, Ill.: Dorsey Press; Georgetown, Ont.: Irwin-Dorsey, 1973), I discovered that I had arrived blindly at what he so ably described as "situation-strategy" analysis of historical events. Wise argued persuasively that "historical ideas don't just grow out of other ideas, nor do they just reflect circumstances around them; instead, they come from precise moments of confrontation between idea and circumstance" (p. 153). Thus, historical figures or agents "refract" rather than reflect reality by "symboling." The merit of Wise's theory and methodology is that they offer "the intellectual historian a way of getting at particulars, and of maybe catching subtleties in the experience of an idea which otherwise could get by the more broad-gauge thematic approach." The point, then, is to trace the careers of historical ideas, watching them most closely at "pivotal moments" as they come under strain and change perceptibly into variant forms.

More specifically, Wise's "situation-strategy" analysis suggests that historians should treat ideas as if they embody strategies devised by human beings to solve problems rooted in particular situations. Ideas do not have a life of their own, fully divorced from the material world; but neither are they merely the rationalizations of men reacting to different environments. Ideas, according to Wise, should be understood as ongoing projects, not as completed and static artifacts of the mind. He urges historians to deal with ideas so as to appreciate their dynamic growth and change. He advocates a view of "mind on the firing line, acting publicly in response to events in the world, and having to face the consequences of those actions over time" (p. 321). In a word, Wise calls for a history—or histories—of ideas grounded in the experience of minds involved with the world.

The study that follows represents an attempt to write history as Wise counsels. I have focused on a pivotal moment in the historical career of the idea of popular sovereignty and its corollary of peaceable revolution. The main characters in the study are true believers, men who tried to hold to the idea no matter the consequences. This stubborn refusal to attend to the dysfunctionality of the idea set off a chain of events marked by tragedy and irony. The story has an inherent interest but also symbolizes important transitions in the history of American constitutional development. Thus, one purpose of the study is to explore the impact of ideology on human behavior. In addition, it seeks to suggest new insights into the course of American history. I trust that readers will share my fascination with both areas of concern. I trust also that this self-styled product of a particular approach to historical studies will not be taken as the conclusive test of the approach.

I accumulated many debts as the study took shape. It began as a doctoral dissertation under the direction of Professor Arthur Bestor, to whom I owe more than I can say for his efforts to communicate his sure grasp of constitutionalism and his sense of historicity. Professors W. Stull Holt, Robert Burke, Thomas Pressly, and Otis Pease—all of the University of Washington—provided wise counsel and early encouragement. Professor William Wiecek of the University of Missouri shared not only a common interest but his research as well, making my task less difficult. Sheldon Meyer of Oxford University Press and Professor Stanley Katz of the University of Chicago Law School read the manuscript and urged me to continue the work. Professors Mark Gilderhus of Colorado State University, Herman Belz of the University of Maryland, Thomas Morris of Portland State University, and David Sloan of the University of Arkansas listened to the arguments and pointed to areas of weakness. These historians did all they could to insure that the final product would measure up to the standards of the profession, but all deficiencies and errors are the result of my own critical decisions.

The American Bar Foundation provided a summer fellowship in 1970 which allowed me to complete the research. The Faculty Improvement Committee of Colorado State University awarded a research grant as well. Professor Harry Rosenberg, chairman of the Department of History at Colorado State University, aided in all possible ways to facilitate the completion of the work. I must also express my gratitude to the staffs of the Special Collections Division, John Hay Library, Brown University—especially Mrs. Mary Russo; the Manuscripts Division of the Library of Congress; the Maine Historical Society Archives, Portland, Maine; and the Federal Records Center, Waltham, Massachusetts.

I have attempted in this essay to throw light on the development of American constitutionalism. In doing so, I have emphasized the role of changing ideas about constitutional government. Part of whatever success I have achieved must be attributed to the admiration and ambition inspired by Professor Arthur Bestor. But admiration and ambition can carry such a project only so far. Through their sympathy and support during the trying periods of writing and revision, Jane I. Dennison and two young men—who took an interest simply because they cared—made the work possible. To them I dedicate the book.

THE BARRICADES

In the history books America has been the story of
those who succeeded, making those who did not,
by implication, non-American, or in the modern
phrase, un-American. The Godly Commonwealth,
the agrarian republic, the small, decentralized
federal government, vanished one by one from the
American scene. But an idea of America remained,
and the continuing process of American
self-definition carried the obligation of doing
justice to the past.

Fred Somkin, *Unquiet Eagle: Memory and Desire
in the Idea of American Freedom, 1815-1860*

Americans have experienced only one major social crisis in the nearly two centuries since the adoption of the Constitution. The lone exception to the general internal peace, the Civil War of 1861-1865, occurred when the South attempted to maintain a civilization based on obsolete principles of social organization. In a brilliant if controversial analysis, Louis Hartz explained the consensus in American history by reference to the truncated character of American sociological, philosophical, political, and ideological spectra.[1] The American colonists were generally drawn from a single social class in the old world and brought with them only the liberal persuasion rather than the full range of European political thought. Thus, with no social establishment sustained by law, no feudal vestiges, and no searing memories of breaking free from burdens of the past, Americans based their social and political system on universal assumptions about the worth and dignity of the average man. How could social crises emerge among a people with so much in common?

Hartz nonetheless noted that until the 1830s a sizable group of Americans feared that the popular nature of politics and government would inevitably culminate in revolution, anarchy, and tyranny. Forming an aspiring but repudiated elite, these Americans issued almost daily prognoses of impending dangers. But as the years passed without incident, without convincing evidence, their warnings were drowned out by a chorus of vigorous catcalls. As Hartz wrote, "If the barricades had been thrown up in 1800 or 1828, the point of Whiggery about [the anarchic and evil propensities of] the people would have been proved and the European pattern would instantaneously have appeared."[2] America would have suffered, as did Europe, recurrent and often violent struggles among various groups contending for power. Fortunately nothing of the kind happened. Instead, American life moved on in its gentle, rippling mainstream, without much more than an eddy or a momentary swirl to disturb the surface. The whirlpool of civil war in 1861 sucked American society into fratricidal conflict as the defenders of consensus forced compliance upon the dissidents.

Liberal Whiggery claimed its patrimony in the United States.

Persuasive as it appears on first impression, the Hartz analysis misses important characteristics of American history. Richard Hofstadter has likened the consensual theme to a picture frame in his analysis of its inherent limitations: "It sets the boundaries of the scene and allows us to see where the picture breaks off and the alien environment begins; but it does not provide the foreground or the action, the interest or the pleasure, the consummation itself, whether analytical or esthetic."[3] The concern of the historian must include both conflict and consensus, rather than one or the other. In this respect, Hartz's claim that liberal Whiggery triumphed in the United States by 1830 fails to carry conviction. Actually a series of minor conflicts that began in the 1830s would lead to the establishment of a new consensus after 1861.

Unquestionably an important contributor to the rising dissensus within the American polity was the clash of ideals relating to human servitude. Negro slavery came to symbolize evil incarnate to the northerners who enshrined the ideal of free labor. Despite wide agreement that the black man had no place in American society, northerners ultimately launched an attack against the southern social order to insure the continuance of the northern free labor society. Conflict erupted because of insistence on consensus.

To understand the northern attack on the South in 1861 requires attention to more than the abolitionist crusade. In fact, a full appreciation depends on an awareness of changing American attitudes and presumptions about people and government during the years from 1830 to 1860. What occurred in the war of 1861-1865 could not have taken place a half-century or even a quarter-century earlier, because Americans in 1810 still cherished a revolutionary ideology that disallowed either tyranny or anarchy.[4] They believed in strong government, but one always controlled by the people. For Americans, the middle way between two extremes had to be followed. Violence as a means of solving social problems seemed counter-productive. Force certainly had to be applied to insure that antisocial behavior remained within the bounds of decency and propriety, but Americans so firmly believed in their control over government that they could not conceive of its using violence against the citizenry simply to maintain itself.[5]

Events of the thirties and forties in their cumulative impact altered that easy conviction among Americans. As conditions changed, as new generations succeeded each other, the American environment, society, and polity assumed new attributes. By the 1830s, Americans of all groups had begun to question the cognitive value of their traditional ideals. This pervasive questioning presaged a new stage in the development of the American nation. Fred Somkin has likened it to the transition between the third and fourth phases in a maturational process that most societies experience: "The generation of the founders . . . knows the cost of what they have achieved; the following generation knows the founders; the third generation lives by tradition; and the last, in token of decay, knows the cost of nothing and believes that it has everything coming to it."[6] During the period of questioning, Americans became increasingly concerned about the maintenance of all that had been achieved since the Revolution. Governments began to use violent means to preserve themselves against irregular efforts to change them. Americans at large came progressively to doubt that any other dispensation could assure the order and security necessary to the enjoyment of liberty. A variety of considerations induced this change in perceptions, from the acquisition of a huge territory populated by alien peoples to the eruption of domestic unrest exacerbating the doubts about the validity of traditional ideals.[7]

The most dramatic of the incidents of domestic unrest occurred in Rhode Island in 1842.[8] Constitutional reformers within the state attempted to change the government without its consent. In fact, the Suffragists under the leadership of Thomas Wilson Dorr acted in open defiance of governmental policies. They denied that American majorities could be controlled by constitutions or established governments. Majorities had the inalienable right to change constitutions and governments at will in the exercise of popular sovereignty and peaceable revolution. This right was guaranteed by Article IV, Section 4 of the Constitution. In brief, the Rhode Island Suffragists argued that the republican guarantee clause of the Constitution had transformed the right of *revolution* into the *right* of revolution—they asserted that revolution was a legal as well as a moral right.

Once the Suffragists instituted the process of reform they discovered soon enough that theory would not always control practice. The supporters of the established government refused to tolerate this unsanctioned usurpation of constituted authority. Whether a majority approved reform or not, the means to achieve it had to conform with existing law. If the Suffragists persisted in their revolution, their only hope lay in success through force. But of course the reformers lacked the wherewithal to stand against the united strength of the state and federal governments. A few months after the suppression of the Suffragist movement, one of the leaders described what had happened. The peaceable effort to exercise "the hitherto undenied Sovereignty of the People has resulted in a complete Revolution . . . & that Revolution has been effected in our case in precisely the same way in which Revolutions in all former Republics have been accomplished. That is to say by an usurpation of power on the part of those in whose hands power has been entrusted. Since the 25⁻ of June 1842 R.I. has ceased to be a Republic."⁹

This Rhode Islander spoke in conceptual terms to characterize the events of the summer of 1842. Where governments suppressed the majority will, republicanism no longer existed. Whereas great numbers of Americans had espoused that ideological view during the years before 1842, within two decades those remaining loyal to it had shrunk to a minority. The first manifestations of change appeared in the national reaction to the Dorr War. Eventually Americans convinced themselves that force was necessary to insure the continuance of the old republic. The character of republicanism changed because of the paradox posed by claiming right in a context of might. The events in Rhode Island, and the responses to them, were symptomatic of the change in attitudes and perceptions.

This study focuses on the Dorr War, the national reaction to it, and the significance of both in the development of American constitutionalism. The presumptions that undergird it are: 1) that the ways people order reality depend on the prevailing ideology; 2) that commitments to an ideological position carry particular imperatives concerning modes of behavior; and 3) that one means of exploring the relationships between ideology and behavior is through an analysis of the conceptions used to order reality. Richard Hofstadter and Karl Mannheim have argued that analysis of the milieu of political action provides important insights into motives and intentions in human behavior.[10] Specifically, it facilitates an appreciation for the role and influence of ideas and ideology. Recent studies have shown that Americans of the first century after independence acted under the imperatives dictated by a paradigm of rules and postulates defining republicanism.[11] Max Weber stressed the utility of employing ideal-types in analysis as the means to penetrate beneath the surface of events and discover their psychological, structural, and ideal significance.[12] Thus the inquiring scholar seeks to enter into the metaphysical or onto-logical world of the historical agents being studied. Constitutionalism, as a form of republican politics, has a milieu worthy of study for the purpose of gaining insight into the developmental patterns of American history. Use of the term developmental should not be taken, however, to indicate a progressive orientation. Instead the intent is to focus at once on the elements of continuity and change in American history. Thus it would seem that an analysis of the Dorr War and the reaction to it can shed new light on the course of American society toward civil war and regeneration in ideal terms.

Within a decade after 1842 the traditional American ideology based on the concepts of popular sovereignty and peaceable revolution had fallen into disrepute. Even when its views were still asserted, the dogmatic tone of insistence contrasted sharply with the older complacent assurance. Venerable principles such as popular sovereignty had become mere catch-phrases, nominalist catechisms, used by politicians in their ceaseless quest for votes. The idea that governments must deal quickly and efficiently with all challenges to their authority gained acceptance as the crisis of the 1850s mounted. Americans no longer insisted on the right and power to decide all vital questions directly for themselves. The Supreme Court, Congress, president, and political parties assumed the role of arbiters.[13] Within another decade, Americans had accepted as practical necessity the state of affairs deplored by the Rhode Islander quoted above. In conceptual terms, the Civil War confirmed the advent of governmental sovereignty in American history. Despite the warning from Rhode Island, or perhaps because of it, "The . . . *Precedent of 1842* . . . [became] a law."[14]

The relationships involved when the microcosm became the macrocosm are even more direct than they appear on first impression. Not only did the events in Rhode Island symbolize changes occurring in the greater whole of the nation, they gave rise to an important Supreme Court decision.[15] The Court's ruling helped first to shift the balance between *might* and *right* within the states. That Americans accepted it revealed their increasing uncertainty about their own ability to determine the *right*. Then, with the Civil War, the Rhode Island decision provided a rationale for similar developments within the nation at large. *Might* settled all questions about social ideals. Even more to the point, Americans finally agreed that governments based on force were as necessary in the United States as they had always been elsewhere. They no longer viewed America and Americans as new and different entities subject to novel principles of development and behavior. Instead America rejoined the world, and Americans became mere men. An understanding of the Dorr War and its aftermath clarifies certain aspects of the course toward that ultimate denouement.

Part I

THE TRIAL

*The making of a constitution paramount is no
act of government; it always exists; it is the
immediate work of God, and a part of nature
itself. . . . Neither can the legislature create a
constitution; since the legislature itself is the
creature of the written constitution, is posterior
and subordinate to it. . . . Neither can the
legislature judge of the necessity of forming a
constitution, or dictate when or how it shall be
formed. To the court is referred to pronounce
judgment; to the legislature, the enacting of
laws; and to the people, the forming of a
constitution.*

Speech by George R. Burrill (1797)

Suppose the case of a State, whose constitution, originally good, had, from the lapse of time and from changes in the population of different portions of its territory, become unequal and unjust. Suppose this inequity and injustice to have gone to such an extent that the vital principle of representative republics was destroyed, and that the vote of a citizen in one county of the State was equivalent to that of six citizens in another county. Suppose that an equal disproportion existed between taxation and representation, and that, under the organic forms of the constitution, a minority could forever control the majority. Why, sir, even under such circumstances, I should bear with patience whilst hope remained. I would solicit, I would urge the minority, I would appeal to their sense of justice, to call a convention, under the forms of the constitution, for the purposes of redressing those grievances; but if, at last, I found that they had determined to turn a deaf ear to all my entreaties, I would then invoke the peaceable aid of the people, in their sovereign capacity, to remedy those evils. They are the source of all power; they are the rightful authors of all constitutions. They are not forever to be shackled by their own servants, and compelled to submit to evils such as I have described, by the refusal of their own Legislature to pass a law for holding a convention.

Speech by James Buchanan (1837)

1.

GENESIS

In the years before 1842 the Rhode Islander Martin Luther was an industrious shoemaker, part-time farmer, and petty trader. Keeping his own shop in the village of Warren, Bristol County, Luther epitomized the independent Yankee who mixed religion with politics in a fundamentalist concoction that made him seem talkative and sharp-tongued, or a simple republican, depending on the mood of the observer. Eastern Rhode Island was in the early throes of the industrial revolution, but there was still room for a man of many callings like Luther. He maintained a home for his aging mother and characteristically minded his own affairs and those of everyone else as well. Nothing about the man set him off from his equally industrious and frugal neighbors, unless it was the gossip about his "very noisy talking" mother who annoyed people by constantly shouting out "Methodist Hymns of which Church she was a fervent Member."[1]

Life changed abruptly for the Luthers in 1842. Like thousands of their peers, they had been caught up in the reform movement sweeping the state. On 18 April 1842 Luther served as a moderator for a special election held under the authority of a constitution approved for the state only by a popular referendum. This election was held to name officers who would put the new People's Government into operation in early May; simultaneous elections were staged under the authority of the old constitution, since the established state government had sanctioned neither the new constitution nor the special election. With his seemingly innocuous act of participation, Martin

Luther projected himself into American constitutional history.

Not only did he assure himself a place in the annals of the republic, Luther exposed himself to unexpected troubles. Within three months he had been harried from the state under threat of prosecution for treason. He established a residence just across the state line in Swansea, Massachusetts, leaving his mother with a companion and two hired hands at the homeplace in Warren. The simple shoemaking Methodist had become a public enemy under the law.

When overt hostilities erupted between the rival governments claiming the sovereignty in Rhode Island, Luther's Warren home became a target for the charter government's military efforts.[2] Old Mrs. Luther found herself near the eye of the storm once the General Assembly invoked martial law on 25 June 1842. On the night of 29 June a detachment of Warren militia invaded the Luther home to capture one of the radical Suffragists, as the defenders of the People's Constitution and Government were called. The inconspicuous shoemaker Martin Luther, and hundreds of other men of similar status, had presumed to lay unwashed hands on the sacred vestments of political and social legitimacy within the state. For that crime they must pay, or the precedent might prove disastrous.

According to subsequent testimony, Captain John T. Child had ordered Luther M. Borden and eight others to seek, find, and apprehend Martin Luther, reportedly in the state visiting his mother. When Borden asked what to do if the Luthers refused entry to their home, Child explained tersely that martial law tolerated no resistance. Accordingly the nine militiamen marched to Luther's home and broke in when no one responded to their knocks. Only Mrs. Luther, her companion, and the two hired men were discovered inside, all in their respective bedrooms. Borden and his fellows refused the requests of the two women to dress in private. They quickly searched the house for fear their quarry might escape. As they swore later in court, they used all possible care to avoid damage to the house and its occupants. But Luther was not to be found. Mrs. Luther complained that she suffered threats and abuse from the militiamen, who, for their part, insisted that they had been subjected to invective never before heard from feminine lips.[3]

From these events came one of the most significant United States Supreme Court decisions of the pre-Civil War period. Within two years the Luthers initiated suits before the federal circuit court in Rhode Island, alleging trespass and seeking damages from the militiamen. Actually, however, the Luther cases were argued on issues far more important than the unauthorized invasion of a private residence. The cases dragged on for five years, delayed for tactical and political reasons, until the Supreme Court finally ruled in favor of the militiamen in one case, while remanding the second for retrial under the principles announced. Both the occurrences and the Court's opinion symbolized the dramatic shift in American political and constitutional thought that was to sanction forcible suppression of southern secession in 1861. Because of its importance in American constitutional development, the Luther decision deserves detailed study. The way begins with the background of the so-called Dorr War of 1842, in which the Luther incident occurred.

Radicalism in the struggle to reform Rhode Island government followed years of patient effort. After 1776 movement succeeded movement as increasingly frustrated men attempted to secure a written constitution and to end the political obsolescence for which the state became notorious.[4] Since 1663 Rhode Island had been governed under the charter granted by Charles II to win the loyalty of his colonial subjects. After independence in 1776, Rhode Islanders tried to emulate their counterparts elsewhere and adopt a constitution incorporating new principles of government. The early attempts failed, at first because of the dislocations of war, and then because of a self-serving political exclusivism. Under the charter, the General Assembly had full power to establish the qualifications for voting and officeholding. By the 1790s freemanship had been limited to those white male adults who owned real property valued at \$133 or who paid \$7 annual rent in tenancy.[5] Beginning in 1729, eldest sons of freeholders had possessed political privileges. This bit of feudalism persisted until after the Dorr War. Despite frauds and threats of violence, the General Assembly maintained the exclusive system and ignored all demands for change.[6] Since only freemen could vote on the question of whether to adopt a new constitution, no request for revision ever received even a fair hearing before civil conflict flared in 1842.

Critics of the charter complained of shortcomings other than the landed franchise. For example, the charter apportioned the General Assembly according to seventeenth-century demographic patterns, which the growth of industrial towns had radically changed. In addition, legislation adopted as early as 1798 barred nonfreemen from service on juries and even from access to the courts, unless civil suits were sponsored by freemen.[7] Reformers warned that a failure to set things right would lead to violence.[8] Their urgings made no impression on the coalition of large farmers and financiers who controlled the state.

The last attempt to bring about reform through legally prescribed means came during the height of the Jacksonian movement during the 1830s. In contrast to the national pattern of reform, however, in Rhode Island it was a group of young Whigs allied with workingmen's associations who fought for reform against Jacksonian Democrats.[9] Although the workingmen launched the movement, the young Whigs soon took control. With some aid from older men, the reform leaders were primarily idealistic lawyers, doctors, newspaper editors, and other professional men, many of whom were qualified freemen. Thomas Wilson Dorr of Providence, a Whig legislator who pushed for banking and public school reforms, dominated these reformers. While most of the leadership was Whiggish, the Constitutionalist movement of the thirties attracted at least some men from all parties. Many of the radical Suffragists of the 1840s began their reform careers as Constitutionalists; thus an analysis of this earlier episode lays groundwork for later events. The issues, the ideology, and the patterns of development during the Constitutionalist crusade provided precedents and practical lessons for the Suffragists in the forties.

Perhaps the most obvious connection between the two movements lies in the man who led both. Thomas Wilson Dorr, scion of an old commercial family, exuded respectability. His background and appearance were hardly those of the typical revolutionary leader. Manifesting a cast of mind similar to if less intellectually isolated than that of Ralph Waldo Emerson, Dorr was well versed in the tenets of English philosophical radicalism.[10] Unlike Emerson, he took pride in his connections with European political radicals. In addition, he believed firmly that principles must be acted upon or discarded. Very much an ideologue, Dorr also viewed himself as a man of action, willing to take the risks and the consequences of his beliefs. Commenting on Dorr's stubbornness that exceeded mere obstinacy, Charles Tabor Congdon described him as "an excellent hater." Congdon added that Dorr looked "as little like an incendiary and revolutionist as any man whom I have ever encountered."[11]

After graduation from Phillips Exeter Academy, Dorr entered Harvard College at age fourteen.[12] According to the reminiscences of his peers, he sympathized with student dissent but took only a minor part in it. His interest lay in history and political theory and naturally led to the study of law after graduation. He returned to Providence and entered the law office of John Whipple, the indisputable leader of the Rhode Island bar and a firm Whig. In addition, Dorr had the advantage of attending a series of law lectures delivered in New York City by the eminent jurist, Chancellor James Kent. By the 1830s Dorr had established himself as a rising young attorney in Providence and had entered politics as a Whig of a strongly philosophical bent. Throughout his career as reform lawyer and politician he stood firmly on the principle of popular sovereignty and could best be described as a Jeffersonian literalist.

As early as 1831 Dorr manifested anti-institutional convictions. In a letter to an English friend, he praised those young
men in all nations who rejected the blind acceptance of social
and political conventions. The only proper stance called for
allegiance to the Jeffersonian postulate that "the actual living
majority of the day possesses the true sovereignty of the country, and have [sic] a right to investigate, review and amend its
political constitution, and to accommodate it to the just demands and necessities of the people."[13] Despite the trials and
pitfalls of a troubled career, he never recanted.

Almost maudlin in his sympathies for the "People," Dorr
nonetheless recognized the need for qualified leadership. As a
firm Christian, he repudiated class politics, always insisting that
the needs of the " 'greatest number' " came first. Thus he
joined the disinterestedness of the Jeffersonian elitist tradition
with the majoritarianism of Jacksonian America. As a reform
Whig, he believed implicitly in constant and continuous progress, even if occasional reverses held back the realization of
"principle in its fullest extent."[14] He denied that men could do
justice individually and directly for themselves. They must
abide the law and respect the rights of others. During the
thirties, he argued that men must seek redress of recognized
grievances through the "slow process of legislation."[15] Only the
experience and pressures of political involvement led him to
modify that position. When he did so, he extended the central
postulate of popular sovereignty and the Jeffersonian gener-
ational imperative to their logical extremes.

Around Dorr clustered a number of young Whigs who shared
most of his assumptions about politics. As primus inter pares,
and because of his inordinate energy, Dorr easily assumed the
mantle of leadership. Only later did it become clear that not all
these Whigs, and very few of the older political figures who
joined the movement, took their political principles as seriously
as Dorr. But from 1833 until 1836, after the workingmen's
associations drifted away from what seemed a futile effort,

harmony and camaraderie prevailed among the Constitutionalists. The group came to be actually an adjunct of National Republicanism or Whiggery in Rhode Island, and most participants placed party interest above immediate reform. Dorr thrust himself into the movement, never realizing that it served for most as a diversion more than a crusade and that the nonfreemen, whose support he assumed, had soon lost all interest. He made the ultimate commitment only to discover that he stood almost alone on the high ground of principle.

In April 1834 Dorr prepared and published an "Address" to the people of the state emphasizing the need for a written constitution to correct the deficiencies of government. He concentrated on the landed franchise, the anachronistic apportionment ratios, and the elective judiciary.[16] Moderate in its recommendations, the "Address" urged the freemen and nonfreemen to undertake reforms that would benefit all people in the state. Dorr denied that these reforms lay within the province of the established government through legislative action. Periodic alteration of the charter by the General Assembly convinced him that its validity had been impaired. Only a constitutional convention drawn from the people at large possessed the authority to lay the foundations for good government. From this axiom, he concluded that all adult male citizens should participate in the reform process, since American principles of government required the consent of the governed. *"Political society could not confer that right or power upon its members by the exercise of which it first came into existence."*

For two years the Constitutionalists worked to obtain pledges of support from candidates running for election by the Whig, Democratic, and Anti-Mason parties. To aid the movement, Dorr founded a newspaper appropriately heralded the *Constitutionalist*, while Charles Randall's *Northern Star* emanated from Warren.[17] When it appeared that competition between the two sheets threatened both, a merger established the *Northern Star and Rhode Island Constitutionalist*.[18] Despite his busy schedule as a Whig legislator, Dorr found time to handle strategy and details that others ignored. By 1836 he listed among his correspondents the leading Whigs of the state, as well as some of the independent Democrats. Most paid lip service to the cause, although the majority followed the lead of Benjamin Hazard of Newport and Nehemiah K. Knight of Providence, who urged caution before making any changes in the venerable fabric of Rhode Island government.[19]

As it turned out, the reformers succeeded only partially in their call for a constitutional convention. The General Assembly authorized one to meet in 1834, but refused to alter either the franchise requirements or the apportionment ratios in the selection of delegates, and it appropriated no funds to pay the expenses. Undoubtedly the entire affair was staged simply to quiet public agitation.[20] Apparently it succeeded in this, since the convention finally adjourned sine die in June 1835 after waiting a year for a quorum.[21] Undaunted, Dorr and the dwindling Constitutionalists turned to the elections of 1836 to recoup their losses.

Their timing could hardly have been worse. In 1836 the two major political parties fought for control of the state. Facing the challenge of the national Democrats led by Martin Van Buren, Rhode Island Whigs lost their appetite for reformist schemes that threatened to divide the vote by obscuring the issues.[22] Thus Whig leaders pressured Dorr and his followers to drop the constitutional question for the time being. Dorr refused, but most Constitutionalists returned to the party folds and hewed the lines drawn by the elders. Charles Randall of Warren reluctantly acquiesced, but complained bitterly that "the Whigs are not true to their friends." Another Constitutionalist-Whig, Dr. John A. Brown, advised Dorr to admit that the movement had been "a complete failure."[23]

In this context, some older Whigs remained firm, although they articulated new fears about the direction of the movement under Dorr's leadership. Charles B. Peckham spoke their minds when he complained about the popular misconception of the purpose of Constitutionalism. "The greater portion hereabouts seem imbued with the belief that our object is to secure unrestricted, unqualified, universal suffrage, and are completely terror-struck."[24] He urged the corresponding secretary to correct these false impressions, warning that otherwise the cause would be lost. Peckham's remarks reveal that the Constitutional movement was riddled by divergent opinions concerning the major issue, broadening the suffrage. Dorr had committed himself in 1834 to universal manhood enfranchisement, with residence and citizenship as the only criteria. Most Constitutionalists rejected Dorr's radicalism. They thought that certain standards had to be maintained. Only intelligent men capable of disinterestedness should have the vote. What good did it do to make reforms if measures were not taken to assure wisdom and moderation? As Van Buren Democrats ran up majorities at the polls across the nation, Whigs everywhere increasingly regretted the democratization of American politics. The situation of the Rhode Island Whigs differed from that of their allies in other states because it required merely that they stand firm to prevent the debasement of the franchise. By 1836 they had discovered that their real interest lay in maintaining the institutions of Rhode Island as inherited from the founders.

Not only did the Whigs and Whig-Constitutionalists lose the elections in 1836, but the reform alliance came apart in the aftermath. With the Van Buren Democrats in control of the nation and the state, Whigs no longer countenanced independent agitation for any reason. The outcome of the elections convinced Dorr even more fully that success in reform required loosening the suffrage requirements for those choosing constitutional convention delegates, persuading the former nonfreemen to vote, and altering the apportionment ratios. Whigs, however, found the prospect of Democratic enfranchisement and reapportionment appalling. Dorr began to receive intemperate letters from Whig leaders across the state ordering him to stop meddling with important matters.

Whigs were particularly incensed by Dorr's appeal to independent Democrats.[25] Such a course had been acceptable when the Whigs enjoyed majority standing, but no longer. Many Democrats indicated a willingness to support new causes after the national panic and depression hit in 1837. Of course, the incumbent Democrats suffered politically from the economic downturn, and Rhode Island Democrats looked for ways to escape the popular reaction. Just as naturally, Rhode Island Whigs preferred to keep the Democrats in an exposed position. Judge William Peckham informed Dorr in no uncertain terms that all thought of reform must be abandoned until the Jacksonian "Tories" were ousted. Only then would the country find relief from the stagnation and decay caused by the "Highhanded and illegal Course which the Administration has pursued."[26] In early 1837 Dorr had to choose between a delay in his plans for reform or an end to his career as a Whig state legislator.

Alliance with independent Whigs, Democrats, and Anti-Masons seemed the only viable course in 1837. The Whig party refused to condone further Constitutionalist activity, and the stigma of economic depression damaged the Democrats' winner image. Dorr struggled to secure a Constitutionalist slate in each election, seeking the strongest possible candidates and depicting Constitutionalism as a new force for reform, prosperity, and good government. Dorr apparently moved away from the Whig Party in 1837 and quite possibly decided at this time to become a Democrat. A cryptic note written in the margin of one of the letters Dorr received from Whigs refusing to run for office as Constitutionalists suggests that he had made the change. " 'So far'! good. V. Buren."[27] His subsequent loyalty to Van Buren and his rapid rise in the Democratic party after 1838 provides further corroboration. Dorr might well have been quoting his new political mentor when he wrote the note. But the evidence is not conclusive. It is clear that he remained a Constitutionalist until the movement died in early 1838.

Whether Dorr deliberately moved into the Democratic party in 1837 or not, the Whigs excommunicated him anyway. When he rejected the advice of Judge John H. Weedon and other leading Whigs to withdraw from his independent candidacy for Congress on the Constitutionalist ticket, and simultaneously opposed a party decision concerning the election of a United States senator, he went too far. The Whigs subsequently forced him out of the state legislature and the party.[28] In response, he renounced the party forever and never again trusted Whigs or Whiggery. As he wrote years later, "Every genuine Whig feels he who declares no principles, or has none to declare, is so like himself, that he can be safely trusted with the keeping of Whig affairs."[29] He rejoiced after a time that he "was delivered from the 'horrible pit and miry Clay' of federalism."[30] His identification of Tories, Federalists, and Whigs was undoubtedly the ultimate condemnation. Political experience had opened his eyes to the implications of much that he had accepted naively as a novice.

Most Constitutionalists returned to party ranks again in 1837. Charles Randall followed the pattern but vowed to support all Constitutionalist candidates who took the field. "If things turn out, as I fear they will," Randall mused, ". . . when are we going to get our men? There will always be some *important election* in the way."[31] In basic agreement, Dorr adhered to his reform commitment in his candidacy for Congress, at the same time extending the range of concern. A written constitution for Rhode Island deserved the highest priority. But he also campaigned in favor of the immediate abolition of the slave trade in Washington, D.C., the right of all citizens to petition Congress and have their petitions read, and against the annexation of Texas.[32] Ideologically Dorr fused local with national issues. He identified political servitude in Rhode Island with physical enslavement in the nation. He argued that all citizens had the obligation to fight against both kinds of slavery. They must organize locally to assure republicanism, nationally to guarantee freedom. Republican slavery of either variety should not be tolerated. Having made the commitment, Dorr stood for reform in its broadest scope in 1837.

He fought hard, ably supported by the other Constitutionalist candidate for Congress, Dr. Dan King of Newport, but
to no avail.[33] The Constitutionalist slate fared worse than in
1836. Dorr concluded that the nonfreeholders and freeholders
of the state preferred "to leave the *foot* set upon their
necks."[34] Nothing remained but to acquiesce and await a more
propitious moment. Proponents of unpopular principles were at
worst tyrants, at best bores. In the meantime political fences
needed mending and other causes beckoned. By 1839 he had
become an influential Democrat, serving as chairman at a
number of meetings and heading a committee responsible for
bringing nationally prominent Democrats into the state to
speak. Defeat in 1837 opened the way to new opportunities.

Again in 1839 Dorr ran for Congress, this time as a Democrat
in harness with his former political opponent, Dutee J. Pearce
of Newport.[35] Despite his new allegiance, he retained his con-
tacts with antislavery leaders throughout the northern states.
Although he refused to act as agent for the American Anti-
Slavery Society in Providence, he reaffirmed his support for the
society's work.[36] Declining an invitation to address the Young
Men's Anti-Slavery Society Convention held at Worcester, Massachusetts, in 1838, he nonetheless dispatched a long message of
sympathy. As Jefferson had done earlier, Dorr argued that only
the younger generation of Americans had the energy and
courage to eradicate a recognized evil; older Americans were
either too corrupt or too timid to act. He urged the young
people to arouse "public opinion" for a massive assault, and
"we shall *move with effect upon the District*." Once "the
centre, the capitol, the citadel of Slavery" had been taken,
slavery would die naturally "in the extremities." The advocates
of equal rights should make it impossible for any northerner to
hold a seat in Congress and sit idly by while some "Southern
aristocrat" denounced the opponents of slavery. Dorr held that
slavery and republicanism could never coexist peaceably. Once
"the People" recognized the dangers to liberty inherent in the
enslavement of some people, the cause would be won.[37]

Time spent reflecting on the frustrations of politics, along with an obstinacy bordering on the absurd, produced in Dorr a quality of leadership typical of religious and political martyrs. His beliefs, deep-seated and firmly principled, altered perceptibly because of the experiences of the 1830s. Aspiring to national as well as state prominence, he clearly yearned for the public position to match his self-image as a leader. However, there is no evidence to suggest that he ever compromised his commitment to the "good old cause" of republicanism and equal rights.[38] Instead he constructed a new perspective. He came to view the nation and the state within similar and rigid frames of reference. Southern slaveowners resembled Rhode Island freemen, despite their differences. Both groups suggested an Americanized Tory gentry, an "Aristocracy." As national Whiggery infiltrated the North and the South, Dorr visualized a vast conspiracy at work to subvert the principles and practices of free government.[39] Aspiring leaders had the responsibility to expose and suppress it.

In contrast, he believed that principle ruled the Democrats. The political situation in Rhode Island that forced him to renounce Whiggery led him to false conclusions about the integrity of Democratic politicians. Since Democrats had provided needed support in 1837 and after (largely because of their own interest), Dorr concluded that they alone espoused his call for a politics of principle. Only later did he learn that politicians of all persuasions practice the art of the possible. Then he discovered a distinction between "Democrat" and "democrat," but for his part, he maintained, "The cause of democracy is infinitely greater than any man, who ever served, or can serve it; and its honors are to be regarded as gifts and not rewards to those who serve it well."[40] As he said, "I am a democrat, and believe that nothing but the loss of my faculties can ever separate me from the faith and practice of democracy." The motto for all democrats was "Sacrifice no principles. Suppress no truths."[41]

Despite his early myopia concerning the Democratic party,

Dorr developed a theory of leadership well tailored for his career in reform politics. Having abandoned Whiggery, he concluded that Whig principles had caused the frustration of the thirties. The mistake had been to try to bring the people to heel, rather than allowing them to institute reform in their own time and way. He came to believe that aspiring leaders could do no more than try to educate and inspire the people to make rational choices, not decide for them. To do otherwise transformed politics into a system of master-slave relationships. He agreed that the people would come to heel for a time, but the inevitable long-range result would be repudiation of the men who subjugated them. Freedom and liberty were the causes and purposes of history, and Dorr never doubted for more than a moment that these would eventually triumph.[42]

From this altered perspective of history, philosophy, and theory, Dorr quickly suppressed his disillusionment caused by the failure of Constitutionalism. He bided his time, pointing the proper directions to those interested in reform and awaiting a signal from the "People" that the time had come to act. He served the cause by guarding those "great branches of Public Liberty" to insure the freedom and public space for action when the moment arrived. All principled men must work "to save the People . . . and to give them the opportunity" to exercise their rights in a free atmosphere.[43] Dorr's mature theory of popular politics mingled inextricably considerations of self-interest and principle, although he refused to recognize even the existence of the former. The hard school of practical politics reinforced rather than modified his optimistic faith that the cause of right and justice would prevail in the end.

Apathy, manipulation, party discipline, and inexperience contributed in due proportion to the failure of reform in the 1830s. Constitutionalists recognized that success would depend on the mobilization of the mass of freemen and nonfreemen alike. In hindsight, they also appreciated the need to coordinate theory and action. The charter government had drained away whatever activism had existed by acquiescing in the demand for a convention. Since the Constitutionalists insisted on reform only through legally prescribed means, they had been powerless to deal with the co-optive governmental strategy. But they emerged from the Constitutional movement indignant at what they took to be willful obstruction of a popular demand and obvious violation of American principles. All this contributed to a new militant spirit among the advocates of reform, in sharp contrast to the patient seeking of earlier years.

In addition, successes in popular reform elsewhere in the nation, through the politics of direct action, provided timely models for Rhode Island.[44] In 1836 Maryland Democrats forced a reluctant Whig government to reapportion the state by threatening to destroy all government. Almost simultaneously, movements led by Democrats in the territories of Michigan and Arkansas created new constitutions without bothering to wait for specific authorization from Congress. In 1838 aroused Democrats in Pennsylvania marched en masse to occupy the state capitol and forced the incumbent Whig-Anti-Mason coalition to respect a Democratic victory at the polls. As Rhode Islanders surveyed these developments, they undoubtedly were struck by the determination of common men everywhere to claim their rights directly.

Not all Americans viewed these new developments with any sense of pride or equanimity. Senator John C. Calhoun of South Carolina feared that American institutions lacked the stability and permanence necessary to a good society. Former Senator John Tyler of Virginia, in response to the Pennsylvania incident, argued, "It is naught else but the precursor of that revolution which is sooner or later to occur."[45] Congress debated for two years before recognizing the legitimacy of the unauthorized transactions in Michigan and Arkansas. Predictions of dire consequences filled the air and the newspapers as conservative men girded themselves for the imminent battle between mob rule and the authority of the law. Just how much the examples of direct action elsewhere influenced the Rhode Island militants of the 1840s is difficult to determine. Some influence was clear from the tendency to claim them as precedents. In contrast, opponents of radical reform made good use of the arguments of the conservative critics of the thirties. In a sense, Rhode Island became the arena for a contest between two different theories of constitutional government.

Change came to Rhode Island in the 1840s only partly because of abstract political considerations, however. The way was prepared not simply by educating competent leaders, but also by a widened recognition among all groups that changed conditions required modernized institutions. Governmental structures and arrangements reflecting the ideas and conditions of the seventeenth and eighteenth centuries had little chance to withstand the pressures and concerns of the nineteenth. By 1840 most reasonable men concurred that the time for reform had arrived. But a widening breach concerning the means of reform ultimately brought civil war instead of consensus. That denouement can be attributed partly to the hesitancy of incumbent groups to accept change, partly to the unwillingness of radical reformers to tolerate further delays. As the situation developed, conservatives perceived radicals as the agents of anarchy, while radicals concluded that any compromise with the conservatives would subvert republican liberty. Thus what began as a movement based on a broad if tentative consensus for reform ended in ideological conflict involving divergent theories of American constitutionalism.

In 1839 and 1840 New York Democrats demonstrated that obsolescence in Rhode Island had gained national notoriety. William Cullen Bryant, Richard Adams Locke, and other Jacksonians sponsored a petition to Congress seeking federal intervention "to free the unfortunate Sons and Successors of Roger Williams." Native white male adult American citizens had been reduced to the position of "Aliens in that *State*." Bryant and Locke reasoned that Congress possessed authority under the republican guarantee clause of the Constitution to require "a government created by the people on the basis of the equal inalienable rights of man."[46] Undoubtedly the New York Democrats were as interested in potential voters as in the infringement of rights, since Van Buren's chances for reelection depended on overcoming the depression syndrome. Nonetheless, the specter of federal intervention and the undeniable cogency of the Democratic critique reinforced the necessity for change in Rhode Island.

Demographic, political, and economic statistics made a nearly irrefutable case for the reformer's critique of Rhode Island government. Only four out of ten adult white male citizens could vote, and those who could not were also still excluded from the jury boxes and courts of the state. Freemen in Providence, a city of 21,870 people, constituted a mere 6 percent of the city's population, while in the tiny southern village of Jamestown they counted 16 percent. Towns with increasing populations had one representative for 2,590 people, while stable towns boasted one representative for 1,074. The state average was 1,512 persons per representative in the General Assembly, but the figures for Providence and Jamestown respectively were 5,793 and 182. The overall impact of these arrangements was that one-third of the voting population, concentrated in the rural south, controlled the other two-thirds living in middle and northern urban areas.[47]

The reasons for these political inequities were largely economic. Rhode Island, like New England in general, experienced tremendous expansion of its population and economy during the three decades beginning in 1820. Between 1790 and 1860 Providence grew in population at the rate of 1,004 percent, while the state average was only 154 percent. In the north, factories appeared almost overnight along the Pawtuxent and Blackstone rivers, drawing men from other areas in the state, nation, and world. As the number of immigrant aliens increased, more and more of the sons of old established families moved to other states seeking the main chance. To illustrate the effects, foreign-born population increased from barely 1 percent of the total in 1830 to more than 16 percent by 1850. Also, by 1840

the number of native Rhode Islanders living outside the state
exceeded that within. Such growth and disruption of the old
social and economic patterns produced tensions not easily resolved in a state as small as Rhode Island.

One result was a burgeoning nativism, evident as early as the
late twenties. In 1829 Whig Assemblyman Benjamin Hazard of
Newport sponsored a report to the General Assembly that fairly
burned with outrage at the rising flood of immigrants.[48] Several
petitions had been directed to the assembly seeking liberaliza-
tion of the suffrage and reapportionment to provide representation for Rhode Island's new citizens. After comparing nonfreemen to enslaved blacks in their common inability to recognize
true liberty and equality once it was granted to them, Hazard
urged the assembly to grant the petitioners leave to depart the
state if they disliked its political institutions. He saw no reason
to destroy sound government simply because of the complaints
of a few demagogues allied with foreigners who could neither
know nor understand the proper principles of government.

Immigrant and native workingmen, in response, joined workingmen's parties, supported the Jacksonian Democrats, and flir-
ted with the Constitutionalists during the thirties. In fact, as
mentioned earlier, workingmen actually launched the reform
movement of the 1830s, although they soon lost faith in its
efficacy. Because of these combined efforts, Rhode Island finally initiated a system of public education, weakened though it
was by the use of its appropriated funds for other purposes. In
addition the General Assembly adopted a lien law protecting
workers' wages. But the assembly and freemen alike refused all
suggestions for modification of the suffrage and apportionment
laws. As Hazard said in his report of 1829, anyone who cared to
do so could qualify to vote simply by purchasing land. No
privileged groups existed in Rhode Island, according to the
standard refrain. But everyone knew full well that by the first
quarter of the nineteenth century the scarcity and consequent
high price of land, combined with the low wages of industrial
labor, assured minority rule. No doubt the political coalition of

farmers and industrialists ruling the state preferred not to experiment when their control was at stake.

Pressures for enfranchisement increased in almost direct proportion to governmental recalcitrance during the 1830s. Although the Constitutional movement failed, it heightened popular consciousness of abuse. One old Whig, a long-time advocate of taxpaying suffrage, told Dorr that reform was no more likely to succeed than it had in the past. Too many of "our Present Freemen violently" opposed any change. Neither the General Assembly nor the freemen would ever initiate a change weakening their power. To secure "a Constitution with the checks and Balances" that proper principle required, "it must Emenate [sic] from the People by their meeting in Primary Assemblies to Chose [sic]—Delegates to meet in Convention." Only "under Such Circumstances [that] every Male Citizen over the age of 21 Years would Exercise his inherent right and . . . bring to Bare [sic] in a great measure the Popular Voice" was there a chance for reform.[49] Old Judge Peckham dropped the idea there, turning his attention to the threat posed by the national Democrats. But the idea of a popular convention representing all the people gained attractiveness as the examples of direct action in other states proliferated and as the existing government failed to respond to demands for relief.

Almost as if calculated to awaken the political eununchs of Rhode Island, the great campaign of 1840 exploded like a time bomb. Whigs across the nation and in Rhode Island took up the practices long used by the Democrats. The effect, although unintended, was inspirational and electrifying. From front porches, store fronts, and stumps in every state, speakers titillated the common man with the design of ravaging his political virginity. Whigs had discovered the expediency of sounding like Democrats. Exploiting the pervasive insistence on loyalty to the republicanism of the Revolution, Whig theorists created "Coonskin Democracy"[50] by transforming ideological imperatives into rhetorical flourishes. As one observer commented, "There was never anything like it before in the history of the country, and there probably will never be anything like it again." The campaign had been "particularly lively" in Rhode Island, and "people who could not vote, more than ever envied those who could." The excitement of the grand event should not be wasted. Rhode Island offered "an excellent opportunity for demagogues, and they improved it."[5][1]

Charles Tabor Congdon, erstwhile law student and unemployed newspaperman, had shrewdly judged the situation. Others able to bear the financial burden of an organizational effort shared his judgment. Thus the Rhode Island Suffrage Association swept into action to exploit the opportunity left in the wake of the "Log Cabin and Hard Cider" campaign of 1840. As Congdon described it later,

> The movement which was to grow to such considerable proportions had a personal and somewhat insignificant beginning. There was a Dr. John A. Brown, a botanical physician, who supplied the people of Providence with root-beer of a pleasant and salutiferous quality. Brown's beer was in demand, and being of a foamy and effervescent sort, it may have had something to do with the ebullitions which followed. . . . when not engaged in building up the constitutions of his patients, the doctor was painfully sensible that the ancient State had no Constitution of its own,—a deficiency which, both as a patriot and as a practitioner, he ceased not to lament. He determined to start a free-suffrage agitation; secondly, he resolved to emit a free-suffrage newspaper; and thirdly, he employed me to edit it. He might have done much better if he had been able to offer a little higher wages; for I engaged to convulse Rhode Island (with the Plantations thrown in) for the modest remuneration of five dollars per week.

Casting about for a name, Dr. Brown accepted Congdon's suggestion to herald the reform sheet the *New Age*, "as we proposed to abolish the work of an age which might be considered an old one."[5][2]

Congdon's satiric account betrays the painful experiences of national civil war in 1861, but no one suspected in 1840 what the consequences of radical reform might be. Instead men threw themselves into the Suffragist crusade determined to adhere to traditional ideas. They intended to carry out the principles of popular sovereignty and peaceable revolution. With spirit and self-conscious pride they identified themselves as the defenders of mankind and human dignity. Manifesting the pervasive fear that they might not live up to the example of the founding generation, the Suffragists and their friends across the nation hoped to convince the world and themselves that the new era had arrived. Ironically, they succeeded in ways far removed from their expectations.

2.

REFORM

*We Know Our Rights, and
Knowing, Dare Maintain Them.*

Rhode Island reformers finally decided to take matters into their own hands. Conditions within the state constituted the classic case described in 1837 by James Buchanan as requiring an appeal to the sovereign power of the people to rectify existing evils in government.[1] Reformers explained the situation from that ideological perspective. As early as 1837 William Peckham had advised Dorr that only "the People . . . meeting in Primary Assemblies" could change the obsolete system of government in Rhode Island.[2] In early 1840 the First Reform Society of New York City circulated an "Address to the Citizens of Rhode Island who are denied the Right of Suffrage."[3] The circular urged the nonfreemen and sympathetic freemen to elect a popular convention to prepare a new constitution. Once completed, the constitution should be submitted for ratification by all the American citizens who resided in Rhode Island. The charter government had no authority to interfere. If the constitution carried by majority vote, the charter government would terminate automatically, and the new regime would move Rhode Island into the modern age of democracy and equal rights.

The New Yorkers ignored some potential legal problems that might arise should the charter government resist the experiment. They glossed over any possible difficulties by asserting the recognized right of American majorities to change governments at will. If the charter government acquiesced, as seemed likely, the change to modern forms would be smooth and uneventful. But if the charter government should resist, insisting on its authority to control the process of reform, the people could appeal to Congress or the Supreme Court for implementation of Article IV, Section 4 of the Constitution, the republican guarantee clause. Since the charter obviously failed to provide the form of government required, and since the reformers could demonstrate that a majority of the people of Rhode Island preferred a better form of government, Congress and the Court would have no choice but to enforce the will of the people. A new legal and constitutional authority would result, in either case, from the exercise of original sovereignty by the oppressed majority of American citizens in Rhode Island.

Within two years the reformers executed the plan laid out in the New York circular. They elected delegates to an unauthorized convention. The convention formulated a constitution and submitted it for ratification in an election approved only by the participants. Asserting that a majority of all adult white male citizens, as well as of qualified freemen, voted in favor of the constitution, the Suffragists tried to erect a government in the spring of 1842. They insisted that lack of formal approval by the existing government was of no consequence. At that juncture, trouble began. The charter government, supported by the coalition of a few hidebound defenders of ancient institutions and a much larger number of men concerned for the maintenance of legal forms, refused to accept the popular referendum. The General Assembly, controlled by the coalition, adopted a new treason statute, launched a massive arrest and detention program, and ultimately proclaimed martial law over the entire state to defend it against what was defined as insurrectionary violence. Indeed, some violence occurred. Dorr and the radical wing of the reformers attempted in mid-May 1842 to seize control of the state and thereby transform a paper into a de facto government. Even before that, however, the charter authorities sought and secured promises of federal assistance if the situation should get out of hand. Thus armed, they acted

energetically to suppress the radicals. Since very few Rhode
Islanders followed Dorr's lead, the crisis ended almost before it
began. With established authority securely in control, the charter government called a convention and supervised the formulation and ratification of a relatively liberal constitution by 1843.
Although not in the way planned by the reformers, the smallest
state finally entered the modern age.

Since the successful reform of Rhode Island in 1843, the
significance of the episode has been disputed. Most commenta-
tors have argued that the events in Rhode Island, although
ambiguous in the short view, nonetheless confirmed the pragmatic character of American constitutionalism. According to
this view, the reformers won the war but lost the battle. Under
the constitution of 1843, the electorate was increased by some
60 percent, and the charge of governmental obsolescence lost
most if not all of its validity.[4] However, such an overall assessment leaves out of account the concerns of the reformers and
the larger meaning of the forcible defense of established authority. It also obscures the importance of the federal intervention
in local affairs and of the Supreme Court decision on the cases
that grew out of the so-called Dorr War. An understanding of
the development of American legal and constitutional thought
requires a more thorough-going analysis of the origins, course,
outcome, and significance of the Dorr War. To argue that the
immutable principles of American government triumphed is to
perpetuate the unidimensionality of a great deal of American
historiography. Instead the episode must be probed for all that
it can reveal about the process of American constitutional
development.

The chapters that follow are designed to perform that function. Chapters 2 to 4 trace the Dorr War in detail, with the
focus sharply on the gradual recognition by the reformers of the
importance of proper theory. The next four chapters concentrate on the national reaction as observed among the general
public, among congressmen, and within the judiciary. Finally,
the Epilogue draws together the lines of analysis and considers

the significance of the Dorr War and the Supreme Court decision on the Luther cases. Throughout, the argument holds that by the end of the 1840s, American attitudes and ideas about free government had shifted so dramatically that little remained of the traditional revolutionary ideology except the forms. Within that new attitudinal context, the Civil War followed naturally when one group of Americans attempted to subvert the established constitutional structure in favor of one more appealing to them. In fine, the Leviathan state had emerged, fully conscious of itself and its imperatives. With that development the American republic was transformed into a constitutional empire.

The radical effort to reform Rhode Island breaks naturally into four phases. The period of initiation ended in May 1841, when the Rhode Island Suffrage Association resolved to go directly to the people. During the following year, constant escalation of both rhetoric and action occurred, until rival governments contested for control of the state in May 1842. The crisis stage was relatively brief, spanning the summer of 1842 and climaxing in the assertion of military supremacy in July and August. Over the next nine months, vigorous political activity showed that all parties were aware of the importance of controlling the new government under the constitution of 1843. Throughout the last three stages of the contest, the issues claimed the attention of people throughout the nation. Advocates of popular sovereignty did almost daily battle with defenders of constituted authority. As Dorr explained later, "It was assumed [by one side] that the People . . . have no right, in any case, to amend their government, without the permission of their rulers." On the other hand, the reformers and their allies presumed that once the popular will had been registered, change followed automatically. The will of established governments prevailed until the people decided otherwise.[5] Far from being an abstract, metaphysical argument, this difference of opinion moved men to violence. It turned on matters of cognitive belief. Thus what began as an argument over proper theory and necessary reform ultimately involved the state in civil war and the nation in a reconsideration of political principles.

Five men met in Providence in early 1840 to form the Rhode Island Suffrage Association, the vehicle for reform in the state. By March they had written and adopted a charter for the organization, complete with a preamble incorporating the theory outlined in the New York circular. Proclaiming that Rhode Island was "destitute of government," the charter asserted the right of all free and responsible citizens to participate in the governmental process. Making their initial appeal "to heaven, for the justice of our cause," the Suffragists planned to petition the General Assembly for a proper constitutional convention. If that failed, they projected a request to Congress "and if need be, to the Supreme Judicial Power, to test the force and meaning of that provision in the Constitution, which guarantees 'to every State . . . a republican form of government.' " Through one means or another they intended to secure their rights as American citizens "from the grasp of arbitrary power." They concluded the charter with a phrase that became the motto of the association: "WE KNOW OUR RIGHTS, AND KNOWING, DARE MAINTAIN THEM."[6]

Carefully delaying all action until after the presidential election in order to avoid partisan complications, the Suffragists pursued their plans after November 1840. They dispatched speakers and agitators to tour the state and found local chapters of the association. They wrote and circulated petitions instructing the General Assembly to call a convention under equitable arrangements. They founded a newspaper, the *New Age*, to promote the cause among the people. The strategy and tactics employed by the association resembled in detail those of the Constitutionalists during the thirties, but the public response exceeded even the most optimistic expectations.[7] Within a few months it seemed clear that public support was overwhelming.[8] The response to Suffragist agitation showed how widespread was the demand for change and reflected the pervasive acceptance of Suffragist theory. As one speaker asked rhetorically, "If the sovereignty don't reside in the people, where in the hell does it reside?"[9] Since the answer was obvious, Suffragists acted to prove their theory.

During the opening stage, the Suffragists had to demonstrate quickly and irrefutably that they had broad public support; they knew that otherwise the new movement would abort as all earlier ones had. In their effort to convey determination and resolution, they inspired predictable charges of violent revolution by government supporters. Suffragist rhetoric exaggerated the scope of their moderate plans, and care was necessary to insure that the public was not put off by the charges and countercharges that filled the newspapers of the state. Charles Tabor Congdon, editor of the *New Age*, wrote soothing editorials, shrewdly exploiting the ambiguity in the idea of revolution as Americans understood it. "There was never any great work in public affairs accomplished—there was never any great truth accomplished but there was a revolution. . . . Quietly—peaceably—and in good order can a revolution be effected in this state, . . . a revolution devoutly to be wished."[10] Rhode Islanders in increasing numbers responded to Congdon's assurances, willing to fix on the promise rather than the threat raised by revolution.[11]

In February 1841 the association moved perceptibly to higher ground in the developing confrontation. A resolution sponsored by the leadership and ratified by a majority in a mass rally in Providence stipulated that if the majority of American citizens in Rhode Island approved a constitution, "it will be then to all intents and purposes, the Law of the State."[12] Certainly the association intended to convince the General Assembly of the consequences of a refusal to call a convention with equitable representation, but the resolution of 7 February had more profound implications also. By May the potential for radical action became clear. When the General Assembly agreed to a convention and altered the apportionment ratios while refusing to amend suffrage qualifications, the association created a State Committee with specific instructions to call a popularly elected convention to meet "at as early a day as possible."[13] Ideology and interest coalesced to move the Suffragists into action on their stated principles.

In theory Suffragism emphasized the majoritarian principle that governments must rest on the consent of the governed. Having committed themselves to the theory of popular sovereignty, the Suffragists had no choice but to refuse any compromise that ignored it. To vitiate the theory by acts even before the process of reform began would have subverted whatever chances the Suffragists had of convincing the nonfreemen that this movement differed from all earlier ones. Many Suffragists had entered politics during the Constitutionalist crusade of the 1830s, and these men knew full well that success depended on broadening the suffrage. Without the active assistance of the disfranchised majority, Suffragism promised little more than Constitutionalism had achieved. Thus the resolutions of 5 May bringing theory and practice into congruity followed naturally from the obstructiveness of the General Assembly and the perceptions of Suffrage leaders.

Threats of direct redress of grievances and the carrying out of such threats require quite different kinds of commitments. Before conservative people act, they need assurances, based on theory and experience, that nothing else will suffice. The Suffragists unquestionably preferred to proceed through legally prescribed means but were forced by circumstances to act otherwise.[14] When the time came for direct action in the summer of 1841, the movement lacked a theory and a tactical plan of action. The traditional American revolutionary ideology was familiar and often eulogized, but as one critic has remarked, it failed to inform people how to achieve what they had in mind.[15] The Suffragists had no articulate theorist or tactician until October 1841, when at last Thomas Wilson Dorr assumed that position. To do so, he challenged and bested Dutee J. Pearce, who had supported the movement long before Dorr took an interest. Thus the first stage and nearly half of the second in the history of the Suffrage movement involved a search for a workable and comprehensive theory of direct action politics. Until October contradictions and ambiguities in the arguments and activities of the Suffragists left an impression of confusion, despite the consistency of purpose.

One contradiction that emerged during the early period concerned an overall tactical approach. The Suffragists resolved in February and again in May to go directly to the people, and yet they continued to insist that they planned an appeal to Congress or the Supreme Court if their political campaign failed.[16] No one explained how to reconcile these two ideas. Also Suffragists held that Rhode Island actually had no government, but at the same time they petitioned the General Assembly to call a constitutional convention. Further, Congdon warned Suffragist zealots not to force a confrontation with the charter government "until we have another and better form to take its place."[17] Finally, while association spokesmen defended revolution as a peaceable process to change governments, letters published in the New Age during the spring of 1841 urged the formation of volunteer militia companies.[18] Of course, these suggestions of force could be justified as defensive, applicable only if the charter government threatened to resist the popular will; but they added to the aura of confusion surrounding the association and its plans.[19] Nonetheless, the resolutions of early May augured new developments that would clarify the ambiguities.

In late June Representative Samuel Y. Atwell of reform-dominated Gloucester read before the General Assembly a report from his Judiciary Committee warmly espousing the latest demands by the Suffragists.[20] Immediately Richard K. Randolph of Newport and William Ames of Providence objected to any departures from Rhode Island's traditional "usages and customs." The majority agreed at least in part and rejected Atwell's proposals by a four to one vote. Atwell warned the assembly that a refusal to listen to the people could only end in violent revolution. Time had run out for the old charter. But Atwell's misgivings failed to move the majority in the assembly from a determination to maintain proper forms when and if change came to the state.

During June the State Committee of the association vacillated, neither acting on its charge to call a convention, nor trying to cool the wrath roused by the arrogance of the General Assembly. On 18 June Congdon printed a letter, forwarded by the State Committee, that announced: "The people—the 'numerical force,' have but to proclaim their will," formulate and ratify a constitution, and then demand that Congress support it under the republican guarantee clause. Still the State Committee delayed the call to action. Instead the divided membership conducted a survey to determine whether a majority of Rhode Islanders approved of the plan. By July nothing had changed, and the initiative returned to the association membership.[21]

Then on 5 July, during a mass meeting staged as part of the Independence Day festivities, the association adopted a resolution peremptorily ordering the State Committee to act as charged.[22] Two weeks later, on 20 July, the call for a convention finally issued, with elections scheduled for 28 August and the convention to meet in early October.[23] All adult male Americans who had resided in the state for one year and the town for six months could take part in the election of delegates. Secretaries and election moderators were charged to keep careful records to certify those elected and to verify the legitimacy of the proceedings. Towns of one thousand people or less could send one delegate, and one more representative was awarded for every additional one thousand people. However, the disproportionate size of Providence caused even the Suffragists to compromise their principle of one man, one vote. Rejecting mathematical precision, they divided Providence into six wards and allowed three delegates from each. The committee proclamation urged all qualified persons to participate, warning that the rival

Freeholders' Convention scheduled for November "is . . . a fraud."[24]

During the next month the Suffragists conducted a campaign to win majority support for the People's Convention. Letters in the *New Age* assured potential voters that the charter government lacked the authority or power to resist. "We are not constrained by force, for we have the power to overthrow it [the charter government], and to erect another on the broad principle of human right. *And this we will do, God helping us.*" The State Committee's major address, "GIVE US OUR RIGHTS, or WE WILL TAKE THEM," breathed moderation and certainty, despite its title. The minority would "promptly" recognize as "the undisputed law of our State" any constitution incorporating proper principles and ratified by a majority.[25] The Suffragists were not yet convinced that they could win majority support, but they never doubted that once won it assured success. No one questioned the Lockean hypothesis that a political majority always had the physical power to insure its dictates.

Old ambiguities and uncertainties about proper theory continued to plague the Suffragists. They assumed that American majorities had the legal and constitutional right to change government at will, especially when ruling minorities refused to redress grievances. Evidence from all sides indicated that the reform movement led by the Suffragists sprang "from the people themselves." If so, and if the theoretical assumptions were valid, a rhetoric of violence was out of place.[26] If in fact the minority supporting the charter had no legal or moral choice but to accept constitutional changes ratified by a clear majority, then the talk of force served only to muddle the issue. One critic aptly characterized the result, noting that "the inconsiderate threats and revolutionary harangues of some of the new Suffrage party, have done more harm to their cause, than any opposition which has been made to it."[27] The critic, Dorr's brother, insisted that majorities had no legal right to trample on the rights of minorities. His critique pointed up a salient consideration in the development of crisis in Rhode Island. As much from their own mistakes as from the reaction of the charter government, the reformers ultimately allowed their principled effort to degenerate into a struggle of might against might. Their unthinking reliance on the rhetoric of violence undercut the legal and moral position they tried to maintain.

But this sequel lay in the future, and hardly a Suffragist allowed such considerations to mar the prospects of success. In the elections a Democratic-Suffragist alliance took shape. Candidates were selected to run for election to both the Freeholders' and the People's Conventions, in the hope of avoiding any difficulties about the ratification of a liberal constitution. The strategy succeeded only in Providence, where all but one of the elected delegates served in both conventions.[28] Elsewhere bitter divisions surfaced. The freemen of the state gave proof in their electoral choices that they had no intention of surrendering without a fight.

In Providence, Thomas Wilson Dorr won a place in both conventions. He had remained aloof from the Suffrage movement during its earlier stages, waiting to see whether the nonfreemen and freemen of the state actually supported it. When requested by the association to address the Newport rally in May, Dorr agreed, "Should I be in Newport on that day." However, his letter of response contained assurances of his individual support for the movement. "I trust that the time is not far distant when every American citizen, having his residence in this State, shall exercise an equal power in its political affairs, under protection of a Constitution proceeding directly from the whole people."[29] Dorr thought it not only the "Right," but also the "Duty," of the majority of Rhode Islanders to reform their government making it more representative and thus more responsive to popular needs and interests. In good Jeffersonian terms, he stated the principles that had guided his political behavior since his earliest involvement in politics during the 1830s.

Mature reflection, pressure from friends, and concern for

proper principles moved Dorr to accept election to both conventions in August. Unquestionably he viewed the People's Convention as the most important development in Rhode Island history since the Revolution. His brother had warned of the consequences if competent leaders failed to take control of the movement. John L. O'Sullivan, an old friend in New York, berated Dorr and other leading Rhode Island Democrats for remaining aloof from the "little Revolution" sweeping the state.[30] These pressures, his devotion to Jeffersonian principles, and the increasing evidence that the people had finally decided to remove "the *foot*" from their necks convinced Dorr of his obligation to step forward.[31] Without doubt, the decision rested on an inextricable combination of interest, ideology, and ambition.[32]

Suffragists discovered during the elections that not even they could escape the contrariness and prejudices of men and follow the dictates of pure principle. Moderators in Providence's Fifth Ward turned away a Negro who tried to vote for delegates to the People's Convention. The ward clerk resigned in protest, and another had to be appointed on the spot. The Suffragists never discovered a solution to the race problem. Until August 1841 the movement condemned all distinctions among citizens based on property, color, or creed. The incident in the Fifth Ward forced a test, and the leadership fumbled in the effort to meet the challenge. Some tried to gloss over the entire affair by arguing that suffrage qualifications must be left to the discretion of the convention and the people. As they said, any attempt at full-scale reform before the convention assembled presented greater problems than those already existing. Others warned that an abandonment of the blacks in Rhode Island would expose the reform movement to the same criticisms its adherents used against the charter government. As it turned out, both proponents of absolute equality and the opponents of any change exploited the Suffragist inconsistency during the remainder of the campaign.[33] The reformers lost valuable support because they failed to stand firmly against prejudice of any

kind. At the same time, they retained adherents who shared the
common American belief in black inferiority.

During the campaign and after the election, the Suffragists
had also to turn aside the barbs of a "Sheep in Wolf's Clothing,"
as Congdon identified Professor William G. Goddard of Brown
University. Pretending to be a Suffragist, Goddard published a
series of letters under the pseudonym of "Town Born." He
disingenuously asked why Providence should not dominate the
state politically as it did in population and economic development.[34] He intended to stir up sectional differences, thereby
isolating the reformers in Providence. He exulted in the emergence of a new political alliance controlling the state, with
capitalist-financiers and their industrial minions displacing the
old coalition of landowners and traders. Goddard's barbs, along
with others of a similar thrust, forced a cautious conservatism
on the Suffragists. Now that a People's Convention had been
sanctioned, Suffrage leaders refrained from any more agitation
than necessary to counter the charges of the opposition. The
new line of argument stressed the need for a coalition of small
farmers and workingmen. To a certain extent, the Suffragist
tactics succeeded.

In October the People's Convention drafted a constitution in
five days and four evenings.[35] Racism provided the only
troublesome issue, and here the delegates compromised. The
constitution provided that nonvoters were exempt from taxation and militia duty. All adult white male Americans who had
lived one year in the state and six months in the town of
present residence would have the right to vote.[36] Frederick
Douglass, the abolitionist ex-slave, described the People's Constitution as "narrow and prescriptive" because it restricted "to a
class of citizens a right which ought to be enjoyed by all
citizens."[37] Caught between the extremes of abolitionism and
nativism, the Suffragists searched in vain for a reasonable solution. They alienated people on both extremes, but finally would
leave the entire issue to the voters. Under the dictates of
popular sovereignty, they found no other choice.

On most problems, however, the People's Convention split rather evenly to follow the lead of either Dorr or Dutee J. Pearce, both Democrats. Dorr, the Jeffersonian idealist, lost almost every encounter to Pearce, the pragmatic realist. Apparently the delegates preferred to attempt the possible rather than to seek abstract truth and adhere blindly to principle. Thus, for example, over Dorr's objections the convention included a clause allowing the legislature to suspend the privilege of the writ of habeas corpus during emergencies. Pearce argued that this power might be necessary to protect social well-being. Again, despite the promptings of Dorr, the constitution said nothing about debtor imprisonment, leaving the legislature free to continue it or discard it, as Pearce advised. However, the independence of the judiciary won the support of an overwhelming majority, as did abolition of the legislature's traditional equity jurisdiction.

The most revealing debate turned on the question of reapportionment. The Suffragist leaders had argued from the outset that ratios fixed by the charter violated proper constitutional principles. In convention, however, they merely revised the ratios and left them permanently set in the People's Constitution. On one occasion the horse-trading nearly got out of hand, as delegates from small towns tried to guard against political domination by Providence. In the end, the convention prescribed a lower house of eighty members distributed among the towns, and a senate of one member from each of the twelve senate districts. Suffrage theorists explained that reapportionment would be no problem in the future, since the People's Constitution provided for its own amendment by simple majority vote of the citizenry. Nonetheless, the departure from the broad principles of human rights asserted by the reformers was apparent. Those principles seemed too vague when the details of practical reform had to be settled.

Before the convention finished its work, a debate over the qualification of voters on fiscal questions revealed the moderation of the majority. Not all citizens, it turned out, would vote on all questions. Only those possessed of personal or real property valued at $150 could vote on fiscal matters. After that resolution the convention decided, with only one negative vote, to submit the constitution to the people without seeking the approval of the General Assembly.[38] For once in full agreement with Pearce, Dorr argued that the convention had formulated a constitution on the basis of positive right. In his view it was absurd to request approval of the process at this point. Similarly Pearce believed that the assembly would simply ignore the People's Convention. The convention accepted the Dorr-Pearce arguments and adjourned until November to allow the people to discuss the constitution and make suggestions for change before ratification. Undoubtedly the Suffragists wanted to elicit some indication of popular sentiment. But the primary goal of an adjournment was to allow to the forthcoming Freeholders' Convention an opportunity to ratify a fait accompli. Peaceable resolution of the Rhode Island controversy remaind a possibility if the charter government and its supporters accepted the legitimacy of the changes incorporated in the People's Constitution. The Suffragists, rhetorical disclaimers aside, could still accept a constitution emanating from the legal convention without sacrificing principle if their demands were satisfied. The movement for reform had not yet lost its pragmatic character. Much depended on the actions of the Freeholders' Convention in November.

Suffragist energy and dispatch resulted in a proposed constitution that even critics admitted was an improvement over the charter. But what mattered was not the quality of the Suffragist achievement. The manner and legitimacy of their proceedings claimed the attention of observers inside and outside the state. Henry C. Dorr, the younger brother of the Suffragist leader, thought the process of reform far too one-sided. He warned his older brother to proceed with caution in the Freeholders' Convention, allowing conservatives to moderate the excessive liberality of the People's Constitution, so as not to "frighten them

from such ... concessions as they might otherwise ...
make."³⁹ Henry Dorr believed that peaceable reform was possible, if only the Suffrage extremists would respect the feelings
and rights of the strong conservative element in the state.

Alexander Hill Everett of Massachusetts found the events in
Rhode Island a "curious and interesting experiment on the
practical working of our institutions." That the reformers had
been allowed to proceed without governmental suppression
proved that "the Sovereignty of the People is not with us, as it
has been in some other countries, a mere name, but a substantial, and practical reality." Everett's letter was written in response to a request from a committee of Suffragists headed by
Dorr. Copies of the proposed constitution had been sent to
prominent persons outside the state under a cover letter asking
the question, "In practice then, what is this right of ultimate
sovereignty in the People?"⁴⁰ Most followed the example of
John Quincy Adams rather than Everett's and refused to commit themselves.⁴¹ While the Suffragist search for national and
authoritative support combined concern about content of the
constitution and about legitimacy of procedure, the latter question had already been recognized as the crucial one.

With the state and national notoriety of Suffragist plans and
actions, the charter government could ill afford to ignore them
much longer. Congdon reported in late October that the "leading and heavy men of the State" wanted a sedition act to deal
with the escalating revolution.⁴² The proposal fell through,
however, because it would plainly aid rather than harm the
Suffragists by making martyrs of them. Since the repudiation of
Federalism in 1800, governmental suppression of free speech,
press, and assembly had been anathema, and political groups
resorting to such expedients usually suffered a fate reserved for
the descendants of Federalists.

More serious dangers threatened the prospects of Suffragist
success. The charter government considered an appeal to the
federal government for aid if the Suffragists became too powerful. The second section of Article IV, Section 4 committed the

United States to aid the states on request to suppress domestic violence.[43] Awakened by this possibility to the double-edged nature of federal intervention, many Suffragists lost their enthusiasm for outside assistance. Congdon tried to minimize the threat involved. As he reasoned, "If first attacked by a minority, we will venture a yankee guess that a Rhode Island majority will not be put down . . . —no, not by all [the] military force of the Union."[44] Congdon's vehemence undoubtedly reflected his awareness that the Suffragists themselves had originally suggested an appeal to a higher authority to resolve the Rhode Island dispute. With both sides arguing that Congress had some power to settle the controversy, the national implications of reform in Rhode Island were becoming obvious. If compromise failed, it seemed clear by late 1841 that local considerations would give way before the national interest in peace, good order, and proper principles of constitutional government. How much would remain of local autonomy was still in question.

When the Freeholders' Convention met in early November, all hopes for compromise dissipated.[45] The committee on suffrage, composed of two Whigs and five Democrats, urged retention of the qualifications based on land and primogeniture and proposed new restrictions on naturalized citizens. In addition to owning a freehold, naturalized citizens would have to prove three years' residence in the state after the date of naturalization. Also, every naturalized citizen wishing to vote would have to present a special certificate issued by the General Assembly qualifying him. Dorr's opposition to these suggestions raised no more than a ripple in the smooth calm of the convention. Only one or two delegates supported his demand for equal rights. If left to the Freeholders' Convention, reform was most unlikely.

Congdon filled the pages of the *New Age* with invidious comparisons between the Freeholders' and People's conventions. The former refused to authorize a secret ballot, with its desired protection against fraud and intimidation. The Freeholder delegates redrafted the proposed declaration of rights to eliminate references to the equality of all men and to popular sovereignty. They did, however, accept an amendment to the suffrage clause enfranchising those men who owned personal property valued at $500 or more. In addition, they approved a clause allowing the state legislature to suspend the writ of habeas corpus. But they refused to enfranchise black citizens and rejected a proposal to allow every freeholder's son who had resided in the state twenty-one years to vote. In one respect, the Freeholders' Convention achieved more than the People's. The state was reapportioned according to population, and the General Assembly was charged to reapportion periodically as the censuses revealed demographic change. In all other respects, maintenance of existing arrangements and institutions characterized the proposed Freeholders' Constitution. After two weeks of tampering to this end, the Freeholders' Convention adjourned until February 1842 to allow the freemen to judge what had been done. Offering an apt commentary on the proceedings, Congdon described them as a repetition of the events of 1834-1835. The freemen and the leaders in the General Assembly intended to "pacify . . . the people" by doing as little as possible. Clearly all hope for reform depended on the people themselves.[46]

Armed with this conclusion, the People's Convention reassembled in mid-November and put the finishing touches on the People's Constitution. The only major change referred the race problem to the people. In the first election under the constitution, voters would be asked whether the Caucasian qualification should be dropped, along with the clause exempting nonvoters from taxes and militia duty.[47] That done, the convention resolved to submit the constitution to the electorate in a special election to be held from 27 December 1841 through 1 January 1842. During the first three days citizens able to attend would cast their ballots in town meetings; the last three days were set aside to allow election moderators to go about collecting the ballots of those persons unable because of sickness or other reasons to appear in town meetings.[48] The Suffragists defended this departure from standard procedure in elections as the only means to insure that all qualified persons participated in the process of establishing a government. They argued that they had merely reinstituted the proxy system used during the colonial period, but actually they innovated, since the proxy system had allowed freemen to vote in town meetings rather than journey to Newport for that purpose. Relying on ingenuity and mis-representation, the Suffragists nonetheless stressed the importance of including as many citizens as possible.[49]

Before adjourning until January, when the votes would be counted and verified, the convention called on Dorr to deliver the closing oration. Already the leading figure in the reform movement despite his belated association with it, Dorr seized this occasion to set forth a proper theoretical foundation.[50] He based his theory on a review of the constitutional history of the state and nation. The fundamental doctrines of American constitutionalism were popular sovereignty and peaceable revolution. Under these principles, popular majorities in the territories, states, and nation could change their governments at will. Governments remained in existence only so long as the people allowed them to stand. Since the people of Rhode Island had never changed the charter, it still provided for "a government of laws." Thus Dorr denied the earlier Suffragist claims that Rhode Island had no de jure government, while simultaneously asserting the right of the people to control government. He intended in this way to refute the charges of violent revolution hurled at the Suffragists. He carefully noted that the People's Constitution did not contemplate anarchy. It contained a provision recognizing the charter as the basis for government if the people rejected the proposed constitution.

Having corrected one misconception, Dorr turned to another. The Suffragists had relied vaguely on the republican guarantee clause of the federal Constitution to sustain their demands. They had discussed an appeal to Congress or the Supreme Court as the ultimate means to assure reform. Dorr rejected this reasoning. A state constitution subsisted only so long as the people of the state supported it. When the people transferred

their support to another constitution, the new regime automatically became the de jure and de facto government of the
state. The only conditions for change were majority approval
and satisfaction of the requirement of republican form. Dorr's
analysis allowed him to deny that either the reformers or their
opponents could legitimately appeal to Congress or the
Supreme Court to settle the controversy over government. The
issue was one that "the people are competent to settle in their
own way, and upon their own grou[n]d." The only authority
Congress or the Supreme Court possessed under Article IV,
Section 4 was to assure a republican form and to aid the states
on request against domestic or foreign violence. Since both the
charter and the People's Constitution satisfied the former, and
since the Suffragists contemplated only political action, no
grounds for federal intervention existed. What mattered was
popular opinion. "If the people give us a majority, we shall
conclude the freeholders; if the freeholders do the same, they
will conclude themselves." In any case, the outcome must be
decided within the state or not at all.

With electrifying clarity Dorr illuminated the theoretical implications of an exercise of popular sovereignty and peaceable
revolution. Yet areas of ambiguity remained. His denial of the
authority of the federal government to intervene stopped short
of abjuring all federal power over such matters. Rather the
federal government must respect the decisions of local majorities, and, of course, national authorities might have to determine which of competing groups actually enjoyed majority
support. Dorr obviously held that numbers alone would decide
the issue. In addition, he assumed far too superficially that a
demonstration of majority support would quell the objections
of rival groups equally bent on controlling the state. By placing
the contest on such a level, he hoped to avoid the problem of
potential violence. By ignoring the intransigence of the General
Assembly and some Rhode Island freemen, the Suffragists
might win by default. On the other hand, Dorr suggested that if
the charter government resisted reform, the people would rise in

defense. In that event, domestic violence was inevitable. No one could predict how the federal government would react. Dorr failed to account for all possibilities in his November speech.

Dorr's theory, like that of Suffragist spokesmen from the outset, focused on current needs and left potential problems unexplored. He, like the others, was so deeply swayed by the necessity and promise of majority support that he never asked what would happen if the minority refused to accept the decision of the majority and had the physical might to prevail. Equating political with physical support, Dorr unwittingly laid his claims of moral and legal rights on a foundation requiring forcible assertion. Since he ruled out Congressional or judicial intervention, he exposed the reform movement to all the hazards of forcible suppression if the Rhode Island majority failed to back ballots with bullets.

For a time, however, Dorr's speech provided a sense of well-being to the members of the Suffrage Association and their friends elsewhere. Changes in the tone, mood, rhetoric, theory, and strategy of the movement were remarkable and signaled the emergence of a more radical leadership. Spokesmen of the movement never again questioned the legitimacy of the charter government, although they continued to castigate its unaccept-able nature. Many Suffragists followed Dorr in disapproving the old idea of an appeal to the federal government, although a serious split developed over this point. "Old Lights" under the leadership of Pearce of Newport and Burrington Anthony and William H. Smith of Providence challenged Dorr's views and urged an immediate appeal to Congress or the Supreme Court to vindicate the People's claims.[51] But the radicals held sway for nearly six months, rejecting compromises and asserting the right of majorities to do as they would with government.

In December the paeans to the spirit of 1776 gave way to analogies to the events of 1787-1788 when the federal Constitution was adopted. The new Suffrage arguments most often asserted that if a majority ratified the People's Constitution, it must go into effect. Before Dorr spoke on 18 November a few had said that resistance by the charter government would constitute violent revolution; thereafter agreement came from all sides. Suffragists looked intently to the future, hardly able to restrain their eagerness to erect the new government. Should the charter supporters dare to resist, the mass of the people would rise majestically and sustain the right to choose. Most Suffragists preferred not to think about possible governmental resistance, so completely had they convinced themselves that it would never occur.[52] Dorr's pleasant prediction that the new government would sustain itself by some inherent moral force swept away all doubts. He believed that a people lacking the determination and will to sustain their own acts could never be free, but he omitted any direct reference to this corollary of the doctrines of peaceable revolution and popular sovereignty. Suffragists in general found it convenient to follow his example.

Euphoria heightened after the disclosure of the results of the election in early January. The Suffragists kept careful records showing an overwhelming vote in favor of the People's Constitution. Nearly 14,000 Rhode Islanders marked affirmative ballots, while only 52 opposed and 9,146 abstained.[53] Based on accepted census tabulations, the Suffragists won an absolute majority of 2,372 out of a potential 23,142 votes. It is significant that a majority of the freemen approved the new instrument of government. If the tally was reasonably accurate, the reformers had scored a major victory. Although subjected to challenge, the election results were unshakable. Even the opposition admitted that a majority of Rhode Islanders had for the first time in history voted to discard the charter and to modernize the state's institutions. Subsequent disputes centered around the meaning of the election, not the accuracy of the vote totals. Suffragists, of course, insisted that the mandate was clear.

In mid-January, the People's Convention reassembled and proclaimed that the People's Constitution "ought to be, and *is*, the paramount law and Constitution of Rhode Island and Providence Plantations."[54] The delegates bound themselves "in behalf of the People whom we represent" to "establish . . . sustain and defend" a new government "by all necessary means." They specifically denied the opposition claim that the huge vote in favor of the constitution had merely tested public opinion on the question of reform. Instead they held that a new constitutional foundation had been laid by the popular mandate, and they intended to respect it.[55] In the context of heightening tensions and Suffragist determination, resistance by the charter government augured civil war. Of course, the resolutions adopted in convention reflected only the attitudes of the delegates. Whether the people for whom they purported to speak shared those attitudes remained to be seen. Dorr and his colleagues never doubted their support. Having won the political majority, they assumed physical preponderance. Thus the stage was set for a confrontation, although the outcome was far from certain because of the unknown reaction of the people.

If the achievements of the Suffragists were legitimized, then indeed the theory of popular sovereignty and peaceable revolution would receive overt recognition. Years later, Congdon described what occurred in Rhode Island in January 1842: "There was no pretense of legality, in the ordinary sense of the word, in their doings. It was simply revolution."[56] But to label the Suffragist activities as "simply revolution" assumes far too much clarity for the idea of revolution. Americans defined that term in various ways. Some referred to the great moral right of redressing grievances through violence because of the absence of any other means of relief. Others, sometimes the same men on different occasions, thought in terms of the inalienable right of political majorities to change government when it failed to satisfy current needs and aspirations.[57] If the Suffragists perpetrated a revolution in January, it was surely of the latter variety. In one sense, it hardly amounted to a revolution. It partook more of the nature of a restoration, in that it established the conditions necessary to the exercise of natural rights by the majority of American citizens in Rhode Island. But the sequel would demonstrate whether Americans actually believed in peaceable revolution.

The Suffragists had acted in accordance with the theory that people could alter government at will by a simple majority vote. They held that American constitutionalism sanctioned that theory, and that it rendered American government unique among the political systems of the world. They argued further that force had nothing to do with the process of change. Only the registered will of the people mattered. Once the People's Constitution was ratified and proclaimed, they had to take the next step and erect a new government. That they discovered a need for force resulted equally from the actions and attitudes of Rhode Islanders in general, of the charter government and its supporters, and of the federal authorities in Washington. Their discovery led to new thought about American ideals and eventually to the clarification of key ideas in the American political tradition.

Be certain of your ground, Dorr's brother advised him in early January. "Your friends have engaged in a most serious undertaking. They have ... taken a position which they may be obliged to maintain by force, and it behooves them to be assured that they are well founded in principle." Because of the issues involved, he predicted that "the matter must be ultimately decided by the citizens of other States."[58] Since the federal Constitution covered the situation, resistance by the charter government would involve Congress and surely lead to the suppression of the reformers. This analysis, remarkable for its insight, proved well founded as the reform movement gained momentum. Suffragists and their friends understood the cogency of the younger Dorr's argument, but had little choice except to press forward.

Fellow travelers in the General Assembly made one final effort in January to settle the differences between the charter government and the Suffragists. On 11 January 1842, Representative Samuel Atwell introduced a bill to repeal all regular election laws and abolish the Freeholders' Convention.[59] The bill was designed to legitimize the People's Constitution. The assembly refused to consider it until a special committee charged to investigate Suffragist activities reported. When his proposal came up for consideration on 21 January, Atwell defended it with the argument that "the people of this State choose to exert their own sovereignty,—which here is not rebellion, but a proper and lawful act."[60] He cited the events in Michigan in 1835-1836 and Congressional acceptance of the legitimacy of Michigan's popularly established constitution in 1837 as proof for his assertion.[61] But his remarks made no impression on the majority, and his bill failed by a vote of 57 to 11.[62] While the assembly had not taken any suppressive steps as yet, the rejection of the Atwell bill revealed an intention to insist on formal and legal niceties as the price for reform.

Atwell's speech in the assembly stated concisely the position espoused by the Suffragists. Almost simultaneously Dorr's brother Henry put the opposing view succinctly in a letter to Dorr and the Suffrage Association. "The spirit of our institutions . . . requires that the people . . . do everything by deputy— that they should not assume to themselves the administration of affairs." American law "left very little for the people to do, in their original capacity. Having elected their officers, their work is done." The younger Dorr believed that American government rested on the theory of divested sovereignty. He predicted that Rhode Islanders would refuse to stand against "constituted authority." In the event that the Suffragists persisted, they "would be like the Chartists of England with a few leaders, and those not the right men to head such an enterprise—& no people—on which you can depend—to support you, at all risks."[63] No one would fight for an abstract principle when the substance of reform could be had simply by conforming to the requirements of legal process.

Reiterating the points made by Henry Dorr, an anonymous memorialist urged the General Assembly to take action to defend the state in late January. It was at best an open secret that the memorialist was Federal District Judge John Pitman, an old Whig who had sponsored a bill before the General Assembly as early as 1811 to drop the property qualification for voting.[64] Pitman realized that the freehold qualification must go, but insisted that the reforms be legal. He warned the General Assembly that "no government can sanction doctrines which are suicidal, which go to its own destruction." The proper relationship between government and citizenry was one of protection and obedience. If the government failed to fulfill "its duties to the citizen," it committed "treason" as surely as the citizen who "wages war against the government." Since 1776, the General Assembly under the charter had legislated for the people of Rhode Island. In numerous ways the people of the state had refused to cast aside the charter for a modern instrument of government. "Who have a right to say . . . [the constitution and laws] shall be changed, when the people say they shall not?"[65] Pitman denied that one group within the population had the legal right to supersede the General Assembly's authority to govern the state.

Pitman also criticized the Suffragists' loose definition of the "people" of Rhode Island. "In a political sense, in which the word . . . is used by political writers, it is . . . applicable only, in a free State, to those who . . . possess the political power."[66] In Rhode Island, that meant the freemen. Using the word as Suffragists did implied that all residents of the state, American citizens or not, competent, independent, and mature, or incompetent, dependent, and licentious, could participate in the governmental process. Yet Suffragists admitted that some residents had no right to vote; they agreed that some restrictions were necessary. Where could a line be drawn? Pitman found little reason to leave this serious matter to the discretion of uneducated and emotional youths, knaves, and foreigners.

He found similar objections to the Suffragist insistence on equal rights and majority rule. The Suffragists seemed unaware that the two ideas were contradictory. Majorities respected no rights other than their own. Because of the universal tendency of majorities to aggrandize themselves at the expense of minorities, constitutions had been developed to control political behavior by defining the qualifications for suffrage and imposing limits on majority rule. Thus constitutions "should not be amendable by a bare majority of the people," or their very purpose would be subverted.[67] Only by maintaining proper forms and respecting the terms of the constitution could majority rule be accommodated with the equal rights of all.

Pitman, much as the Dorrs, placed his analysis within a larger frame of reference. He agreed with Henry C. Dorr that American constitutionalism rested on the theory of divested sovereignty. But he leaned toward Thomas Wilson Dorr's insistence on state rights and prerogatives within the federal system. He denied that American citizenship conferred any special rights or status in Rhode Island. If it did, then the people of Rhode Island had no authority to decide for themselves how to structure their political institutions. "This is, indeed, consolidation! Where then, are State rights?" Pitman agreed with the elder Dorr that the suffrage qualifications, as all other constitutional questions except the requirement of republican form, had to be settled within the state: "It belongs not to Congress, nor to the Supreme Court of the United States."[68] Only the courageous actions of the level-headed majority of Rhode Islanders and their representatives in the General Assembly could save the state from revolution and chaos. Judge Pitman cautioned against either permissiveness or reactionary obstruction. Obviously what he wanted was energetic government fulfilling its obligation to satisfy the needs of the citizenry. That he tended to emphasize the rule of law as command was evidence of the heightening tensions in Rhode Island.

Pitman and the younger Dorr articulated a counter-theory that had nearly as much historical authenticity as that asserted by Dorr and the Suffragists. Since 1787 Americans had disagreed about whether the Constitution established majority rule or minority rights. In terms of political experience, the framers undoubtedly meant to maintain a balance between the two, a balance conceptualized in the idea of ordered liberty under the rule of law. But from the time that Jeffersonians battled

Federalists over where the accent should lie, on liberty or on order, Americans had fought over this question. In the context of the rising ideological dispute in Rhode Island, Henry Dorr and John Pitman stood firmly on the need for authority and order within any polity. Thomas Wilson Dorr and the Suffragists argued that order was not possible without liberty, and that liberty was possible only if the people controlled their governments. Henry Dorr and John Pitman, speaking for the charter supporters, saw in the Suffragist reliance on the doctrines of popular sovereignty and peaceable revolution a direct threat to social and political stability within the state and the nation. On the other side, Suffragists perceived tyranny behind the governmental insistence on adherence to proper forms. The ideological differences could not be compromised, and violence threatened to engulf the state. Whatever the outcome, differing groups would regret the creation of a precedent of violence that might subvert the entire American experiment in free government.

Suffragist radicalism in Rhode Island drew the fire of conservatives across the nation, not just those within the state. The Rhode Island incident seemed the last and most dangerous in a series of political disturbances increasing in frequency and violence after 1830. As such, it appeared as the logical result of a trend pregnant with evil for the American experiment. Prophecies of chaos, murder, and rapine proliferated as the reform movement escalated in rhythm and intensity. Charter supporters glimpsed vast conspiracies at work beneath the surface of events. Ironically, most Suffragists thought only of affirming the fundamental premise of American constitutionalism, the right of the people to change government at will. Their rhetoric and recommendations sounded more reactionary than revolutionary. Rather than innovation, they postulated a reinvigoration of old ideals. They had no intention of subverting the American way or American constitutionalism; in fact, they gloried in both. Yet they came to represent to many Americans a direct challenge to all that had been accomplished during the years since the Revolution.

PEACEABLE REVOLUTION

A gentle, a peaceful, a voluntary
and a deliberate transition from one
Constitution of government to another.

Indignation and fear marked the debates in the General Assembly through the winter and spring of 1842. Yet the majority realized that the massive vote in favor of the People's Constitution demanded respect for the reform sentiment within the state; to ignore it might bring on the violent revolution foreseen by Samuel Atwell. In late January the assembly accepted Atwell's amendment to the legislation calling the Freeholders' Convention. The amendment authorized all persons enfranchised by any constitution proposed by the Freeholders' Convention to vote on the question of ratification.[1] The assembly hoped to prove to the people that reform was no longer in doubt and to indicate to the delegates in the Freeholders' Convention that the charter and the landed franchise must go. By accepting the will of the people, the charter government could direct the process of change and insure its legitimacy.

By early 1842 it appeared that the reformers had won the battle to move Rhode Island into the modern age. If controversy erupted now, the stakes would be very different. A reasonable man might well have concluded that the end was in sight. Surely the Suffragists would accept the substance of reform offered belatedly by the established government rather than stand on abstract principles. Having convinced the public and government of the legitimacy of their demands, the Suffragists in all likelihood would submit to the rules of organized

society and accept the authority of the government to oversee
the reform process. After all, since the adoption of the Constitution in 1787-1788, this pattern had repeated itself endlessly
in American constitutional development. Reform agitators had
launched crusades to secure recognition of just demands. After
convincing the people and the government of the practical
wisdom of satisfying the complaints, the reformers had always
moderated their rhetoric and actions and had cooperated with
reasonable men to make the changes necessary for a good
society and social harmony.[2] American reform had been pragmatic, piecemeal, and peaceable, as much from the acquiescence
of government as from the attitudes of successive waves of
reformers. Who would expect men interested in reform to
become the agents of its obstruction?

But Suffragists, particularly the leaders, were not average
men. More than any of their contemporaries or their intellectual
ancestors, the Suffragist leaders were ideologues. Rather than
accept the government's pledges of reform, they stood on the
belief that American majorities could do as they willed with
government. Since the people had already ratified the People's
Constitution, no acts of the repudiated charter government had
any bearing on what must be done. To stop after the people had
registered their will and meekly supplicate the old government
for confirmation of acts done by the people themselves violated
the fundamental principle of popular sovereignty. The Suffragist leaders viewed the situation in early 1842 and discerned
disturbing implications in any compromise with the charter
government. That government, "having inclined but not bowed,
in granting the inevitable emancipation as an act not of justice
but grace, . . . sought to maintain its absolutist principle by
conceding reform without accepting anything like democratic
authority."[3] Convinced of this conclusion, the Suffragist
leaders preferred defeat to surrender.

Suffragist obstinacy convinced the charter authorities and
their supporters that Suffragism was merely another term for
anarchy. If the reformers prevailed in their absurd resistance,

Rhode Island would be condemned to endless squabbles as group after group pushed their demands by claiming to represent the people. The very existence of government was at issue. Without respect for constituted authority, government would not rest on the rule of law to assure ordered liberty. Instead the will of the strongest would prevail. By February 1842 the practical reform movement in Rhode Island had metamorphosed into an ideological crusade with the defenders of two conflicting theories of American constitutionalism locked in combat. Institutional formalism and political majoritarianism had finally come to direct confrontation in the United States.

Conclusive evidence that reform had ceased to be the cause of conflict in Rhode Island appeared in the proceedings of the Freeholders' Convention in early February. Rejecting Dorr's motion to adopt the People's Constitution, the convention nonetheless used it as a model for change. In fact, the final Freeholders' Constitution resembled the People's in liberal tone and provision. The only major differences between the two instruments offset each other. The Freeholders' Constitution established a flexible apportionment system based on decennial censuses; it extended the franchise, but discriminated against naturalized American citizens by incorporating the restrictions suggested in November; and it banned slavery from Rhode Island, but failed to make any provision for the trial by jury of alleged fugitive slaves. On the other hand, the People's Constitution perpetuated the recognized anachronism of constitutionally prescribed apportionment ratios, guaranteed the suffrage on liberal terms to native and naturalized citizens alike, said nothing at all about the institution of slavery, and granted trial by jury to those accused of being fugitive slaves.[4] In other respects, the two constitutions were so similar that acceptance of one as opposed to the other seemed of little moment.

Yet the Suffragists mounted an intensive campaign against the ratification of the Freeholders' Constitution.[5] They argued that the discrimination against naturalized citizens and the vague provisions concerning public access to the clam beds, fisheries, and other natural resources of the state rendered the constitution unacceptable. Undoubtedly Suffragists were sincere in both objections; but the vehemence and pointedness of their opposition must be explained on other grounds, for the Freeholders' Constitution amounted to a virtual surrender. Under its terms, amendments to fulfill the Suffrage program could be carried with ease. In some areas, notably reapportionment, the government men had accomplished much more than the reformers themselves could boast. Unquestionably the Suffragist response was dictated by ideological imperatives.

Having won the battle, with the war in the balance, the Suffragists refused to compromise either "principle or conscience." Both required that they stand resolutely behind the People's Constitution as the concrete expression of the popular will.[6] A mandate had been given; it must be enforced. There was no reason to accept the government's belated offering and every reason to reject it. If the people accepted the Freeholders' Constitution, then change would come from above, bestowed by an omnipotent though benevolent government. The authentic act of the people in the ratification of the People's Constitution would have been in vain. That the people would ratify the Freeholders' Constitution, just as they had the People's, assured its legitimacy, but the act of doing so would subvert the principles of republicanism. Popular sovereignty and peaceable revolution would be exposed as little more than trifling political aphorisms, with no practical significance aside from their propaganda value. When they considered the effort since November 1840 and the responsibility they had to protect the revolutionary heritage of all Americans, the Suffragists actually believed they had no choice. Either the people or the government possessed the sovereignty. Responsible Americans abhorred the second possibility, and the Suffragists stood as defenders of the faith.

When the Suffragists insisted that the People's Constitution was the law of the state, what had been a reform movement in

1840 changed into an ideological crusade. Predictably, many who had been warm and vigorous supporters turned away in disgust. Men like Martin Stoddard and Jacob Frieze, both Democrats and Suffragists from the outset, repudiated the association because they believed that reform, not ideological consistency, was the objective.[7] Other men left for reasons not so commendable. William Sprague, a former governor and a Democratic fellow traveler, had been among the most influential sympathizers until early 1842. In February, even before the Freeholders' Convention completed its labors and provided the assurances of reform, Sprague traded his support for the Freeholders' Constitution for election by the General Assembly to the United States Senate. Abraham Payne insisted that the machinations of men like Sprague ultimately split the Democratic party, produced a new alignment of men and parties with the emergence of a Law and Order coalition, and led directly to the rapid decline of the Suffragists from an absolute majority to a mere plurality.[8] Samuel Atwell had also wanted the Senate seat. Sprague won the contest only by cooperating with his former political enemies, abandoning the rump Democrats grouped around Atwell, Dorr, and Thomas F. Carpenter. Payne argued that if Atwell had won, the Democratic-Suffrage alliance would have held firm and guaranteed the success of the struggle to establish the People's Constitution. As it was, however, Sprague's acceptance of a political deal insured that the "same class of men who controlled the State [before 1842] have continued to guide its policy from that hour to this."[9]

Political machination and massive disgust at patent foolishness both played a role in the ultimate defeat of the Suffragists. One scholar holds that the Suffragists were too radical for their "genteel" and agrarian sympathizers, and too conservative for the potential "plebeian" and urban mass of supporters.[10] Thus a firm coalition never developed, and defeat was inevitable from the outset because of the anachronistic political ideology of the Suffragist leaders.[11] To win, the Suffragists needed to promise more than enfranchisement and political equality. But they waged their entire campaign on that basis, refusing to condone class or interest-group politics. If anything, this modern critique of the Suffragists merely reinforces the conclusion that their movement must be explained as an ideological crusade to vindicate a theory of American constitutionalism. Its very failure enhances its importance as the last stand of an older philosophy of government against the practices of modern politics.

At the height of the struggle over the Freeholders' Constitution, the judges of the Rhode Island Supreme Judicial Court issued a public letter castigating the Suffrage movement for proceeding "without law." The letter warned that efforts to erect a government under the People's Constitution would "be treason against the State, if not against the United States."[12] Congdon responded to the charge with the admission that the Suffragists were acting without regard for positive law, but he denied that they disregarded all law. Actually they already had laid the basis for a new law, resting it on proper principles of right and justice. Accusations of treason against those who had the support of the majority of the people, the source of all law, were plainly absurd.[13]

Chief Judge Job Durfee held to his argument, however. All through March he traveled about the state delivering public lectures and charging grand juries in a prepared speech that sounded the alarm against anarchy. His remarks hardly varied from the thoughts developed earlier by Henry Dorr and John Pitman, although his prestige as chief of the high court added weight to his conclusions. In addition, he clarified certain points in dispute. He agreed basically with Henry Dorr that Congress had the authority to decide the issue in Rhode Island. Article IV, Section 2 of the Constitution, the territorial integrity clause, prescribed that "no new State shall be formed or erected within the jurisdiction of any other State, without the consent of the State legislature concerned, as well as of Congress."[14] Beginning with a literal and sophistical interpretation of that clause, Durfee insisted that any constitutional changes within a state required the approval both of Congress and of the existing state legislature. From that conclusion, he went on to deny the applicability of the so-called Michigan precedent suggested by Atwell and others in resolving the Rhode Island question. In 1837 Congress had merely waived the irregularities that occurred during the process of creating a state government. No state government had existed or its consent to the waiver would have been required. Once established, state governments could only be changed with their own and Congressional consent.

Durfee thought that any other approach raised theoretical difficulties impossible to overcome. Only "corporate" peoples had "the capacity to receive and exercise sovereignty," since "a Sovereign will" was by definition "a unit," having no "existence independent of law." Thus, to divide sovereignty was to "destroy it." The quickest and easiest way to achieve that result was "to pass . . . [sovereignty] to the unorganized mass" of the people. In few words, Durfee developed a theory of revolution that denied its occurrence among reasonable men. If only a corporate people could exercise sovereignty, and then only through the forms of law, clearly popular sovereignty and peaceable revolution were logical absurdities. Durfee's analysis reduced revolution to a change of government instituted by designated representatives exercising the divested sovereignty of the people. According to his view, Americans had not committed revolution in 1776, at least in the usual meaning given to the term. Instead they had acted in their corporate capacity through the means of law to change their government in certain respects. Durfee stated forthrightly the institutional theory of American constitutionalism, putting in sharp relief the points of difference from a political theory.[15] Having done so, he concluded with the assurance that rational people would rally to his view.

One Suffragist described Durfee's oration as a "floundering speech" denouncing Suffragism as "a lawless combination of a few . . . to put down the legitimate government."[16] The judge had ended with the admonition that "the State now offer[s]

you all you ask; and if you do not take it now you never can."
While they ridiculed the judge, Suffragists nonetheless caught
the implications of the warning. As one man remarked, "The
Tory party will do anything and everything they can do and will
attempt many things which they cannot sooner than recognize
the right of the people at large to make and alter their government at will."[17] From the towns visited by Durfee came
requests from Suffragists for references to authorities to refute
the judge's arguments. To answer the requests and to defuse the
dangerous potential of such a statement from a man of Durfee's
stature, Dorr arranged to publish a statement signed by nine
lawyers of high standing in the state who accepted the political
theory of the Suffragists. On 14 March the *Nine Lawyers'
Opinion* appeared in pamphlet form and was quickly distributed
throughout the state.[18] More than a mere refutation of Durfee,
Henry Dorr, and Pitman, the pamphlet incorporated a mature
statement of Suffragist constitutionalism.

The *Opinion* paralleled Dorr's speech of 18 November 1841
before the People's Convention, but the argument was smooth-
er, with an eye for detail and logical consistency. For the first
time since the contest began in 1840, Suffragist theorists held
that even if an existing constitution prescribed the mode and
means of its own amendment, the people retained the right and
authority to act at will. "By the Sovereign Power of a State we
understand that supreme and ultimate power, which prescribes
the form of government for the People of the State. By the
Republican theory of this country this power resides in the
People themselves." Talk of indivisible sovereignty and corporate capacities merely evaded the important considerations. To
change either the national or a state constitution, the people
had the inalienable right to "proceed in the mode and manner
they deem most proper." No one could deny the validity of this
principle, the basic premise of American constitutionalism.

As proof, the *Opinion* pointed out that "the [national]
Constitution was not made by virtue of any call or power from
the then existing Congress or General Government, but the

voluntary unauthorized act of the several States" under a mandate from the people. It really mattered little whether the
"General Government" was described as "the creature of the
States, or the People of the States." To hold one way inescap-
ably asserted the other, so close was the control of the people
over their state governments. In support of its contentions, the
Opinion quoted extensively from the letters and speeches of the
framers of the national Constitution. Judging by the thrust and
general character of the argument, and by the frequency of
quotation, James Wilson of Pennsylvania more than his contemporaries had anticipated the needs of later generations of Americans in the struggle to perfect democratic government. Stressing Wilson's formulations of proper theory in his speeches and
lectures of 1787-1792, the Suffragist lawyers asserted that
American constitutionalism had transformed revolution into
" 'a gentle, a peaceful, a voluntary and a deliberate transition
from one Constitution of government to another.' "[19]

Repeating Dorr's earlier precaution against viewing an appeal
to Congress or the Supreme Court as a panacea, the *Opinion*
exhorted Rhode Islanders to stand behind the constitution they
had adopted. This message could be taken in two different
ways. Either the people should arm themselves in preparation
for forcible defense of their handiwork, or they should ignore
the charter government's obstructionism and proceed with the
establishment of a proper republican government. Undoubtedly
people read the *Opinion* to suit their own pleasure. Dorr and
most other Suffragist theorists had not yet perceived the possible costs of ambiguity. No prominent spokesman made any
serious public effort to solve the difficulties caused by the
fallacy of asserting right in the context of might. Whether
events would have taken a different course had Dorr more
thoroughly comprehended the subtleties of James Wilson's
theory of peaceable revolution cannot be conclusively determined. However, his subsequent failure to clear away the confused fog obscuring the difference between a Lockean right of
revolution and the Wilsonian *right* of revolution certainly con-

tributed in large measure to the fiasco in the summer of 1842 that bears his name.

The vote in late March on the Freeholders' Constitution confirmed what had become increasingly clear since January. The Suffragists, allied incongruously with the few hidebound charter defenders, defeated the constitution by the narrow margin of 8,698 to 8,013. Only a strong showing in Providence County, where the Suffragist-Charterite alliance polled two-thirds of the vote, produced the numbers necessary to overcome the favorable response throughout the rest of the state.[20] The Suffragists had jeopardized reform because of considerations they deemed far more important. Of greater significance, however, in less than three months their support at the polls had declined by over 5,000. If the trend continued, the decision to defend the purity of principle would be their undoing. Although Suffragists refused an analysis based on such crude standards, events confirmed that judgment.

Immediately after the election, the General Assembly's select committee reported that partisanship had obstructed the effort to reform Rhode Island's government.[21] Atwell promptly introduced a resolution to submit the People's Constitution in a legal election for possible ratification. By 59 to 3, the assembly quashed this conciliatory effort, rejecting simultaneously a bill to extend the suffrage by a vote of 52 to 2.[22] One contemporary argued that enactment of either proposal would have solved the Rhode Island dilemma, but this was naive optimism.[23] Both the Suffragists and the charter government supporters insistently rejected any suggestion of compromise. Nothing augured a change of attitudes in April; if anything, the determination to prevail stiffened on each side.

On the same day the General Assembly adopted a new treason statute christened the Algerine Act by Congdon.[24] The act prescribed fine and imprisonment up to life for any one of multiple offenses involving an attempt to establish a putative constitution for the state. Specifically, the Algerine Act made it a treasonable offense to serve as candidate for office, officer of government, election judge, or town meeting moderator under a fraudulent constitution.[25] With this measure the charter government gave final warning that its authority must be respected on pain of prosecution for treason. At the same time, the government blocked any appeal by the Suffragists to Congress or the Supreme Court. Before that could occur, the Suffragists had to establish a government, complete with representation to claim the Rhode Island seats in Congress. Any attempt to do so exposed the challengers to state prosecution. The Suffragists found themselves nicely boxed in by the government's strategy.

Clearly some action by the charter government had become necessary to avoid default. Even with the Algerine Act on the books and with the increasing numbers of defections suffered by the Suffragists, People's candidates took the field and campaigned vigorously for office in the April elections. At the same time, men ran for office under the charter, and the competition for votes was high.[26] Dorr spent most of April trying to complete the list of candidates, but the problems increased as the government pressure intensified. After unsuccessfully sounding out the leading Democrats, he finally decided to run for governor himself.

In spite of frustrations, which he dismissed as temporary, Dorr allowed the euphoria of partial victories to blind him to the rough times ahead. Old Sullivan Dorr urged his son to reconsider and to withdraw from his candidacy for governor. He expressed great pain at the prospect of a son's engaging in "acts calculated to bring the State into contempt, arrouse [sic] passions which you cannot allay and (which God forbid) produce civil strife attended with bloodshed and murdering." Dorr rejected such entreaties. He thought the Suffragists "in fine spirits and ready to sustain their friends against all Algerine edicts, whether passed by the General Assembly or otherwise."[27] In fact, Dorr reasoned, the recent comical legislation actually benefited the cause by rousing the indignation of the people and bringing new votes to the side of right. Dorr doubted that "there will be more than a paper-war." The Algerine Act was "the last experiment on the People" by a repudiated government too cowed to do more than threaten that the act would "be enforced *by and by*. They meant it merely to frighten the common sorts of folks," he taunted. The Suffragists had merely to stand "firm and determined" to "succeed gloriously." Dorr's optimism blithely waved aside all unfavorable signs and warnings.

Suffragist complacency in the face of imminent peril stemmed from the same source as the ideological crusade itself. Not only had the charter government waited too long to offer the changes demanded, but it also delayed action against the Suffragists until few believed that anything could or would be done. Suffragists and many of their opponents shared the view that so long as the majority of the people supported the People's Constitution, the government dared risk nothing. That their alleged majority dropped to a plurality by early April did not disturb the Suffragists. They pointed out that the empty threats of the charter government were bound to confuse some people. However, once the People's Government took office in early May, the people would rally. Then the Algerines would be forced to accept what they could not prevent. From this per-spective, the Suffragists wanted nothing but the nerve to triumph.

At this critical juncture, before the elections were held, Gover-nor Samuel Ward King requested federal intervention, thus raising a local controversy into a national concern. Composed of two prominent Democrats, John Brown Francis and Elisha Reynolds Potter, and one influential Whig, John Whipple, the mission to Washington secured interviews with President John Tyler and leading members of Congress.[28] The three charter emissaries couched their requests in terms certain to arouse the well-known fears of southern men about the Suffragist insistence on the equal and natural rights of all men and the iron rule of majority will. A number of southerners, including President

John Tyler, immediately accepted the premise that locally determined laws must be strictly enforced "to prevent negroes [from] revolutionizing the south."[29] Having properly prepared the way, the supporters of the charter government intensified their pressure on President Tyler and southern congressmen to secure a federal guarantee and thus regain the upper hand in the struggle against the Suffragists who seemed to enjoy local majority support. Ironically, firm state rights Democrats such as John Tyler sanctioned this redressing of local political balances by calling to bear the power of the federal government.

Facing the possibility of presidential compliance with the charter government's request, the Suffragists dispatched Dr. Brown, the association president, to protect their interests.[30] Brown and the charter delegation subsequently returned to Rhode Island, each side convinced that it had succeeded in its mission.[31] But the charter government had the proof and published it in the *Providence Daily Journal* on 15 April, just days before the elections. Along with a proclamation warning the people against further involvement in Suffragist schemes, Governor King made public a private letter from President Tyler pledging federal military assistance in the event of hostilities. The president explained that he thought the need for troops unlikely but left no doubt that he would act with vigor to aid the charter government against the rebels. With this blank check as insurance, Governor King and the General Assembly had the freedom to act as they saw fit to protect established authority.[32] Local majorities, if indeed the Suffragists still enjoyed one, were meaningless when the power of the nation weighted the balance.

Actually Dorr had advance notice that President Tyler favored a peaceable resolution of the dispute but would support the charter government at all costs.[33] Dr. Brown's complacent reports that Tyler dared not intervene had obviously been supplanted by other and more reliable sources of information. To counter the government success in the appeal to President Tyler, Dorr wrote frantic letters to leading Democrats in Congress urging them to restrain the president from his reckless, despotic course.[34] A number of these men sent encouraging letters of sympathy for Dorr and the Suffragists.[35] Most cautioned the reformers that the president could not order troops to the state unless the Suffragists resorted to violence. Thus, the Democrats urged Dorr and his supporters on to victory only if the majority of Rhode Islanders stood firmly behind them. If, on the other hand, rumors that the people "are fleeing you" were true, wise and expedient men would not risk an attempt to assume the sovereignty of the state of Rhode Island.[36]

Senator Silas Wright, Jr., of New York, took considerable pains to check the radicalism of the Suffragist leaders. He politely but firmly repudiated Dorr's theory of peaceable revolution as an inalienable right. When an existing constitution prescribed the means of its own amendment, those seeking change must respect its prescriptions. Wright thought that Dorr's theory would unsettle all government within the nation, and he wanted nothing to do with it. In fact, although he responded to Dorr's appeals because of the demands of friendship, he wanted little to do with the Rhode Island incident or the Suffragists themselves. He instructed Dorr to "*burn* this and my former letters" to avoid any possible ill effects from even this long distance association. And by all means, he advised the Suffragist leader, since the president had yet to issue a military order, "if the people are not with you do not provoke it."[37]

Cautious and conservative advice characterized the letters Dorr received from the Democratic congressmen. These men understood that if the president decided to intervene, Congress could do little, even if the will existed. The president was the commander-in-chief, and the Enforcement Acts delegated to him the discretion to act on requests from states for assistance under the domestic violence clause of Article IV, Section 4.[38] All hope for the Suffragists lay in their ability to demonstrate absolute majority support within the state and in their claims to moral and legal right. Knowing all this, few congressmen encouraged Dorr toward an adventurous course.

Yet Dorr interpreted the letters in a very different way. His answering letters to Senators Levi Woodbury of New Hampshire and William Allen of Ohio revealed the ambiguity of his position and his tendency to misread the situation.[39] He correctly characterized Tyler's letter as asserting the argument that once government existed "the sovereignty is in the governors, and not in the governed." He meant by this that Tyler accepted the idea of divested sovereignty that Henry Dorr, John Pitman, Job Durfee, and the charter government adherents espoused. In addition, Dorr stated clearly the Suffragist claim that a majority of the people had the right and authority to alter government to "establish a Republican Constitution, in such manner, and at such time as they deem expedient." This was "the right of the People, even where an existing Constitution prescribes a particular mode of procedure for amending the Same." He held that force had nothing to do with the process of reform, unless the repudiated government attempted to resist. In that event, "the People will act on the defensive; but they will protect themselves, and maintain their Constitution, as they have a right, and are bound in honor to do."[40] From this conclusion he reasoned that Congress must and would support the people in their defensive effort. Never doubting his popular majority, he was oblivious to the warnings he received from Washington. He listened only to the assurances that he was right.

Letters from private persons expressing unqualified approval of the Suffragist activities reinforced Dorr's tendency to read what he wanted into the blandishments of the Democratic congressmen. Abolitionist Louis Lapham of Fall River, Massachusetts, promised Dorr three hundred armed men on short notice if the charter government in league with President Tyler declared war on the Suffragists.[41] Lapham's letter hardly merited the credibility of those from the Democratic congressmen, but Dorr used it and others like it as guides for the interpretation of the rest. He completely failed to understand the constraints on Congress. Rather than stating how Congress could restrain the president, he criticized the Democrats in

Congress for failing to act. He thought they were abandoning the Suffragists in Rhode Island because the state was small and thus politically unimportant as compared to New York, Ohio, Massachusetts, or Pennsylvania.[42] Instead of thinking constructively, he carped at the Congress and drew sustenance from private letters similar to Lapham's. By the time Senator Wright's blunt message arrived in late April, Dorr had concluded that Suffragist maneuvers in Rhode Island would force the Democrats to act at the national level.

Meanwhile some Suffragists tried to check the euphoric radicalism. They urged Dorr to sponsor a petition requesting an investigation of the Rhode Island controversy by the United States Senate. The petition should prove beyond cavil that the majority of the people had approved the People's Constitution and that the charter government was threatening civil war with the assistance of the president.[43] But Dorr rejected the proposal. Instead he relied on the private expressions of support that came in from outside the state. One New Yorker assured him that if "John Tyler attempt[ed] to carry into execution the threats contained in the letter to King," New Yorkers by the hundreds would "stand by you *and with you* if necessary."[44] Warned against a resort to violence, urged to maintain a position of moral strength in the face of governmental oppression, Dorr refused to be persuaded. He persisted in the belief that a political majority always had the physical power to prevail.

President Tyler's letter appeared in the press at an opportune moment. With the election at hand, it exerted a significant influence on the outcome.[45] To add to the impact, the *Providence Daily Journal* published on election day a letter purloined from the files of the Suffragist State Committee.[46] Although unsigned, the letter was probably written by Samuel Atwell. In it the author declined to accept election to any office under the People's Constitution and specifically warned the State Committee that an attempt to establish a People's Government would result in federal intervention and civil war. He proposed a truce between the opposing forces until a compromise could be negotiated. As he said, reform of the state's obsolescent government was far more important than a meaningless Armageddon in defense of the cause. But this fellow traveler had little influence in either camp.

The April elections showed a further decline in Suffragist support. Dorr polled 6,604 votes for governor, as compared to 4,781 for the incumbent Governor King, and 2,363 for ex-Governor Thomas F. Carpenter running as a reform candidate. Since Carpenter had urged the repeal of the Algerine Act and the legal ratification of the People's Constitution, Congdon argued that Suffragism had actually won a majority again.[47] Nonetheless, real differences separated Carpenter and his supporters, who voted only in the legal elections, from those who chose Dorr in the unauthorized elections under the People's Constitution. The other side could claim victory on the ground that a majority had voted in the legal elections. Moreover, even accepting Congdon's claim, 8,963 out of a potential 23,000 voters did not constitute a majority. Therefore observers outside the state doubted that the Suffragists would have any chance of victory if they tried to take over the state in May. Suffragists, of course, saw only the effects of governmental abuse in their reduced electoral count. All that would change once the People's Government restored the state to order and decency.

Once again elections failed to resolve the controversy in Rhode Island. For the second time the Suffragists actually lost. But they followed the example of the charter supporters in January and rationalized the outcome rather than admit defeat. Since neither side would surrender or compromise, it is clear that only superior force could have restored a semblance of good order to the state after the events of the first three months of the year. As inauguration day approached, the charter government gave signals that it intended to act at last. Governor King convoked the General Assembly in special session and recommended measures looking to preparedness. Encouraged by the decline of

Suffragist support and the pledge of federal assistance, the government strategists thought it safe to proceed.

The General Assembly complied with most of King's requests. A Board of Councillors was created to advise the governor. The assembly declined to authorize volunteer militia companies, because of the fear of standing armies, but approved the formation of special "police companies" in Providence. In addition, the Riot Act was amended by the deletion of the hour's delay usually required between its reading and the use of military force to break up riotous assemblages. Finally, the majority in the assembly refused to call another constitutional convention until the Suffragists agreed to give up their mad schemes. Spokesmen explained that all hope of compromise dissipated when the Suffragists rejected the Freeholders' Constitution. The authority of government must be vindicated before talk of reform would be in order. To demonstrate firmness, the government published warnings that the Algerine Act would be strictly enforced if the Suffragists persisted. Everyone agreed that the time of truth had arrived.[48]

Inaugurations took place as scheduled on 3 and 4 May, the People's Government first as usual. The Suffragists celebrated in Providence, while the charter government remained in Newport.[49] Almost immediately Governor King instituted a strategy calculated to reduce the Suffragists to impotence without outraging the public sense of decency. People's officials were arrested, arraigned, and indicted for treason under the Algerine Act, and then released under peace bonds restraining them from further illegal acts.[50] Whether those arrested would ever be tried was not clear, since the charter government preferred to win at the smallest cost. The plan nearly succeeded.

In contrast to the united charter government, the People's Government broke into warring factions. Dorr and the radicals urged an immediate seizure of power.[51] Pearce, Anthony, William Smith, Walter Burges, and the moderate majority opposed that course. The moderates won the argument but had no program of action to substitute for the radical plans. As a result

the People's Government neither asserted its claimed prerogatives nor adopted any kind of policy capable of maintaining at
least the status quo. Instead confusion reigned during the period
of 5-16 May, probably the most important few days in the
entire Suffragist crusade. The People's Legislature contented
itself with the repeal of the Algerine Act, the enactment of an
unenforceable revenue measure, and the adoption of resolutions
charging the governor to request the state seal and the public
records from the charter authorities.[52] Instead of acting to
defend its supporters from Algerine justice, the legislature com-
missioned the incumbent judges and most militia officers to
remain in office. Finally, Governor Dorr was instructed to
communicate the change of government to the president, Congress, and the governments of the other states. Following this
flurry of meaningless activity, the legislature adjourned until
early July. Leaving Dorr with the responsibility to solve the
difficulties, but with no authority to act, the People's representatives went home.

Moderates in control of Suffragist affairs planned to follow
the example set by the charter government and appeal to
Washington for a solution to the Rhode Island controversy.
Outvoted and overruled, Dorr decided to go to the national
capital himself, although he had no faith in the idea. Actually
he had no choice, since the majority of Suffragists agreed with
the moderates. Brown, Pearce, Anthony, and one or two others
were already in Washington when Dorr left Rhode Island. The
People's governor had reason to doubt the effectiveness of the
moderates in the important task of neutralizing President Tyler.
Perhaps he could help. Meanwhile, vigilante groups in Woonsocket and elsewhere protected People's officials from arrest
and imprisonment or peace bonding.[53]

Dorr went to Washington not because he expected to find
succor there, but because he had lost faith in the ability of
others to represent the People's cause.[54] In addition, the trip
would prove to the moderates that the only hope for success lay
in vigorous action within Rhode Island. It might also provide

the opportunity to fortify friends in Congress who must some-how restrain President Tyler. The decision to make the trip did not reflect any change of strategy or belief on the part of the People's governor. He left Rhode Island convinced that the Suffragists must implement the will of the people by creating a government of fact as well as right. He returned to the state strengthened in that conclusion.

En route to Washington, Dorr urged those in Providence to "stand firm" and "strengthen our men."[55] Let them know that all would end well if only they had the courage to prevail. People's officials under arrest should refuse peace bonds. To accept them meant that "our Legislature will be broken up." Submit to arrest, stay in jail, and await the rising of the people. "There are too many outside for them to remain inside prison walls." To Bradford Allen, commander of the People's militia, he dispatched orders to hold the troops on alert, "ready for action at very short notice." Allen was also to sound out the United States artillery officer in Providence. "See if he is right. We may want his guns." These recommendations and military orders indicate clearly that Dorr viewed the Washington mission as incidental to the plans for establishing a government of right and fact. The objective must be won in the state or not at all. He planned to act as soon as he had satisfied the demands of the moderates by demonstrating the futility of an appeal to Washington.[56]

In Washington, Dorr received an audience with the president. He described Tyler as a pleasant man, but one who wanted "a head for his place."[57] The president lacked any principles that Dorr could discover. He found it easy to understand how Dr. Brown had been deceived. The Suffragists had erred only by failing to appeal to Tyler's vaulting ambition to be president in his own right. Had they given an early commitment to support him in 1844, they would have won the support he bestowed on the Law and Order men backing the charter government. Dorr believed that a deal had been arranged in April. Although no such arrangement ever existed, he argued that this alone would explain Tyler's departure from the principles of state rights. Dorr lacked an understanding of the special concerns of a southerner fearful of precedents that might undermine the slave system. Righteously indignant at the presidential affront to Suffragist principles, Dorr left Washington convinced that Tyler could only be moved by the force of national popular support for the Suffragists.

On the other hand, congressional Democrats gave Dorr a warm and encouraging reception. After numerous discussions, he finally caught a glimpse of the hard problems the Suffragists faced. Some southern Democrats condemned Suffragist principles because they "might be construed to take in the Southern blacks, and to aid the abolitionists." But the true friends in Congress, those who exerted "the moral & intellectual weight," all "urge us to go on, with one voice," fearing only that "our strength might not hold out." He did not expect to win majority support in Congress, but the Suffragists would never need it. They must rely on themselves and the justice of their cause. If they moved as one man, with no faltering, the charter government could not withstand them, even if the president and other "Tories of the rankest sort" intervened.[58] As he had predicted, the trip to Washington changed nothing.

Yet indirectly there were positive benefits. While in Philadelphia and New York, Dorr made "personal application for military aid" in the event of a federal invasion of Rhode Island. From the enthusiastic responses, he saw no reason for despair among the Suffragists. "God bless our friends of all kinds. Without them the Small State of Rhode Island could do little against the General Government. With them, it can maintain itself successfully."[59] He had always thought that the "People of the States" would respond to the needs of the popular majority in Rhode Island. Now he was even more certain. He vowed "to return to Providence as soon as possible, and . . . forthwith call on the military to protect me and others from arrest under the Algerine law."[60] Already President Tyler had been forced to moderate his earlier stand against the Suffragists.

Alarmed by "the fear of an American War of the People against the Government," the administration would soon come to terms.

For four days Dorr sojourned in New York City, enjoying public dinners in his honor and seeking assurances of military support if needed. At Secretary of State Daniel Webster's instigation, the agents of the two rival governments met in a secret conclave to try to arrange a compromise.[61] Neither side had any authority to approve a binding agreement, but Dorr refused even tentative terms. Most of the others present recommended a truce until a prepared case could be brought before the federal courts to determine the legal government of Rhode Island. Until the case was decided, the Suffragists were not to act on their claims, and the charter government was to suspend the Algerine Act. Following a decision, the victorious side would proclaim a universal amnesty. Dorr insisted that as the properly designated governor of the state, he could not barter away the sovereignty of the people. Governor King and his council ultimately took the same position.

On 16 May 1842 Dorr returned to Providence amidst rumors of his impending arrest and of forcible resistance by the Suffragists.[62] Dorr's most trusted adviser, Aaron White, Jr., cautioned him against precipitous acts. The government was prepared. Federal reinforcements at Fort Adams made a seizure of power unfeasible. The troops would be in Providence "within a few hours after an outbreak."[63] White urged delay, since the Suffragists gained in strength every day. But Dorr was carried away by the assurances of private persons outside the state. This time he resolved to make no further concessions.[64] If the moderates were not convinced now, they never would be. The People's Government must defend itself against usurpation. Nothing short of that would do.

Holding pledges of military support from Pennsylvania and New York, Dorr sought to secure more. He wrote to the governors of Connecticut and Maine on 13 and 17 May asking for commitments. He discussed the possibility of federal intervention, describing it as a direct violation of the Constitution. All pertinent clauses in the Constitution applied only in the event of rebellion against a legitimate state government. In the case of Rhode Island, federal assistance belonged rightly to the People's Government against the tyrannical charter usurpers. Moreover, Dorr denied that the domestic violence clause of Article IV, Section 4 was intended to authorize federal suppression of "peaceable, orderly assemblages of the People, as in our case to decide new forms of government." Nor could the charter government legally invoke federal power against "the actions of the Legislature under a Constitution" ratified by "a great majority" of the citizens of the state. If some objected to the validity of the claims of the People's representatives, a proper test "in a legal manner" existed in the "modes of redress open to every citizen, without the intervention of a dictatator [sic] and without a resort to the sword." Let the challengers prove their case if they could. Their refusal to take their claims to a court of proper jurisdiction gave the lie to their objections. Certainly they should not be allowed to suppress the only legitimate government of the state by bringing to bear the military might promised by a misguided president.[65]

Dorr's argument was ingenious. Despite his earlier rejection of a legal test to validate the People's Constitution, he now insisted that those who objected to the constitution had no other option but to go to court. Certainly his situation dictated much of the reasoning. Claiming to act as the legitimate governor, he intended to assert his prerogatives and to defend the state. He proposed doing that even if it brought federal intervention and civil war. He refused to accept the status of challenger, basing his contentions on the mandate given by the people. In January the charter government had been deprived of all lawful authority in the state, except as caretaker to maintain order until the People's Government assumed the sovereignty in May. Dorr had delayed consummation of his duty to the people only because he desired a peaceable resolution of the controversy. But the usurpers would neither surrender nor press their claims before the proper tribunals. Clearly bent on forcible retention of state property and accouterments, the charter supporters refused to respect the law. Dorr saw no alternative but to suppress them.

Dorr's admission that legal means existed to test the legitimacy of the rival claimants to the sovereignty was most important. Since only legal and constitutional rights were involved, the proper test must be legal and constitutional. That clearly meant a hearing before a court of appropriate jurisdiction. At the point of a resort to violence to assert the will of the people, Dorr finally recognized that his purpose might be accomplished another way. At last he grasped the potential of the theory of peaceable revolution that James Wilson had developed during the founding period.[66] Properly applied, Wilson's theory eliminated the need for violence in a free society. Unfortunately, however, Dorr's insight came too late to affect the course of events in Rhode Island during the summer of 1842.

4.

SUPPRESSION

*The first instance of military
sovereignty asserted in the Union.*

Hundreds of sympathizers watched on 16 May 1842 as Dorr
raised the sword presented to him by his New York admirers.
They heard their choice as governor pledge to stain the weapon
with the blood of usurpers if the People's Government was
attacked. Governor Dorr proclaimed his obligation to put the
new government in possession of the sovereignty delegated by
the "People" in January. He called the citizens of Rhode Island
to rally to the standard of right, justice, and popular sovereignty. "It has become my duty to say," he warned, that if
federal troops "shall be set in motion by whatever direction . . .
against the People of this State, in aid of the Charter Government, I shall call for aid . . . from the city of New York and . . .
other places." Assistance "will be immediately and most cheer-
fully tendered to . . . the People" of Rhode Island. "The contest
will then become national and our State the battleground of
American freedom."[1] At the risk of civil war Dorr invoked the
right and power of the American people to control their governments.

On 17 May he ordered militia companies from Woonsocket,
Gloucester, and Pawtucket to march to Providence prepared for
battle. As his forces assembled, he laid plans to capture the state
arsenal in Providence and distribute the weapons among loyal
Suffragists.[2] He expected that this would precipitate war, but
he felt that any conflict would be short. The charter government dared not try to suppress the people, even with the help

of the federal government. By morning of the following day, the right would prevail. Once again American principles would exert their purifying force to restore the republic in all its simple virtue.

In the great tradition of American reform, Dorr sought to invoke the regenerative power of American ideals. Since 1776, through the Jeffersonian revolution of 1800, and into the era of Jacksonian Democracy, Americans had recited their catechisms based on the trinity of equal rights, the rule of law, and republican principles of government. But over the years, much had changed that Dorr failed to take into account. Perhaps the most conspicuous difference between the founders of the republic and Dorr's contemporaries was one of attitude toward the legitimacy of established institutions. In the early period, when all was in flux and in the process of becoming, Americans believed in their ability to control their own destiny. Institutions were merely human contrivances, designed and constructed to satisfy the needs of their creators. One constitution of government had no more sanctity than another. Choices were made on the basis of utility and in conformity with the aspirations and ambitions of the living majority. By 1842, however, the flexibility and openness of the American situation had been virtually eliminated by increased consciousness of special interests. Too many Americans identified their well-being with the maintenance of social and political arrangements grown sacrosanct with age and familiarity. To expect the third and fourth generations to respond to the example of their ancestors simply placed too much faith in the uniqueness of the American character. Dorr and the Suffragists were naive men who called Americans to a reaffirmation of the glorious ideals of the past, failing to understand how men and their cultural creations change.

Sometime after midnight on 17-18 May, against the wishes of every other Suffragist leader, Dorr and a small army of volunteers vainly tried to capture the arsenal in Providence. It was forewarned, reinforced, and impregnable.[3] Fortunately the attack aborted when the cannon borrowed from the Providence military academy failed to fire. Discouraged and frightened, the People's militia marched back to headquarters in Burrington Anthony's home without a shot fired by either side. If the cannon had not flashed out (because the touch-holes were corroded), the volunteers drawn up in an open field around the arsenal would have been slaughtered by the dozens. The windows of the fortresslike building fairly bristled with rifle barrels.[4] After marching the men out of harm's way, Dorr ordered them to disperse and regroup outside the city. Then he abandoned the field to the usurpers.

The People's governor had no intention of surrendering. On 19 May he instructed People's Colonel Henry D'Wolf to hold a position in Woonsocket and prepare for another assault on the arsenal. The original attack had failed for want of organization and timing. Proper care would eliminate the problems. D'Wolf was to "disregard the resignations of the timid members of our Legislature, and all attempts to divide our friends, & to compromise our rights."[5] The governor intended to return to assume command himself that evening, and he predicted victory. Everything depended on taking the arsenal, since so many of the people needed weapons. Undaunted by adversity, he still believed the cause of right must triumph.

Wiser and cooler heads prevailed, however. D'Wolf and others convinced Dorr that persistence meant disaster.[6] The people refused to rally, and the charter government obstinately refused to surrender. More and more People's officials resigned their positions in protest against the resort to violence. Rumors spread of a compromise incorporating the suggestions reportedly made in the New York conference.[7] Although the government gave no sign of a willingness to negotiate, Suffragists preferred to consider alternatives rather than to take the field and expose themselves to danger. With Dorr outside the state, the Suffragist volunteers scattered in disarray; the government rounded up all identified leaders and called for federal assistance. The People's Government seemed about to disintegrate.

Actually the reformers had never succeeded in erecting their government. The aftermath of the attack on the arsenal revealed the weakness of their forces. Anticipating a glorious rising of the people, the radical leaders found themselves deserted by many who had stood firm until the trial by force. Although thousands remained loyal to the cause, they rejected violence to support it. White warned Dorr against any further adventures, pointing out that he had been right all along. The Rhode Island majority wanted its rights, but not at the price of civil war. As White said, "I verily believe that if you were to come on with 1000 men to aid the Suffrage Party just now, you would have to fight Suffrage men just so completely have the minds of many been turned by recent misfortunes."[8] Unable to deny White's conclusion, Dorr grasped more fully the fallacy of asserting right in a context of might.

Meanwhile the government arrested and indicted men for treason against the state. True bills issued from a South Kingston grand jury against Joseph Gavitt and Sylvester Himes, both former members of the Suffragist State Committee as well as of the charter General Assembly. Other indictments followed, against Dorr, Pearce, Seth Luther (the old labor radical), and the few others caught in the government net.[9] But the legal prosecution paled in significance when compared to the persecution by other means. Government spokesmen alerted the community to the threat to property. The town watch in Providence became an instrument of "military despotism." Mayors refused requests to use town halls for meetings. Citizens were advised to arm and form militia companies in preparation for the impending war. Laborers and mechanics lost their jobs because of "honest difference[s] of opinion." Calculated boycotts and vicious conspiracies proliferated in the determined campaign "to break down honest tradesmen, who are not of . . . [the charter] party." In the greatest abuse of all, the government employed "scores of pimps and farmers in the disreputable business of espionage." Not even "the domestic sanctuary" escaped defilement by the supporters of law and order, all "without the color of law, under false pretenses." Congdon warned that these depredations would surely produce the war they were intended to prevent.[10]

Governor Dorr prudently remained outside the state, traveling about from New York to Maine. He enjoyed gracious treatment wherever he went. But nothing could "alleviate the slow death . . . I am dying. God save our poor People in Rhode Island." Conflicting advice came from friends across the nation. Representative Edmund Burke of New Hampshire urged Dorr to stand firm. There was no reason to worry about federal intervention. President Tyler had "no right to act as the arbiter between two political parties and decide by military force."[11] Burke's advice countered that of John L. O'Sullivan, who urged a truce and a compromise. O'Sullivan submitted a set of resolutions to the legislature of Connecticut, requesting that state to intervene and act as the investigating agency to determine which side had a majority in Rhode Island.[12] But it was far too late for that kind of reasonable solution.

Dorr stated as his first premise that he would never compromise. On the other hand he could not fight alone. He urged White and others in the state to "keep our men together for God's sake." Those Suffragists opposed to violence must work with others "to keep up the forms of the Constitution till the next election of members of Congress." Since the people would not fight, they must vote. By electing congressmen, the supporters of the People's Constitution could secure vindication. Dorr himself thought that the military actions of the Algerines justified the refusal of "any Patriot in Rhode Island [to] throw away his arms."[13] But all that mattered now was to hold together until the congressional elections the following year. Men might "differ as to what are the 'necessary means' for maintaining" the constitution; but even so, "the peacemen ought to cease from denouncing the force men and all go along together as far as they can in harmony."[14]

Painfully aware of his own responsibility for the situation of the reformers, Dorr used all his persuasiveness to promote reconciliation. He devised new strategy as the situation unfolded, never changing his determination to hold to the constitution. He had no choice but to remain in exile and do what he could to sway national public opinion against the charter government, President Tyler, and the tyranny of governmental sovereignty. Warrants had been issued for his arrest and extradition, but none could or would be enforced.[15] His plans called for his return to the state in early July to reconvene the People's Legislature. Having tried force, he proposed now to rely on politics as a means to secure justice. Grasping at straws, he seized on the predictions of Representative Edmund Burke: "You may rely on it, when this question comes before the House, as it will if a single drop of blood is shed by the U.S. soldiers, that the friends of the People will not be confined entirely to our party." Dorr came once more to believe dogmatically in the political approach as opposed to the forcible assertion of right. The United States Congress would exact harsh punishment on those who threatened to " 'shoot . . . [people] *down because they wanted to vote!*' "[16]

Dorr's acceptance of the political strategy worked a gradual but profound change in the theory of the Suffragist movement. It remained an ideological crusade, but no longer one seeking its fulfillment through violence. Actually the violence of the movement was more in the nature of "spillover" from the socialization of ideological conflict, as men aligned themselves on opposing sides.[17] Once the radicals learned that Americans rejected the vision of regeneration through an imposed consensus, they focused on the essential problem. If American constitutionalism assured rule by the consent of the governed, and if a republic made no place for the concept of governmental sovereignty, it followed that violence used by either side in a political struggle threatened the moral foundation of the constitutional order. Neither the rising groups represented in new political majorities nor those minorities favored by institutional arrangements could be allowed to topple the system simply to guarantee their own interests. While the Suffragists continued to act on an eristical rather than a dialectical view of politics, they began to see that the conflict was properly a juridical one. However, the radicals themselves had come close to destroying the kind of constitutional politics they idealized by producing a confrontation they could not hope to survive. Because of their own errors, the Suffragists under Dorr's leadership might well appear in the annals of America as "the *first* indirect agents in bringing about the very first overturn of Democratic Institutions that has ever taken place in any State in our Union."[18]

During late May and most of June Suffragist agitators in Rhode Island continued the campaign as best they could. Leaderless and much weakened by governmental and private persecution, Suffragism nonetheless remained a viable force within the state. In fact it gained new strength from the abuses against its adherents and the new level of argument stressing moral and legal right. Governor King and his council bombarded President Tyler with almost daily demands for federal intervention.[19] In the minds of these men, the test of American institutions was at hand. They convinced themselves that Dorr intended another attack as soon as he had collected an army in other states and had reorganized his band of criminals and degenerates claiming to be the "People of Rhode Island." That kind of attitude, prevalent among the supporters of established government, proper political principles, and the rule of law, jeopardized any hope of success for Dorr's new political strategy.

In Washington the president and the secretary of state observed the Rhode Island situation with trepidation. Tyler had already dispatched Colonel James Bankhead to collect intelligence, and his reports arrived as punctually as the charter government's appeals. Colonel Bankhead disagreed with Governor King's analysis of the situation, however. Secretary Webster visited the state briefly and returned to the national capital convinced that Bankhead was right.[20] The Suffragists had actually given up the fight, Webster told the president. The vast majority had never intended to resort to violence to achieve their objectives. Very likely they had become the victims of their own rhetoric, losing the ability to distinguish between propaganda and commitment. Webster thought the agitation would continue until the Suffragists under arrest and indictment were released. He favored a compromise and an amnesty. Everyone admitted that the charter must be exchanged for a written constitution, and that the suffrage would have to be broadened.[21] It made little sense to prolong the agony in the state merely to prove one side or the other right in a foolish dispute over abstract principles.

In their weakened condition, Suffragists nonetheless continued the struggle for right. Some suggested compromise, but the majority refused. They also realized the importance of President Tyler's hasty act of pledging to aid the charter government against all challenges. As Aaron White reported, Rhode Island had succumbed to "the will of John Tyler and the force of his standing army."[22] Dorr sought frantically for proof that federal troops had taken part in the defeat of the Suffragists.[23] Although the most he could show was that Fort Adams had become the strongest United States garrison on the coast, he persisted in the belief that only federal power protected the repudiated charter government from the oblivion it so richly deserved.

Benjamin Colwell, who had joined the Suffragist movement after the ratification election in January, urged the people of Rhode Island to act in support of their *"second Declaration of Independence."* He compared the suppression of the People's Government to the restoration of the monarchy in English history. Americans everywhere should realize the importance of the issue. He concluded that "the Rhode-Island question has now become a national one." Every true democrat and responsible citizen must be "as much interested in the principles upon which rest the legality of the Suffrage movement, as Rhode Island is. If an oligarchy under the semblance of Republicanism can govern Rhode-Island, it may govern everywhere else."[24]

Tyranny came in different guises according to circumstances, but its character was always the same. Although he repudiated violence, Colwell thought an abandonment of Dorr and his principles at this point might undermine the American republic beyond repair.

Governor King immediately ordered the arrest of Colwell as a subversive. The pamphleteer fled the state rather than submit.[25] Precisely what effect such exhortations as his had on public opinion is undetermined. Some people responded, either by announcing their allegiance to Dorr and the People's Constitution or by joining volunteer militia companies and marching about proclaiming their intention to protect the People's Legislature when it reconvened in early July.[26] The town of Chepachet became the scene of boisterous activity as armed men and curious onlookers swelled the population. White urged Dorr to call the legislature to meet in Chepachet rather than Providence.[27] The little town was located near the Connecticut border, a safe refuge in the event of a government attack. In addition the spirited hostility of the people in northwestern Rhode Island and the presence of the volunteer militia companies assured the People's legislators the peace and tranquility necessary to conduct public business. Dorr accepted White's advice and made an appropriate change in his plans. On 24 June he crossed the border into Rhode Island and established himself in Chepachet to prepare for the meeting of the People's Legislature.[28]

When he returned to maintain the formalities of government, Dorr entertained a lingering hope that the people would rally and force the charter government to abdicate. Some still urged him to act with energy. *"Our cause has at no time looked more favourable of success.* In my opinion your person will be as safe in R.I. as elsewhere," wrote the commander of militia at Chepachet. Burrington Anthony told Dorr that a thousand men could be raised in Providence in less than twenty-four hours, although when requested to prove it he could manage only forty-five altogether. But White's warnings against such tactics

convinced Dorr that the political strategy was preeminent. He
returned to the state to insure that "our Constitution can be
kept alive till the next Congress, [when] our members will no
doubt be received, and our government recognized."[29]

These disturbing developments had a profound effect on the
Law and Order men. Already frightened by the thought of
Dorr's return, the assemblages of armed men and the reports of
stolen ammunition and gunpowder raised their fears to a level
requiring action. Appeals to Washington became increasingly
frantic. When Dorr issued his proclamation on 25 June urging
the people to "sustain" their government "by whatever means
necessary," the government men lost all perspective.[30] The
ambiguity of Dorr's intentions and the demonstrated passivity
of his supporters rendered the situation anything but volatile,
but men in positions of authority thought otherwise.[31] The
General Assembly declared martial law over the entire state.
Overleaping the obstacles presented in the body of American
law and opinion, the charter government's act was "the first
instance of military sovereignty asserted in the Union."[32] In
effect, the necessary precedent for the modern positive state
had been established.

In pursuance of the new policy, Governor King ordered the
militia to muster for action and dispatched a last-minute appeal
for federal troops. From all appearances, state and federal
forces would soon take the field to drive the People's governor
and his minions from their supposed stronghold in northwestern
Rhode Island. The militia responded with alacrity, and the mass
of Rhode Islanders acted as Aaron White had predicted they
would. Accepting the assembly's action and the governor's
proclamation as final proof that the state had been invaded by
an alien force aided by traitors within, people from all walks of
life leaped to their arms in the defense of life, liberty, property,
homes, and political legitimacy. Armageddon had come, and
now the defenders of law and order must do battle for the
cause.

In Chepachet, Dorr waited in vain for either the arrival of

members of the People's Legislature or the direct popular action
he half-heartedly envisioned. But what he saw was a rising of
the people against him and all that he stood for. The regular
militia remained loyal, and literally thousands of troops assembled in Providence. The newspapers carried notices of more
resignations by People's officials and embittered condemnations
of Dorr's activities. It appeared from the complaints that the
People's governor alone was responsible for the chaos about to
consume Rhode Island. Few men aside from White knew exactly what Dorr intended. The overwhelming majority assumed,
as have all historians of the Suffrage movement, that he was
bent on civil war.[33] The evidence demonstrates, however, that
Dorr had learned a hard lesson in mid-May. Since the people
would not fight, and since the cause was just, they must vote. In
late June it seemed they would not even do that, preferring
security and stability to the defense of principle. But even more
appalling from the perspective of a man who trusted above all in
the integrity and spirit of the people, the majority repaid with
hatred this reminder that they were the sovereigns of the state
of Rhode Island.

Nearly every Suffragist leader aside from Dorr took the
position in late June 1842 that the assembly's call for another
constitutional convention to meet in September was a viable
compromise. Two days before the assembly invoked martial
law, the legislation authorizing the convention won approval.[34]
Walter S. Burges, Edward Farmer, W. M. Webster, William
Simons, A. W. Davis, and one or two other prominent Suffragists published a broadside in support of the convention and
deprecating Dorr's efforts. "Law & Order, justice and political
Equality are no longer enemies," the broadside proclaimed.
"Who will fight for *any form*, when the substance can be gained
by peace?"[35] The rhetorical question came with little grace
from men who had caustically condemned the only possible
answer just four months earlier. The new convention could
hardly achieve much more than the Freeholders' Constitution
had offered. In fact, the Suffragists accepted in June what had

outraged them in March. The difference, of course, was one of perception and experience. No longer able to hold out for principle when the mass of people voted with their arms for compromise, the Suffragists surrendered. Dorr stood almost alone at Chepachet, but he was confident that the trimmers would soon repent their sins against principle and the people.

By 27 June Dorr knew he had lost. The people would neither fight nor stand firm. He denounced the men who accepted the government compromise. "We have a Constitution, which has been rightfully adopted by a majority of the *whole* People. When the same majority shall repeal it, it will rightfully be abrogated."[36] Nonetheless, he agreed that the majority should decide the course of action for the People's Government. If the decision was to use the new convention as a means to legitimate the People's Constitution, so be it. He denied the need for additional confirmation, but he would not oppose the majority will. He asked for evidence concerning the desires of the majority, however, and in addition he wanted assurances that the men with him in Chepachet would be allowed to return to their homes unharmed. Once convinced on both counts, he would issue the proper orders and proclamations.

Late in the afternoon of the same day, still without the assurances, Dorr finally decided to give up. He ordered the militia to disband and the men to return to their homes.[37] Actually the number of armed men at Chepachet never exceeded four hundred, and a considerable proportion of these were merely onlookers.[38] Disconsolate at the failure of the political strategy as well as the earlier military one, Dorr once again went into exile. He had learned that Rhode Islanders wanted nothing to do with military adventure. He suspected that they would not even approve a political effort to sustain the right. These disappointments forced him to seek yet another means to restore the public faith in the principles of popular sovereignty and peaceable revolution. But more important, he himself finally understood the meaning of those principles. Whether failure alone explained Dorr's superior insight, or whether adversity called forth the kind of hard thought necessary to understanding, he devoted the next seven years of his life to an analysis of American constitutionalism that produced the most brilliant exposition by any American theorist since James Wilson.

The charter battalions arrived in Chepachet on 28 June. By that time, the only sign of activity was two small boys playing around the half-finished bulwarks on the hillside just out of town. Government censors had refused to allow the publication of Dorr's dispersal order, and the troopers were anticipating a hard fight in the "storming of Acote's Hill."[39] But the peaceful countryside was disturbed only by the din of the invading army. People stayed out of sight. The only casualty of the Chepachet campaign, aside from the men who suffered the usual rigors of camp food and hard drink, was a cow. Government troops executed it by mistake, perhaps revealing their actual impressions of Suffragists. The battle of freedom against tyranny never took place, since the defenders of freedom no longer knew which side to join.

As if to complete the farce, President Tyler ordered federal troops to intervene on 29 June, two days after Dorr had absconded.[40] That same day charter troops guarding a bridge in Pawtucket to hold back the expected hordes from Massachusetts fired into a harassing crowd. The shots wounded two men and killed an innocent bystander. The next day Colonel William P. Blodgett led a troop of militia into Massachusetts to extradite a fugitive "by authority of the bayonet."[41] A dead cow, an innocent man killed accidentally, state boundaries violated by military force, constitutional principles reduced to absurdities, and men fleeing their homes to escape arbitrary arrest and imprisonment—these were the results of the correlative decisions to revolutionize Rhode Island and to impose martial law. The spiritual and intellectual carnage transcended the boundaries of the state, as the entire nation felt the shock of the Dorr War. Just which side had injured itself most was by no means clear, and unfortunately the record was not yet complete.

Governor King and his council instituted exact enforcement of the Algerine Act under the summary processes of martial law. Normal constitutional guarantees of procedure became irrelevant for the mass of Suffragists and their sympathizers. Well-to-do leaders like Dorr, Brown, Smith, Harris, Pearce, Atwell, Anthony, Burges, Simons, and White escaped the heavy-handed procedures by posting bail or leaving the state. Others as lucky as Martin Luther emulated them.[42] But the rank and file, the little men Dorr called to fight or to vote, stayed to pay the consequences. These men, "the People," discovered by experience the costs of daring to claim the heritage of the American Revolution. The two Suffragist newspapers shut down their presses because of the official and unofficial harassment.[43]

Within two months the crisis was over and a semblance of order had returned. Hundreds of men had been arrested, interrogated by a special commission, and either held for trial by the civil authorities or freed.[44] No one was tried or executed under martial law, but no one enjoyed the benefits of the great common law procedural rights of notice of cause, habeas corpus, reasonable bail, counsel, and speedy trial, which provide the foundations for American law. Perhaps it would be unreasonable to expect men in positions of authority to retain the intellectual and emotional balance needed to insure those rights when the social and political order itself has been threatened. On the other hand the ringing defenses of martial law made by prominent men hardly bespeaks a commitment to those great rights. As Richard Randolph and Henry Anthony said, martial law was actually less rigorous than ordinary law because it allowed informal questioning of men without the usual consequences of incarceration and delay. No one much bothered about the three or four hundred men who served time without knowing exactly why, uncertain even whether they had the right to protest their arrest and imprisonment.[45] One New York civil libertarian lawyer offered his services to the accused. But the hostile reaction among government supporters per-

suaded him to return to his home and stay out of other people's
affairs.[46]

By mid-July, all the prisoners had been interrogated. Indictments began to issue on 25 August from a Newport grand jury,
although the alleged crimes had been committed in Providence
or Chepachet.[47] Finally, on 30 August, Governor King changed
from temporary to indefinite his earlier suspension of martial
law. The next day elections were held for delegates to the
constitutional convention.[48] Since the Suffragists abstained
(the leaders were trying to capitalize on the reluctance of the
people to vote), the Law and Order coalition won a complete
victory. The Algerine Convention then drafted and submitted
for ratification a constitution incorporating almost literally the
provisions of the repudiated Freeholders' Constitution. The
only innovation was borrowed from the People's Constitution.
A special clause referred to the people the question whether
blacks should have the franchise on the same terms as whites.
Most expected easy ratification of the Algerine Constitution,
now that martial law was suspended indefinitely over the state;
all doubts were erased when the General Assembly undercut the
Suffragist abstention strategy by requiring only a majority of
those voting to ratify.[49] With the election in November, Rhode
Island finally entered the modern age.[50] Suffragists were not
certain that it differed from the old.

By January 1843 Rhode Island boasted a new constitution that
enfranchised blacks and whites and apportioned the legislature
on the basis of population. In addition, after one abortive
effort, the state suspended the treason trials until some indefinite future date. Many people believed they would never be
held, and, in fact, very few were.[51] The state was fairly buzzing
with the antics of a lively political campaign that made 1843
seem like 1840 all over again. The victors in the contest would
win the right to erect the new government in May, a privilege
far more important than the honor associated with it. The
Suffragists had repented their decision of the preceding summer

to abstain from politics. They joined with the rump Democrats left over after the formation of the Law and Order coalition, and everyone hoped the new alliance would bring them into power at last in the April elections. Once ensconced in Providence, they intended to convoke a convention to declare the People's Constitution the fundamental law of Rhode Island.[52]

At least the loyal Suffragists adopted that strategy. Others regretted this rehash of matters better left forgotten and called for Democratic control of Rhode Island under the Algerine Constitution. But Dorr's prestige among the faithful remained high, and he would accept nothing less than the decision of a convention. He admitted that the proposed convention could not be controlled once it met. "But there is no danger that a popular Convention, freely elected, will undo what has been already done, or substitute any other form from that which now embodies the collected will of the State."[53] The responsibility of the true democrats and Suffragists was "to save the People . . . , and to give them the opportunity to defend . . . themselves." As for himself, "I adhere to the People's Constitution, and to the right to enforce it; and I wish to stand or fall by it. But I have no power to establish it without the aid of the People, who will not fight." He concluded that "they must then vote, or be lost; for reliance on aid from abroad, or from the Supreme Court, or on Congress is deceptive. Resolutions without action are vain and unprofitable."[54]

Still in exile, Dorr used all his influence to control the political efforts in Rhode Island. By January 1843 he had tried force and met disaster; adopted a political strategy based on an appeal to Congress, only to see its prospects destroyed at Chepachet; and had come full circle back to the localist position stressing popular access to the ballot box. He realized fully the implications of the new tactics. If a majority of Rhode Islanders participated in the April elections under the Algerine Constitution, its legitimacy could never again be challenged, so the Suffragists would risk much in taking part. Dorr had decided to take this course only after it became clear that nothing else would do. He could see no opportunity for an appeal to Congress; private aid from abroad never came; and to rely on the Supreme Court of the United States exposed the Suffragists to the possibility of having to respect an adverse decision.[55] If the people were free to choose as they desired, he had no doubt that the People's Constitution would win. But politicians like Dexter Randall, Samuel Y. Atwell, Dutee J. Pearce, and other visible but not confessing Democrats might spoil the bright prospects. These men sought only the main chance, refusing ever to rise to the demands of principle. Dorr warned his followers to watch them closely.[56]

Even without considering the complicated strategy Dorr outlined, the Suffragist-Democratic alliance faced problems enough. The Algerines had adopted a conciliatory stance designed to bridge the social divisions and increase their vote. Now that the radicals were isolated and ostracized, the better course was surely to temporize and thus restore social harmony under the new constitutional edifice. In February the assembly granted amnesty to all former Suffragists who recanted. Government spokesmen correctly observed that virtually every reform demand had been fulfilled. If enough people supported what remained of the program, it could easily be achieved piecemeal by amendment. With the electorate increased by more than 60 percent, who could doubt that the majority ruled?[57] Meanwhile, the social pressures continued, and many Suffragists had to choose between political principles and work, trade, and social acceptance. Branded as anarchists and power-hungry demagogues, the Suffragist-Democrats stood little chance of victory.

As it turned out, they did lose, but the election was closer than anyone had really anticipated. Only eighteen hundred votes separated the contestants in a turn-out of over sixteen thousand.[58] His faith in the character of the people badly shaken, Dorr charged the loss to collusion, manipulation, and proscription. But the lesson was painful in its clarity. "The Suffrage majority will not fight nor vote; and, we may ask, what will they do? What remains for them to do?"[59] Another year of

"Algerine oppression and misrule" lay ahead, with no hope for an appeal to Congress or a convention of the people. Some men, rather than turn out to vote, hid in "haymows, and in cellars under barrels."[60] The performance had been so abominable "that I think we could select from the whole lot a set of slavish, abject, poor-spirited creatures who would do credit to the serfdom of Russia, and who ought to be attached to the soil, and sold out and transferred with it, in its various changes of ownership." White was already convinced. Experience in the Suffragist crusade "has taught me thoroughly that little dependence is to be placed on the spirit and character of men for the security of Freedom."[61] As he had said in November 1842, "I cannot perceive that our American & Republican minds are made of much sterner stuff in R.I. than in Poland or Mexico."[62] The outcome of the election provided evidence beyond question that Americans, like all other men, preferred security and safety to honor.

Having learned much about human beings in general, and about Americans in particular, Dorr's initial reaction was a pessimistic retreat from all his earlier beliefs. But within a few days he regained his faith, the old conviction that had sustained him since the Constitutionalist struggle of the 1830s. There was no need for despair. "The cause is as true and great as ever, and should inspire every man with renewed devotion, come what will." Those who claimed the right to lead the people must "once more in hope . . . bear right onward."[63] The obligations of duty were unclear. He could not decide whether to surrender to the Algerines for the punishment "laid on by might, and not by right," or to remove to another state and begin a new life. But "while a plank remains to stand upon, let our Party strive to maintain their footing."[64] Dorr's mind had been nourished on the belief in progress and the perfectibility of man; he simply refused to accept the possibility of error in these premises. The optimistic democrat as always, Dorr sought once more a means to reconcile faith and practice.

For the next several months, the Suffragists searched for a new strategy to replace those that had failed in the past. Dorr thought of nothing else, devoting his attention to the evolution of tactics that not only suited the principles of popular sovereignty and peaceable revolution, but also took into account the crippling weaknesses of the American character. Retaining his belief in the politicism of Jefferson and the radical Whigs, Dorr had also to make room for the institutionalist critique of John Adams and the conservatives, who began with the assumption that men rarely live up to their potential. Synthesizing these two divergent credos, Dorr arrived ultimately at the Wilsonian constitutionalist position.[65] The significance of the position is that its juridical thrust allowed Dorr to reconcile the principles of popular sovereignty and peaceable revolution with the theory of judicial review. It took time to fill in the details of this subtle view of American constitutionalism. Over the interim, Dorr struggled with the difficult theoretical transitions required to achieve the ultimate synthesis.

Dorr was overwhelmed with tactical suggestions made by Suffragists determined to keep the cause alive. One man thought a secret election of People's congressmen the best way to get the Rhode Island question before Congress.[66] Aaron White preferred an appeal to the Democratic National Convention in 1844. If the friends of the Suffragists in other states would elect exiled Suffragists and sympathizers as delegates, the Convention might adopt a platform pledged to the affirmation of popular sovereignty and the recognition of the People's Government. White warned Dorr not to return to Rhode Island. The Suffragists had risked all in the effort to overturn the oligarchy in the state. They had accomplished a great deal, since the good portions of the Algerine Constitution incorporated Suffragist ideas. But the achievement had earned for them "the vengeance of our adversaries." The oppressed people of Rhode Island could not and would not protect them. Their only hopes were "God's good Providence & our own wits." And yet, he wrote, "popular good will is in our favor . . . & we ought if we

can to give it some permanent & tangible effect." The best way
to do that was by nationalizing the crusade through an appeal
to the Democrats assembled in convention. They should not
give up now. But they should keep in mind that "honor has
been secured, & now let us guard ourselves as well as we can
against the danger we have incurred." A few lethal death-kicks
remained to the vanquished Rhode Island "Aristocracy."[67]

Dorr rejected both these plans, although he included parts of
them within the larger strategy he devised. In May he resolved
to return to Rhode Island and force the Algerines to try him for
treason. "I enlisted in the cause not for success, but to assist in
carrying out what was right and just, if possible." It followed
that "I ought not to avoid the consequences of what I have
done or failed to do." Later he would take comfort from the
truth that "any hardship that I may be called upon to endure
will be laid on by might, and not by right."[68] His misfortune
did not reflect on the validity of the cause, but the failure of
"the party with whom I have acted" which "suffered the right
to be trampled underfoot." Impervious to the advice of his
friends, Dorr meant to satisfy his honor and at the same time to
set in motion a plan to reconfirm the principles of popular
sovereignty and peaceable revolution.

Trial by the Algerines opened the way for an appeal to the
United States Supreme Court. A number of national issues were
involved, and Dorr had no doubt that a proper case could be
made when the time came. The problems associated with the
strategy were twofold. First, the Algerines might simply ignore
him. Having defeated him, they might choose to destroy him
through humiliation. White warned Dorr to consider the consequences to the cause if the Algerines acted so shrewdly.[69] On
the other hand, Dorr's fragile health almost subverted the
plan.[70] He could do nothing about his health, except wait for
recuperation before submitting to arrest in October 1843.[71]
Once in the grasp of his enemies, he insisted on an immediate
trial to serve as "the occasion of diffusing more light among the

People upon the important questions in the controversy." His "real offense consists in an earnest if ineffectual, support of the great doctrine of popular sovereignty and equal rights, which lies at the foundation of our republic, and which cannot be impunged [*sic*] without impairing the freedom of every individual citizen." As he said, "In such a Cause it is . . . an honor to endure hardship."[72]

Prominent national lawyers offered their services to Dorr during late 1843 and early 1844.[73] When the time for trial came, however, Dorr was forced to act as his own counsel. He was assisted by Samuel Atwell, Walter S. Burges, and George Turner of Newport.[74] Atwell planned to argue that treason was an exclusively national crime, since the Constitution defined it explicitly. But the illness that took Atwell's life shortly after the trial prevented him from appearing, and Dorr argued the treason issue himself. He failed to make a good case because he had not prepared for it. He spent little time worrying about the defects of the argument, however. All that mattered was to raise the issues and thus lay the basis for an appeal to the United States Supreme Court.

Dorr's second line of defense was an insistence that he had acted throughout the controversy in Rhode Island as the legitimate governor. The people of the state had voted overwhelmingly to establish the People's Constitution. No one had been able to dispute the majority vote in January 1842. Under that constitution Dorr, as the only candidate, was elected by the people to serve as governor. He denied that he could be tried by courts acting under a later constitution for crimes allegedly committed against the repudiated charter. Even if the Algerine Constitution was now legitimate, the charter government had not been so after the election on 4 May 1842. Thus crimes defined only by the charter General Assembly did not have any validity at law. Actually, Dorr pointed out, the People's Legislature repealed the Algerine Act in early May. But even if it had been on the books, it more properly applied to the actions of the officials of the charter government than to his own. The entire argument rested on the contention that American constitutionalism sanctioned the exercise of popular sovereignty in peaceably revolutionizing an existing government. Dorr intended to force the court to rule on that specific point. If he won, all well and good. If not, the ground was readied for another appeal to the Supreme Court.

Dorr's conduct of his trial indicates that he had finally accepted the view that the rights asserted in 1842 were legal rights. Thus they could be asserted and defended in a court of law having appropriate jurisdiction. He had surrendered nothing of importance when he accepted an approach emphasizing the judiciary. The Suffragist majority had refused to fight or to vote. Dorr hoped to establish an institutional defense of public liberty by invoking the judiciary to enforce decisions made by the people themselves in authentic exercises of their inherent sovereignty. Once again he convinced himself that the cause of right would prevail. This time it was because judges had no choice but to respect the right of self-government guaranteed by the Constitution.

As Dorr anticipated, the Algerine Court ruled his defenses unacceptable. Chief Judge Job Durfee, the man who had lectured enthusiastically against the Suffragists in 1842, instructed the jury, "Wherever allegiance is due, there treason may be committed. Allegiance is due to a State, and treason may be committed against a State of this Union."[75] As for the second argument, Durfee held that courts and juries must presume that constitutions and governments exist. Both must be taken as they are, "and where the plain letter of the law prescribes . . . [a] course, that [courts and juries] . . . are bound to pursue." Only legislatures, as the depositories of sovereignty within all polities, had the political power to decide between rival constitutions and governments. Durfee also denied that courts had the authority to resolve disputes about the outcome of elections. Courts must hold themselves aloof from political controversies such as those concerning elections or the changes of government. Otherwise, he pointed out, "neither the people nor the Legislature would be sovereign. We should be sovereign, or you [the jurors] would be . . . and we should deal out to parties litigant . . . sovereignty to this or that, according to laws of our own making." Warning against any penetration of that political thicket, Durfee ended with the reminder that "sovereignty is above Courts and Juries, and the creature cannot sit in judgment upon its creator." Bound to know and respect the constitutions under which they exercised their functions, courts must presume the sovereignty of all existent governments.[76]

The jury followed the judge's charge and entered a verdict of guilty. No one recognized the specious quality of Durfee's argument, the willful refusal to consider the meaning of popular sovereignty. Few people saw any way to correlate that principle with the claim that judges must resolve disputes concerning its exercise. It had taken Dorr four years to reach a position reconciling the two. It took the American judiciary another century to discover the logical consistency of Dorr's argument when viewed from the perspective of republicanism and self-government.[77] That the Rhode Island court and the majority of the people of Rhode Island found the theory somewhat ambiguous should not be surprising.

George Turner moved for an immediate retrial, stating seventeen objections to the obvious bias of the judges and the jurors. The court heard the argument in late May, and then ruled the request out of order. Under the circumstances and the applicable law, Dorr had been tried as fairly as possible. To accept his claim that trial must be held in the county where the alleged crimes occurred would not be fair because of the state of public opinion in Providence. To try Dorr in that city or county guaranteed acquittal; if in Newport or elsewhere, conviction followed as naturally.[78] The accused had had his day in court and must abide the sentence the court imposed. Judge Durfee said nothing about a possible appeal to the United States Supreme Court, except to deny that federal courts had any jurisdiction over matters reserved to the states. In all cases, the states must possess the authority and power to defend themselves against usurpers of public authority. Already convinced of that postulate, Durfee's rulings in the Dorr treason trial were perfunctory.

Before sentence, the judge gave Dorr the customary opportunity to speak in his own behalf. The obdurate People's governor repeated most of his defense arguments. He accused the judges and the jury of patent bias against him and against the proper principles of American law and government. From such a court no one could expect justice. At the same time it was clear that "the process of this Court does not reach the man within. The Court cannot shake the convictions of the mind, nor the fixed purpose which is sustained by integrity of heart." In indignant protest he told the judge he would not "exchange the place of a prisoner at the bar for a seat by your side on the bench." He knew that right would triumph. The American people would not allow such travesties to occur. They would rise to reclaim the heritage of the Revolution. "From the sentence of the Court, I appeal to the People of our State and of our country. They shall decide between us. I commit myself without distrust to their final award."[79] With that assertion of his unquenchable faith, Dorr submitted to the sentence of life imprisonment in solitary confinement at hard labor. He entered prison unrepentant on 27 June 1844.

Dorr remained in prison for exactly a year.[80] During the interval, he perfected his case for appeal to the Supreme Court and assumed some direction of the Luther cases as well.[81] Martin Luther and his mother had instituted suits in 1843 and 1844 as agents for the Suffragists to secure a decision on the issues raised by the Dorr War.[82] Later Dorr neglected his own case and devoted full time to the Luther actions. He had concluded that those two cases more comprehensively covered the ground necessary to a full hearing and a meaningful decision on the principles of popular sovereignty and peaceable revolution.[83] For the next five years, most of his time and energy were used to guarantee a proper resolution of the controversy.

Meanwhile, Dorr finally won the hearts and votes of the people for whom he had sacrificed so much. Almost on the day he entered prison, a liberation campaign began. After nine months of agitation a coalition won the election in the spring of 1845 on the pledge to liberate Dorr. Since he refused to recant or to accept any form of release that implied admission of guilt, the liberation coalition in control of the General Assembly sponsored an unconditional amnesty.[84] Dorr emerged from prison amidst celebrations that reconfirmed his faith in the people and his principles. His victory was a limited one, however. Until 1851 he had no political or civil rights. Nonetheless he devoted himself to the eradication of errors that had crept into American constitutional and political thought. As he aged, and as his health worsened, he intensified his efforts, almost as if he knew he would die with his work unfinished.

Dorr's predictions of the triumph of principle and right joined dogged belief with sharp awareness of the price for misjudgment in political affairs. Aaron White had warned him earlier that the Suffragists might win a reputation as the first indirect agents of tyranny in the United States.[85] Certainly the course of events in Rhode Island tended to corroborate that assessment. White also discussed the obligations incurred by those persons responsible for the Dorr War. They had served the cause of right. Thus they had a tentative claim to a place among "hundreds of martyrs for the rights of Man." Probably they would appear in the history books as "the apostles of liberty in these trying times."[86] But they could not be certain. Nor could they afford to rest on their doubtful laurels. Too much was at stake. Indeed, their reputations and the fate of human liberty were so entwined that one affected the other. They must continue the fight to insure that "the Rhode Island *Precedent of 1842* . . . [did] not become a law."[87]

In the years after 1844 the Suffragists and their friends elsewhere struggled to fulfill their mission. The effort led the Rhode Islanders far beyond the confines of their small state. Ultimately the people of the other states, the Congress, the federal courts, the political parties, and the historical traditions of the nation were affected. As Dorr had intended in the summer of 1842, the Rhode Island contest became a national crusade. As such, it forced a reconsideration of fundamental beliefs concerning the nature and future of Americans and America.

Part II

THE TESTING

As our constitutions are superior to our legislatures;
so the people are superior to our constitutions.
Indeed the superiority, in the last instance, is much
greater; for the people possess, over our constitutions,
control in *act*, as well as in right.
The consequence is, that the people may change
the constitutions, whenever and however they
please. This is a right of which no positive institution
can ever deprive them.

James Wilson, Speech of 26 November 1787

The revolution principle—that, the sovereign power
residing in the people, that they may change their
government whenever they please—is not a principle
of discord, rancor, or war; it is a principle of
melioration, contentment, and peace.

James Wilson, "Law Lectures" (1791)

THE DEMOCRACY

*Democracy is not, never was, and never
can be, the government merely of numbers.*

John Quincy Adams's diary entry for 21 May 1842 expressed
foreboding. "The news of the bloodless termination of the
Rhode Island war was this day received. The ignominious flight
of the spurious Governor, Thomas W. Dorr, has postponed the
heaviest calamity that ever befell this nation; but I scarcely dare
yet rejoice."[1] Adams's comment characterized the reaction of
one large group of Americans to the seemingly radical threat
posed by the Suffragists to order, liberty, and stability. For
years members of the group had been predicting civil conflict
because of the increasingly popular nature of American politics
and the decline of standards for political behavior. The events
of the 1830s, spreading from South Carolina to Maryland, to
the frontiers of Texas and Michigan, and back to Pennsylvania
and Rhode Island as the 1840s opened, seemed to indicate that
the anticipated rebellion had begun. Pressed by these events and
by the arguments of the radicals responsible for them, Adams
and his group strove to articulate a political philosophy that
would assure the maintenance of the traditional republic. They
defined a republic in terms that placed institutional supports
under existing political and social arrangements. Forced onto
the defensive, traditionalism was transformed into a conservative ideology at odds with the mythic vision of the Suffragists
and their friends.

John Louis O'Sullivan, editor of the *Democratic Review* and
an old friend of Dorr, expressed the radical view of the Rhode

Island contest. He described it as "one of the most interesting that have arisen within the period of our national history, and one essentially involving the very fundamental principles of our entire system of American institutions, and American political ideas." O'Sullivan had no doubt about the correctness of Dorr's stand. The majority of Americans believed in "the right of the people to alter their form of government at pleasure." That principle clearly placed the Rhode Island Algerines in the wrong. They had committed "real moral treason against the State" and the nation in their forcible suppression of the Suffragist martyrs. Americans would rally to the standard of right, and would aid the Suffragists in the struggle to vindicate the People's Constitution and Government.[2]

Domestic conflict in the United States had finally produced an ideological division that was total in its pervasiveness.[3] Adams and the conservatives accused the Suffragists of willful refusal to abide by the traditional principles of American society and government. No mere argument over the means to achieve commonly defined ends, the Rhode Island contest was a life and death struggle concerning the nature of a good society. Suffragists and fellow travelers shared this total ideological perspective. They, too, saw their adversaries as exponents of unacceptable social and political ideals. Because of the character of the division, the American people had to choose between the conflicting ideologies.

The national reaction to the Dorr War indicated that great numbers of Americans had lost their faith in the revolutionary ideology of the earlier years. Another large group feared the consequences of this loss of faith. Spokesmen for both sides responded to the felt need to clarify the issues, and for a few months the debate monopolized the press and all public forums, with obvious influence on the political process. When discussion proved inconclusive, the ideological contest was removed to Congress and ultimately to the United States Supreme Court for resolution. This chapter and the three that follow analyze the reaction to the Dorr War in detail, tracing the process of argument and settlement and assessing the extent of change in attitudes and ideology. In the aftermath of the debate the American people reached new conclusions about political theory. The new theoretical position emphasized the maintenance of stability and liberty while simultaneously expressing the indwelling *"Volksgeist."*[4] Traditionalism, translated into a conservative institutionalism, displaced liberal or radical politicism as the basis for constitutional government.

Newspapers across the country reflected the ideological division forced by the Dorr War. Editors lined up behind their colleagues in Rhode Island according to political persuasion and intellectual position. Francis Blair's *Washington Globe* reprinted without change the caustic critique of the Algerines made by Congdon and the Suffragist polemicists. Horace Greeley's *New York Tribune* followed the line laid down by Henry Anthony and other government defenders.[5] Elsewhere the lines firmed up and held, as each side described the degenerate tendencies of the other. The *Galveston Weekly News* reported in November 1845 that democracy "consists in affording an asylum to the oppressed of all nations—the territorial extension of the blessings of civil liberty, and the immediate liberation of Gov. Dorr."[6] Greeley put the other side as pungently. If Suffragist theories won acceptance, "all Courts, all laws, all Constitutions, become the merest frostwork, which the next breath may dissipate, or which a bushel of votes, collected by a peddler on his rounds, may utterly set aside."[7]

The ideological division spawned conspiracy theories on both sides. J. B. Jones, editor of President Tyler's political mouthpiece, the Washington *Madisonian*, warned Americans of an alliance between abolitionists and egalitarians to subvert the established institutions of the country. The Suffragist theory of peaceable revolution flew in the face of "the uniform practice of the country for fifty years, and the best settled principles of constitutional law." Jones was convinced that a plot existed to overthrow "the Constitutions of the Southern States as well as the Federal Constitution." He thought that only the decisive action by the charter government, supported by President Tyler, had averted revolution. He called Americans to stand in watchful readiness against a resurrection of the conspiracy. Only if the people showed their determination to support the legitimate governors of state and nation and rejected the absurd theories purveyed by the Suffragists and fellow traveling Democrats would "the perpetuity of our noble institutions . . . be established beyond cavil."[8]

Jones's conspiracy theory assumed as affinity between advocates of equal rights and abolitionists that in reality did not exist.[9] However, men responded not to the realities of the situation, but to its radical potential. Henry Clay of Kentucky stressed the same relationships that disturbed Jones and many other southerners. Clay traced the troubles to the visionaries within the Democratic party who exhibited "a spirit and bearing disorganizing and dangerous to the permanency of our institutions." He agreed with President Tyler's insistence that the failure to act against the anarchic and revolutionary disturbances of the 1830s laid the foundation for the radicalism in Rhode Island and the nation in the 1840s. Unless halted, the spread of Suffragism "would overturn all social organization, make revolutions—the extreme and last resort of an oppressed people—the commonest occurrences of human life, and the standing order of the day." He knew of no way that government could be changed without its own consent, short of "forcible . . . revolution." Clay was most concerned about the impact of Suffragist principles in the South, where racial considerations were so important. If Suffragism prevailed, "the whites will be brought in complete subjugation to the blacks." Clay rejected principles so absurd in their implications that they afforded no security for established institutions.[10]

Others took up the themes developed by Jones and Clay. In early July John Whipple of Providence, Rhode Island, warned in a speech that the events in the state had been merely "the beginning of that struggle which was to rage throughout the country. The fire that was kindled in Rhode Island was to spread to Maine and Georgia; the battle to become national." Later in the year, John Quincy Adams raised his voice in a public lecture intended to refute the theories espoused by Suffragists and their friends. Adams chose for the occasion a speech he had written in 1840, the year of the great electoral campaign announcing the advent of majoritarianism. In a diary entry he explained the frame of mind that impelled the self-righteous outpourings from conservatives across the country. "Jesus Christ went about doing good—I would do the same."[11]

Adams maintained a cool, rational tone in his address, and he developed a thesis lucid in its focus on the probable impact of Suffragism. "Democracy is not, and cannot be, the government merely of numbers." Resting his analysis on the works of the great Whig theorists of England from Sydney and Locke to James Burgh, he argued that the "Social Compact" originated in the union of the sexes, creating a social order based on the family. The "will or vote of every family . . . [belonged to] its head, the husband and father." Thus, the qualified voters in any society "can never amount to more than one in five of the whole." Relying on the view that only independent persons should exercise the franchise, he hoped by this conception of the organic structure of societies to demonstrate the absurdity of the Suffragist claim that all persons must have a voice in government. "The social compact which constitutes a sovereign state is a compact not only of individuals, but of families." Proper principles required that both be considered when the details of society and government were under review.[12]

From that base, Adams described the polity as an organic union growing from mutual accommodations arrived at over long periods of time. Only fools would attempt to impose a new order leaving out of account the ancient customs of the people. Adams urged Americans to structure their theories in accordance with the centrality of the family in decent societies. He explained that democracy in the United States had always rested on this institutional arrangement. The Constitution of

1787, and those adopted in all the states since 1787, had always been intended to shore up the social supports for free government. Only institutions such as family, church, school, and community provided the social framework that assured a place to every person within the society. That meant essentially that numerical majorities were not allowed to infringe upon the rights guaranteed to discrete groups within state or national constituencies. Constitutions were artifices, meant to endure for all time and to guarantee a proper social order. Adams warned that liberty without order ended inevitably in anarchy. He closed his speech with an exhortation for all Americans to return to the principles of the founding period. The great American experiment in government depended on a restoration of the rule of reason and law, "the work, not of eternal justice ruling through the people, but of man—frail, fallen, imperfect man, following the dictates of his nature and aspiring to perfection." Adams reminded Americans of the only good and common cause, "the cause of *our Country*."

Adams's lecture differed from other commentaries by conservative Americans only in its rational moderation. Most of the others exploited the emotional and irrational fears aroused by the perceived threat to established interests. Federal District Judge John Pitman described the People's Constitution as a monstrosity "conceived in sin and brought forth in iniquity, . . . the fruitful parent[s] of so many abominations." Associate Justice Joseph Story approved wholeheartedly of Pitman's intervention in this inherently political dispute, absolving him of any imputations of ethical misconduct in so doing. Story wrote, "If ever there was a case that called upon a judge to write and speak openly and publicly, it was the very case then before you."[13] Story, Pitman, Adams, Clay, Whipple, Jones, and Tyler sought to convince Americans that something had to be done to preserve the glorious American experiment in free government from the dangers of excessive enthusiasm and vicious principles.

Conservatives found Suffragist constitutionalism most disturbing because of its indeterminancy. The Suffragists closed ranks after early 1843 to argue that the republican guarantee clause of the Constitution sanctioned the principles of popular sovereignty and peaceable revolution. At minimum the Suffragists contended that numerical majorities could do as they chose with government. They recognized no limits on majoritarianism except the prevailing sense of political decency and the enlightened self-interest in maintaining the liberties of all men. The conservatives, on the other hand, believed that self-government worked only so long as the people respected the need for legal forms. They reacted with horror to the Suffragist claim that numerical majorities had the inalienable power to establish a new legality more suitable to current needs and interests. Aware of the popular attraction of the arguments of their adversaries, the conservatives realized that they had to articulate an opposing theory that reconciled popular sovereignty and peaceable revolution with order, regularity, and stability. They had to convince Americans that the inherently evil nature of all men necessitated institutional restraints for the preservation of a good society. Americans must be made to understand that they differed not at all from other historic peoples. Governments based on the myth of a virtuous citizenry violated all the sound principles discovered over the course of history. The Suffragists had succumbed to a visionary enthusiasm that promised only chaos because of the interference with the natural order of things.

A counterconspiracy thesis originated in the heat of the battle within Rhode Island. Dorr and Aaron White expounded it initially, and others took it up and elaborated upon it. White caught its purport in his remark that Rhode Island experienced in the summer of 1842 "a complete Revolution . . . in precisely the same way in which Revolutions in all former Republics have been accomplished." He defined a revolution as "an usurpation of power on the part of those into whose hands power has been entrusted." The Suffragists were the "indirect agents" of that revolution, and thus had the responsibility to insure that it failed. White had no doubt that Algerines everywhere would seize the occasion to subvert the free institutions of the country.[14]

White's characterization of the events in Rhode Island reveals the parallels between conservative and radical thought. He, too, appealed to history and tradition to construct the proofs for his arguments. The major question was a definition of sovereignty. "Is it divine right of the Ruler or the People? If it is as our Algerines say in the Ruler why then we are where our Ancestors were under the Tudors and Stuarts."[15] Relying on many of the same theorists that Adams used for opposite purposes, White called Americans to a defense of their revolutionary traditions. He thought the Rhode Island Algerines, northern capitalists, and southern slaveholders had formed an unholy alliance designed to suppress those "who try to make . . . Slaves expect their rights." Unless good men everywhere united, the nation, as Rhode Island before it, would cease "to be a Republic."[16]

Suffragists stated flatly that federal intervention in Rhode Island in the spring of 1842 violated American constitutional principles. Most assigned less than honorable reasons for President Tyler's actions. Then, in September 1842, William Goodell raised the conspiratorial implications of the Suffragist critique to a conscious level. Goodell described the "Rhode Island controversy" as more than a "mere local concernment." Actually it touched "vitally, and harshly, the great interests of liberty and law, of religion and rights, not only in Rhode Island, but in the whole country." If Americans failed to perceive the potential danger, they might "unconsciously rivet their own fetters." Goodell proposed the thesis that southern aristocrats had allied with their northern counterparts to reduce "Northern freemen" to the status of slaves. Americans must look to their liberties or suffer the consequences.[17]

John Tyler of Virginia was the major villain in the Suffragists' conspiracy theory. Incongruous as it appears, Tyler emerged as a Machiavellian figure capable of a deviousness and wile that hardly suited his plain, straightforward character. Dorr insisted that Tyler hoped to win the presidency in 1844 by appeasing the Law and Order men of Rhode Island and the nation.[18] No doubt Tyler was ambitious. But his actions resulted more from his fears for the future of the Union and his concern for proper principles than inordinate ambition. He expressed sincere regret that he had to order federal intervention to preserve order in Rhode Island, but he saw no alternative.[19]

In 1844 President Tyler explained to Congress the necessity for federal action in Rhode Island two years earlier. As President, he had been required to enforce the laws as they existed. Article IV, Section 4 of the Constitution and the Enforcement Acts of 1795 and 1807 imposed on him the responsibility to defend any existing state government from attack.[20] He denied having had any discretion to decide whether political opposition to existing governments was legitimate or illegitimate. All that had mattered was that Congress had recognized a government by seating its representatives. Until Congress indicated a change of opinion, the president must act to assure respect for its dictates. Tyler noted that the charter government had remained throughout the contest the only recognized government of Rhode Island. As such, it had rightfully demanded federal support when the Suffragists resorted to violence to achieve their objectives. Tyler had never found it necessary to order the troops to take the field, but he had been ready to do so if the circumstances required it.

Tyler's response to the Dorr War depended as much on his conservative beliefs as on any logical requirements imposed by his office. In terms of precedent, President Martin Van Buren had refused to provide federal aid to the government of Pennsylvania in 1838 during the so-called Buckshot War.[21] The situation in Rhode Island in 1842 differed little from that in Pennsylvania in 1838. The attitudes of the man occupying the presidency made the difference. Van Buren followed a neutral course, refusing to intervene in state affairs unless the situation got completely out of hand. He explained that political disputes must be settled locally if self-government meant anything at all. Tyler reacted negatively because of his concern about the spread of Suffragist principles, and because he wanted no precedents established by the acts of the Suffragists. He chose active support of one group rather than neutrality. In doing so, he proved the validity of Van Buren's arguments against such a course. Despite Tyler's disclaimers, he realized that federal intervention played a significant role in the outcome of the Rhode Island contest.[22]

The opposing conspiracy theories spawned by the Dorr War were symptomatic of changes occurring within American society. Conservatives perceived a citizenry running out of control and threatening the future of the republic. Radicals caught the vision of an aristocratic elite bent upon transforming the republic into an oligarchy. As third and fourth generation Americans tried to put the events into perspective, they discovered ambiguities and contradictions in their traditional beliefs that required resolution. One group stressed the open-endedness of the revolutionary traditions established in 1776 and 1787. The other warned that society could not exist without a conservative respect for established arrangements which helped men to define themselves and their positions. The former invoked the right of political majorities to decide the future for themselves, while the latter argued that the human condition was one of determinacy and organic dependence. The mass of Americans refused to choose one or the other of these views. However, more came to accept the idea that men were the victims rather than the makers of history. If one side could win the political and legal argument, it seemed certain that the American people would acquiesce. With so much at stake, neither side left a stone unturned in the search for the means to prevail.

Nonetheless the traditional revolutionary ideology endured the challenges of 1842 and the debates of 1842-1845. In fact, the events of 1846 in New York revealed the continued American reliance on direct action concepts.[23] The New York incident resembled in nearly every way the Rhode Island episode of four years earlier. In violation of the existing state constitution the reformers called a convention, reapportioned the state, and successfully established a new constitution. But in New York the reformers controlled the state government throughout, and they won. Although they succeeded, their actions intensified rising conservative fears.

During the early stages of the New York reform effort, conservatives appealed to the state supreme court to force the reformers to respect the state constitution's provisions concerning its own amendment. On 14 April 1846 the court ruled that the people of the state had the power to change the constitution at will.[24] According to the logic of the decision, it made no difference whether the state constitution provided for amendment by legislative action or by popular referendum. All that counted was that a majority of the people approved a change, or a call for a convention, in a special election held for that purpose. The court held that the legislature had no authority to alter the constitution. It could only propose amendments to the people and must abide the popular decision. The legislature could not refuse to accept an amendment or a new constitution ratified by the people. In short, the New York Supreme Court approved the principles asserted by the Suffragists in 1842. The decision confirmed the argument that political control insured acceptance of disputed constitutional principles. The legitimacy of the politicist view of American constitutional government was proclaimed.

Two years after the New York incident, a similar situation developed in Ohio.[25] Democrats in that state organized a boycott of state government to force the Whigs and conservative Democrats to accept their reform demands. Before the contest ran its course (ending in compromise), the United States Supreme Court delivered its decision in the Luther cases.[26] One observer noted the importance of the decision to put an end to the radical disturbances spreading throughout the nation. "The whole country may congratulate itself upon a decision which confirms and assures the great principle of liberty regulated by law."[27] In his view, institutional imperatives had finally received due recognition in American government. No doubt the decision exerted considerable influence in the campaign to convince Americans of the need to surrender traditional beliefs for new ones reflecting modern conditions. That meant that the simple republic must give way before the positive state, a new republican empire.

Before they put all their hopes on a decision by the United States Supreme Court, some Rhode Island Suffragists carried their cause to Congress. They did so by requesting the Democratically controlled House of Representatives to investigate the federal intervention in local affairs during the spring and summer of 1842. For about a year after the investigation began in early 1844, it took a prominent place in public and congressional discussion. All this occurred while other Suffragists were perfecting the legal cases to test the validity of Suffragist theory. Divisions in Congress paralleled those across the nation. The debates revealed a broad awareness of the significance of the Rhode Island question. The winners of the contest would decide the future of the nation.

By 1845 few Americans remained as certain of their own unique character and of the novelty of their experiment in government as they had been in 1800. The nation had been founded as something new, a repudiation of all historical experience in social and political matters. Since both the people and the government differed so radically from other peoples and governments, it followed that Americans would have to develop new principles to order and conduct their affairs. This conclusion rested on scientific, political, economic, and sociological postulates reflecting the intellectual revolution of the seventeenth and eighteenth centuries.[28] But as time passed, and as an American establishment developed in place of the repudiated European institutions, it was no longer possible to insist that Americans had escaped from the determinism of history.[29] By the opening of the 1840s Americans were becoming convinced that the earlier assessments were incorrect. The advent of domestic strife, threatening the historic achievements Americans celebrated in their institutions, forced a reconsideration of political and social theory.[30] Symptomatic of the process of new thought was the national reaction to the Dorr War.

After nearly a century of experience with the vague generalities of the Constitution and traditional ideals, Americans involved in the Rhode Island debates showed a realism that contrasted sharply with the earlier romantic assertiveness. Frankness and candor in argument by both sides underscored the impression that the United States as a nation, and Americans as a political people, had reached a crossroads in constitutional development. The choice was between governmental or popular sovereignty, since the two could no longer coexist. Americans could cling to their revolutionary heritage of voluntarism and local autonomy, as the Suffragists urged, or they could take the path of other peoples in other times and create a great empire. The United States could become a respectable, even a heroic nation, or it could remain a conglomeration of jealous states. Organic unity could triumph over particularistic multiplicity, or vice versa. With the pervasiveness of the idea of an American continental destiny, the final choice was hardly surprising.[31]

6.

THE CONGRESS

The next tribunal & the only proper
& constitutional one is the U.S. Congress.

Until the 1830s, Americans worked out their ideological conflicts through the political process. After the transformations of
the late Federalist period and the "revolution of 1800," most
understood that success in the political arena carried with it the
power to decide all questions in the United States.[1] The Jeffersonians and their Jacksonian heirs joined traditional ideas about
popular control of government with the novel achievement of a
party system and thereby circumscribed the freedom of action
of both voters and officeholders. Although most Americans
failed to perceive the actual relationships, a rising number grew
restless under the lines of control imposed by machine politics.[2]
In the wave of Jacksonian Democracy at the opening of the
thirties, Americans everywhere began to assert their right to
participate in government and to decide for themselves who
should rule. This political phenomenon very likely reflected a
burgeoning awareness that the old America was rapidly disap-
pearing with the advances of industrialism and the growth of
population—developments that tended to reduce the availability
of opportunities for men to better themselves. Out of the
awareness of these changes grew the popular demand for a
politics capable of reopening the roads to success and facil-
itating the release of individual, creative energy.[3]

Since the decisions of Congress came more and more to
affect the extent of economic and political opportunity, control
of Congress became increasingly important. The disputes of the

years from 1815 to 1836 are best seen as part of a power struggle between North and South, with the West coming gradually to hold the balance.[4] As established groups lost battles in the political arena, they turned to constitutional exegesis to assure their interests. That trend had barely gotten under way by the mid-1830s when the outburst of populistic radicalism gave it additional impetus.[5] Debates in Congress and in the public media revealed the tendency of concerned men to define all problems in administrative rather than political terms. The reason, of course, was that, whereas politics inevitably involves the unpredictable, administrative procedures allow for control and rational settlement; effective administration limits the range of choices in the solution of problems to those means calculated to protect the integrity of the existing arrangements.[6] Southerners concerned about slavery, northern capitalists worried about a proper business climate and continued expansion, and established elites fearing the push from below joined in a demand for the maintenance of sound principles of government to effect their objectives. They hoped in that way to hold back the changes that otherwise threatened to sweep away the social and political order they thought acceptable.

Just as the demand for rational administration under an established consensus on government began to attract political leaders, the Rhode Island Suffragists launched their ideological crusade reasserting the principles of popular sovereignty and peaceable revolution. The advocates of administrative rationality recognized from the outset the threat posed to their version of a good society by the indeterminacy of Suffragist constitutionalism. They saw the movement as another but more dangerous manifestation of the equal rights radicalism that spawned abolitionism and communitarianism. The Rhode Island revolution had to be suppressed or the entire nation would suffer the consequences. By June 1842 that conclusion had secured a firm hold on the minds of conservatives everywhere. Over the course of the next few years, its grip strengthened rather than weakened.

In reaction to suppression locally, the Suffragists concluded that an appeal to Congress was the only means left to win the constitutional struggle. They knew that it was "the Democracy of the whole Country" on trial in Rhode Island.[7] They girded themselves for a hard fight to insure that the "Rhode Island *Precedent of 1842* . . . [did] not become a law."[8] Their appeal to Congress was based on a relatively novel interpretation of the republican guarantee clause of the Constitution. Suffragists held that Congress had to look beyond the superficial aspects of mere form when implementing that guarantee. They defined republicanism as self-government under the imperatives of politicist majoritarianism, popular sovereignty, and peaceable revolution.[9] Members of the conservative coalition forming in Congress resisted this effort to involve Congress on the side of radicalism. After losing the opening round, they waged a retreating action that accomplished a good deal more than initial victory could have promised. The Suffragists naively assumed that to win a debate carried the day for them. But they discovered in the end that "resolutions without action are vain and unprofitable."[10] Still, the Rhode Island debates and Congressional reports served to clear the atmosphere for a judicial resolution of the question in contention. In the wake of the Dorr War and the national reaction to it, American constitutional thought veered sharply to the right, and institutionalism won acceptance within the nation at large.

During the spring of 1842 Dorr sought frantically to rouse Democratic friends in Congress to action against the threat of federal intervention. In May he reluctantly journeyed to Washington himself to add what he could to the demands made by Brown, Pearce, and others. Some members of Congress reacted with advice and encouragement. For example, Senator William Allen of Ohio introduced a resolution calling for an investigation of President Tyler's conduct.[11] Senators John C. Calhoun and William C. Preston of South Carolina stalled discussion of the proposal until Allen lost his self-control. The Ohio senator blurted out charges that the president had conspired with a repudiated and tyrannical minority to suppress the majority will within Rhode Island. At that juncture, Calhoun and Preston demanded a full debate of all the issues. They could hardly afford further delay because of Allen's accusation of an abandonment of state rights principles. Other adherents of this school of thought followed the lead of the South Carolinians, displaying a lack of concern about federal intervention in local affairs until after Allen's sensational outburst. However, by the date assigned for special debate (late May), Dorr had already returned to and departed Rhode Island and the resolution died on the table. The incident was significant because of what it revealed about the new state rights position: So long as federal intervention worked to preserve the status quo, the high priests of the old school held aloof. The advent of domestic radicalism had strange effects upon traditional beliefs.

Even earlier, a few congressmen had communicated directly with Dorr and expressed attitudes similar to Allen's. Senators Thomas Hart Benton of Missouri, Levi Woodbury of New Hampshire, Silas Wright, Jr., of New York, Perry Smith of Connecticut, Allen of Ohio, and Congressman Edmund Burke of New Hampshire took a grave interest in the proceedings in Rhode Island. These Democrats assured Dorr that President Tyler would not dare to send troops to the state without congressional consent, a condition impossible to fulfill unless violence occurred.[12] They concurred with the Suffragist claim that the People's Constitution had become the basis for government. They argued as well that the charter government had no right or authority to oppose the establishment of a People's Government. All subscribed to the opinion expressed by Woodbury that "if your people, who have never yet pleased to make a Constitution for themselves, have not a right to do it when and how they please, the whole fabric of American liberties rests on sand and stubble."[13] The New Hampshire senator specifically denied that the legislature under the charter had any discretion in the process. Since the charter contained no provision for its own amendment, and since it had become obsolete when independence was declared in 1776, only the people of Rhode Island could legitimately erect a new governmental structure. The congressmen joined in Woodbury's recommendation that the Suffragists persist through "constitutional means" until the People's Government became the de jure as well as de facto government of the state.

Senator Wright extended the analysis of the Rhode Island situation in order to clarify the position taken by the congressmen. He stressed the absence from the charter of any provision for its amendment, underlining Woodbury's reminder. Then in blunt words, Wright denied Dorr's claim that a majority of the people of a state could alter a constitution at will despite the existence of provisions prescribing the means to be used.[14] Wright's realistic analysis should have modified Dorr's enthusiasm, but the Rhode Islander preferred other, more facile exhortations to action.[15]

Actually the congressional Democrats lacked the means to act on their beliefs in the summer of 1842. No way had yet been found to get the Rhode Island question before Congress, short of a special investigation of the president's conduct. While some men were prepared to support such an extreme approach, too many believed in executive independence and discretion. In addition, since the president's mere pledge of aid had proved sufficient to swing the balance in Rhode Island, there was never an overt act for Congress to investigate. The promise of succor from Congress depended upon the ingenuity of the Suffragists in devising a way to present their claims in an official manner. It took more than two years to discover how to achieve that objective.

The first strategy had called for the election of People's congressmen in 1843; but when the People's Government failed at Chepachet, another plan had to be devised. Then the Suffragist-Democratic coalition planned to accomplish the same purpose by winning the election of 1843 held under the authority of the Algerine Constitution. Once again the reformers lost, and all hope of congressional action seemed gone. But Dorr refused to give up. He finally acted on a suggestion made as early as April 1842 that the Suffragists petition Congress to investigate the events since 1841.[16] While awaiting trial for treason, the People's governor drafted a memorial subsequently approved by the Democratic minority in the state legislature. The memorial protested executive interference in local political affairs and demanded congressional action to determine the "legitimate" government of Rhode Island.[17] If successful, the strategy held the potential to reaffirm proper principles if not to reestablish the People's Government.

When it came before the House of Representatives, the Rhode Island memorial stirred a debate that ranged broadly. The House referred it to a special committee, chaired by Edmund Burke of New Hampshire, for investigation and report.[18] Burke requested and obtained authority to call for persons and papers, but hesitated to ask that the committee be authorized to hold hearings in Rhode Island. He thought the balance of power in the House much too close for the risk.[19] Even the limited powers requested caused the conservatives to protest bitterly against congressional usurpation of state and executive authority. Their complaints were phrased in technical language, but the point of the objection was clear. Congressman Henry Y. Cranston of Rhode Island ascribed the entire proceedings to the idiocy of the Suffragists and their friends who indulged "wild theories about universal liberty, and all that sort of thing." The House should dissociate itself from the foolish notion that the "people, at all times, and when, and how they pleased, might change their form of government."[20]

Burke contented himself with the authority to investigate, to call for persons and papers, to request all the information the president had about the events in Rhode Island, and to report to the House any recommendations the committee found suitable.[21] Dorr was unhappy about the failure to bring the committee directly to Rhode Island for hearings, but he had to acquiesce. He dispatched specific instructions to Burke from

Newport Prison on the conduct of the investigation and the content of the report. The central points should be "the right of the People of R.I. in the Case proposed," and whether they exercised that right "by voting for their Constitution." Burke should begin with the *Nine Lawyers' Opinion* defining "popular sovereignty," look carefully at Dorr's speech of 18 November 1841, and then survey all the "papers in the Case of *Martin Luther* v. *Luther M. Borden & others.*" Dorr listed the names of prominent Suffragists who must be interviewed. In addition, Burke should secure one or two of the most principled Suffragists to serve as aides to the committee. Under the limits of authority granted to the committee, every effort must be made to present a complete record to demonstrate the legitimacy of the Suffragist theory and actions.[22]

Dorr told Burke, "The greatest fact of all is the vote of the People for the Constitution." Aaron White had the records to prove that the People's Constitution won an absolute majority of all citizens as well as of freeholders.[23] Dorr confessed that a few bad votes had been accepted in Newport, but he pointed out that even the Algerines admitted the validity of the overwhelming majority. The records had not been widely publicized because the charter government had threatened to use them as a guide to prosecution under the Algerine Act. White would send them on, or would come to Washington himself to help in the conduct of the investigation. With all the evidence on their side, Dorr could see no reason to doubt that the final victory was at hand.

From 29 February to 3 June 1844, the Burke committee met irregularly on seventeen occasions to take testimony or discuss the evidence.[24] Aaron White, Welcome B. Sayles, John S. Harris, Colonel James Bankhead, and Captain John B. Vinton appeared for personal statements. Most of the testimony was taken by deposition before authorized agents in Massachusetts.[25] The committee followed Dorr's instructions in most respects. Two questions dominated the discussions. Was the People's Constitution legitimate? Did President Tyler unconstitutionally use the military power of the nation to suppress it? The Democratic majority on the committee overrode all minority objections to the first question and merely verified an earlier conclusion on the second. The tone and content of the majority report indicated that principles and not actions constituted the fundamental concern.

Burke predictably became the workhorse of the committee. He drew all the resolutions and the final report, conducted the debates concerning the creation of the committee and the possible acceptance of its majority report, kept all the records, and made all the decisions concerning the committee's work. He complained about the burdens imposed on him, but was "willing to make any sacrifice in this great cause." However, he had warned Dorr earlier that most Democratic congressmen lacked the backbone for a real fight. They "have . . . very little of the pure spirit of Democracy. We are a little too far from the People, to feel its purifying influence."[26] Burke regretted Dorr's decision to return to the state to be tried for treason. Much better to remain free and continue the struggle for the cause, "the great principle of free government." He thought that the trial of a man who merely affirmed his belief in the Declaration of Independence and the Revolution was "the foulest blot that has ever yet fallen on the bright escutcheon of the Republic." He vowed to conduct the investigation and prepare the report in a way that would place Dorr's principles forever "beyond controversy."[27]

Burke's Report, as it came to be known, included 968 pages of documentation and 86 of conclusions and resolutions. The minority, under the leadership of John A. Causin of Maryland, submitted a conflicting report that had 131 pages of documents and 38 of conclusions.[28] The former condemned John Tyler for usurpation and reaffirmed the Suffragist principles of popular sovereignty and peaceable revolution. Burke stated categorically that the People's Government had displaced the charter and remained the de jure government of Rhode Island until after the election of 1843 when the people acquiesced in the

Algerine Constitution. He did not urge the restoration of the People's Constitution. Throughout he stressed the need to educate Americans on the proper principles of American constitutionalism. On the other hand, Causin sustained the president's actions, castigated the Suffragists as revolutionaries, and insisted that the charter government had remained de jure until displaced by the new establishment under the Algerine Constitution of 1843. Causin held that governments could only be changed with their own consent. Otherwise there would be no security, stability, or permanence in government. In his view, the guarantee clause of the Constitution obligated the federal government to protect state establishments against any unauthorized efforts to undermine their authority. Thus he urged the House to commend President Tyler for the faithful execution of his duties under the Constitution.

The two reports were submitted in early June, just days before Congress adjourned during an election year. As a result, both were ordered printed but their consideration by the House was postponed until Congress reconvened in the fall.[29] That the Democrats failed to exploit a useful campaign document indicates that opinion was split over the issues raised in the report. Burke himself did not run for reelection in 1844, but he remained a fervid Democrat. It seems clear that timing and concern about the reaction to the report led him to postpone its publication. In addition, Burke unquestionably felt that the report should be used for educational purposes and not as a mere campaign circular. Its bulk and style of argument hardly fitted it for mass consumption. Much more good would result if the report became the authoritative statement of American constitutional ideals and principles. Burke aspired to be a leader of the people rather than a mere politician.

Burke actually departed from Dorr's instructions in important ways. First, he made no pretense that the committee or Congress had the authority to resurrect the People's Constitution after two years of oblivion. Second, he stated straightforwardly that the massive participation in the election of 1843 legitimated the Algerine Constitution. Dorr had never admitted that the People's Constitution had been displaced. But after reading Burke's report, he acquiesced. Having done so, and having secured the confirmation of Suffragist principles embodied in the resolutions Burke offered, Dorr waited impatiently for Congress to take some decisive action. Not much happened. When Congress debated the reports, all the old complaints were aired by both sides. However, the majority preferred to debate the matter and leave action to others.

Burke's resolutions began with the assertion "All power is inherent in the people." By that he meant that the people "have . . . an inalienable and indefeasible right to alter, reform or abolish their government . . . as they may think proper."[30] The Rhode Islanders had claimed no more than their constitutional rights when they repudiated the charter in favor of a constitution of their own making. They had exercised the same prerogatives when they registered and voted under the Algerine Constitution in April 1843. But the final act that legitimated the current constitution of the state did not affect the criminal culpability of President Tyler and various federal officers who had aided the charter government in the suppression of the People's Constitution and Government in May and June 1842. Burke called for censure of all involved. He warned that Congress must do at least that much to protect the revolutionary and democratic heritage of all Americans.

Members of the conservative coalition in Congress savagely attacked Burke and his resolutions. Lucius Q. C. Elmer of New Jersey blamed the Democratic majority for perverting the principles of the Declaration of Independence and the Constitution. He argued that Dorr had voluntarily incurred both moral and legal guilt by abandoning peaceable agitation and attacking the Providence arsenal in May 1842. Civil war had begun with that act. Elmer denied even a semblance of cause for that outrage, since the charter government had already offered to institute the reforms demanded. No one questioned the right of desperate people to try to escape from the chains of tyranny. But who thought that any American government could be described as tyrannical? The patience and moderation shown by the charter government made the Suffragists seem like willful children lacking any sense of decency and fair play. Elmer wanted them laughed out of Congress.[31]

Elmer added substance to his critique in an analysis of the principles of American government. He argued that Americans had surrendered even the great moral right of revolution when they ratified the Constitution in 1787-1788. That instrument provided for popular control of government and for its own amendment should the need arise. Within the Union, the federal government had the supreme power to oversee the operations of government at all levels. The major responsibility of the supreme government was to insure that all political activity was legitimate and lawful. No residuary sovereignty remained with the people after 1787. By the act of ratifying the Constitution, they willingly submitted to its prescribed forms and procedures and the statutes adopted in pursuance of its terms. In 1842 some few deluded men in Rhode Island had assumed the right to resist a lawful order issued by their state government and corroborated by the president. In doing so, they committed revolution and transformed themselves into common outlaws. The only reward they deserved was a trial before a proper tribunal so that sentence could be imposed as required.

Henry Williams of Massachusetts condemned Elmer's doctrines as anti-American. He accused the New Jersey representative of too much association with aristocrats and monarchists. It was absurd to deny the right of revolution in the United States. The nation had begun with the exercise of that great right. Americans would never surrender it simply to satisfy the qualms of a few theorists and aristocrats. Self-government meant the right of revolution to Americans. Elmer's contention that the president must sustain every existing government would subvert all that Americans believed proper. Williams thought the Rhode Island situation ought to be viewed in perspective. The Suffrag-

ists had merely defended themselves against governmental oppression. If treason was committed, the supporters of the
charter government were guilty. Williams doubted that the
Congress or the American people would trade their revolutionary heritage for the tyranny of the Dorr War.[32]

These exchanges characterized the debates in Congress. Once
the points had been made, both reports died on the table. Dorr
emerged from prison in the summer of 1845 already aware that
the congressional strategy had produced little if any benefit.
Principle had been upheld. The arguments for right had been
publicized more extensively. Still rhetoric and unenforced
resolutions amounted to a pyrrhic victory at best. Frustrated
once again, his obduracy merely increased. He refused to believe
that properly informed Americans would ever allow such a
travesty as that of the summer of 1842 to become a precedent.
There had to be a way to awaken them to the dangers involved.

Actually Dorr had concluded even before the Burke Report
was debated that Congress might refuse to act. Hence he set
afoot two additional tactical initiatives designed to produce
practical results. While acting as the supervisor of the Burke
Committee from Newport Prison, he tried to commit the Democratic National Convention of 1844 to the defense of the
principles of popular sovereignty and peaceable revolution. His
interest in the convention indicated that he still believed that
only a political settlement for the Rhode Island question was
possible.[33] He had initially considered the idea in early 1843
when he had the option of attending the convention himself.[34]
But his decision to submit to arrest and trial forced a change in
plans. Thus in the spring of 1844 he prepared a set of resolutions for introduction by the Rhode Island delegation in alliance with Ohioans at the convention.[35]

In Baltimore the convention never seriously considered
Dorr's proposals because of the objections raised by Calhoun
and the southerners. Calhoun thought them subversive of good
order. In addition, he warned that if the Democrats adopted
them, John Quincy Adams would lead the Whigs in an assault

on southern state governments. Better to avoid the entire subject.[36] As a result, Dorr's resolutions were postponed in the interest of party unity during an election year. In great outrage, Dorr insisted that the "pretext of avoiding all 'new issues' " frustrated his efforts to convince the Democrats in 1844.[37] He tried again four years later, with more success. At least, the Democratic candidate in 1848 ran a campaign built around the principle of popular sovereignty applied in the territories.[38] Unfortunately, however, the principle no longer meant all that Dorr had in mind when he used it.

In the struggle for right, the Suffragists had relied in turn on direct action, violence, and political machinations. Nothing had worked. In 1845, after the publication of Burke's Report, they had gained no ground. In fact, they had lost much over the interim. Ironically, almost every American admitted the theoretical authenticity of Suffragist principles, but very few stepped forward to defend them. Since 1841 the Suffragists had called incessantly for a return to the ideals of the founders of the republic. They saw themselves as the guardians of the true American faith. Yet every day brought increasingly bitter denunciations of the reformers as anarchists and demagogues bent on the destruction of the American way. How can this disparity of perception be accounted for? Which, if indeed either, had a base in reality?

Actually both conceptions were accurate. The Suffragists were the intellectual progeny of the revolutionary generation. In 1776 the first Americans "fought in the name of a revolution, a first creation, that they had not instigated."[39] They repudiated not only the connection with the British Empire, but the total world-view of Europe as well. In conceptual terms, they intended to cut away the artificial social, political, and intellectual order created by Europeans in America. Once that had been done, the "natural" order of things could prevail; America and Americans could become what "Nature and Nature's God" had decreed for them. In their terms, the Americans in 1776 consummated a counterrevolution rather than a revolution. That is, they destroyed history and its artifacts so that what should exist naturally could emerge. The Suffragists conceived of their movement in a similar fashion. Their conception of the "modern age" had an Adamic quality about it that belied its progressive implications. Their belief in progress rested on the assurance that immutable principles would prevail with no recognition that principles change, as well as conditions, over time.[40] They intended to reestablish the natural order perverted by history and locked in by the artificial institutions of mid-century America. They, too, were counterrevolutionaries. They defined the natural order they sought in concepts bequeathed them by the founding generation.

Great numbers of Americans reacted with horror to Suffragism because they identified the American way by reference to existing institutions. They saw those institutions as the concrete manifestations of the American spirit and environment.[41] Thus when Suffragists proclaimed that America was not being "true to itself," Americans recoiled from this threat to their very identity.[42] That they misconstrued Suffragist conservatism for progressivism did not affect the validity of their conclusion. Indeed, the Suffragists would have destroyed the American way as it existed in 1840. Seen from this perspective, the Suffragists were revolutionaries. Determined to recreate the older America of formlessness and near anarchy, Suffragists threatened to deny American history just as their forebears had denied European history. Little wonder that they failed; Suffragism was an anachronism.

Very few understood these relationships in 1845. The opponents of Suffragism continued the effort to see that it failed. Dorr and the Suffragists struggled against increasing odds to defend their vision of America. Failure in Congress and the political convention provided the incentive for new thought. After careful consideration Dorr concluded that the judicial strategy had been the best one all along. He had changed his mind considerably since his conviction for treason in 1844. The utility of transforming the Rhode Island political question into a litigable issue dawned on him as all other avenues were closed. To do so involved still further drastic alterations in theory. This last creative effort produced a mature understanding of the Wilsonian doctrines of popular sovereignty and peaceable revolution. By 1845, for Dorr as for many other Americans, the United States Supreme Court had truly become the court of last resort.[43]

7.

THE JUDICIARY

Judges always stick by the Govt. right or wrong.

The ideas of popular sovereignty and peaceable revolution developed side by side with the notion of judicial review. The earliest proponents of the three ideas found no conflict among them. As James Wilson said, if errors were found in government, the judiciary could correct them by upholding the Constitution; if in the Constitution, the people could act. Alexander Hamilton expressed a similar theory in the *Federalist* when he described the judges as intermediaries between government and people, although he rejected Wilson's conception of peaceable revolution.[1] A committed institutionalist and an early advocate of government as administration, Hamilton viewed a constitution as an artifice intended for eternity. It violated logic and common sense to construct a constitution and then leave it to the whims of transient majorities. Constitutions were designed to guarantee security and stability for property and rights. To function properly, they required more permanence than absolute majoritarianism allowed. Hamilton concurred that all proper governments rested on the consent of the governed, but he denied the right of the people to change government at will. Changes must be made in accordance with the procedures outlined either in the Constitution itself, or in the laws adopted under its auspices. Thus, while Hamilton and Wilson agreed that courts had the authority to set aside unconstitutional governmental acts, they disagreed about the power of the people.

Other Americans, who misunderstood Wilsonian constitutionalism and repudiated Hamiltonian institutionalism, also distrusted the judiciary. Years of experience with colonial, imperial, and Federalist-controlled courts had taught that judges were subordinate members of the executive department of government. During the Jeffersonian period, Americans widely assumed that political control of government implied the right to install acceptable men as judges.[2] Such a view, of course, jeopardized the theoretical accomplishments of the founding period.[3] How could there be an independent judiciary to function as the third balance-weight in the perfect constitutional mechanism if political majorities changed the judges as the wind shifted? As in all political matters, Americans professed allegiance to new ideas but acted in old and trusted ways. An independent judiciary meant to most people that the judges shared the prevailing political philosophy. When judges opposed dominant opinion, Americans complained bitterly about the usurpations of appointed officials exempt from political control. Only gradually did Americans discover the importance of a judiciary staffed by impartial and competent men.

Public attitudes toward the judiciary were more important in the United States than elsewhere because of the unique function assigned to the judges. Many scholars have shown that questions resistant to resolution in the political arena came finally to rest before the bar in some American court. Moreover, if the decisions obtained through trial and review failed to satisfy the parties, the common response was an appeal to the Supreme Court of the United States. Grounds were easily manufactured to support federal jurisdiction, and the federal courts up to the Supreme Court invited appeals despite often patent fabrications of such jurisdictional grounds. Even so, the majority of Americans during the pre-Civil War period refused to recognize Supreme Court decisions as conclusive. The practice of submitting to that high tribunal's pronouncements evolved slowly over years of dispute and experience. Acceptance of judicial supremacy came as part of the movement toward administrative rationality. It had gained ground by 1840, but had yet to win widespread approval because many Americans still believed that judges reflected individual and class biases in their decisions. Until that belief decayed, the argument over the judiciary would continue.[4]

Americans had reason enough to suspect the judiciary. American courts reflected the interests of the groups controlling government. This happened in other countries also, but the superior powers of American courts made for worse abuses here. The contributions of the courts to the rise of free enterprise and corporate capitalism in America are well known. Their early protectiveness toward vested interests is equally striking. The legalistic thrust of American thought allowed the judges to influence if not to control political, economic, and social development.[5] Political thought took the character of a progressive constitutionalism, and constitutional law served to bridge the gap between ideology and reality. Depending on the time and circumstances, constitutional law was understood to express either the indwelling spirit of the American people or the positive aspirations of the prevailing majority. Eventually the Supreme Court gained the authority to decide which definition applied.[6]

The constitutional struggle in Rhode Island made an important contribution to the establishment of judicial supremacy in the United States, although that hardly seemed likely in 1842. The Suffragist leaders never really trusted the judiciary. Suggestions of an appeal to the courts appeared very early, but not until all else failed did the Suffragists overcome their dislike for the conservative bias they discerned in the decisions of most judges. Then they convinced themselves that courts had no choice but to uphold the principles dating from the Revolution. They thought that conservative men always chose the old solutions for new problems, failing to take into account the concern of conservatives to preserve intact what exists. What existed in 1842 differed greatly from what had existed in 1776. Calling the judges to protect the American revolutionary heritage, the Suffragists invoked the power that destroyed them. In this way, they prepared the way for judicial absolutism.

From the outset, one group of Suffragists introduced new ideas in the guise of traditionalism. They argued that the guarantee clause of the Constitution set up legal rights defensible in courts.[7] Political rights deserved as much protection as property rights. The law of contracts applied to both. Rights were rights, whether to material objects or to intangible relationships. Actually American constitutional law distinguished between controversies involving tangible objects and those relating to abstract political considerations. In a series of cases ranging from *Marbury* v. *Madison* in 1803 to *Decatur* v. *Paulding* in 1840, the Supreme Court had held consistently that litigation required a contest over concrete, possessory rights.[8] Claims to sovereignty hardly satisfied the prerequisites. But legalistic Suffragists countered that the Constitution provided explicitly for self-government. Denial of that right created a litigable issue. That their argument flew in the face of numerous precedents changed nothing. Centuries of error could not gainsay right.

Radical Suffragists rejected this theory until after reliance on direct action, violence, and politics failed. Dorr, White, and others held to the old view of limited judicial power. Their arguments derived from what has been called the doctrine of political questions. Courts applied existing law, whether statutory or constitutional. They did not make law, nor could they change law simply through interpretation. This mechanical view of jurisprudence reflected the distrust with which most Americans viewed the judges, seeing them as interested agents rather than impartial arbiters. Few Americans could explain how courts could make law and simultaneously respect the decisions of the political branches of government. Hence the tendency was to deny all law-making power and to conceive of judging as the application of known laws to particular sets of facts. That most Americans also accepted judicial review meant that they conceived of the review function in the same terms. Judges merely placed the offending act of government alongside the pertinent clauses of the Constitution. If the two conflicted, the act must fall. Political questions were not amenable to this mechanical approach. It followed that courts could not resolve them.

Radical Suffragists denied the authority of courts to resolve political disputes because of their concern for the principles of popular sovereignty and peaceable revolution. If the people had the inherent power and the inalienable right to change government at will, it made little sense to require confirmation by the courts. Instead, the courts must respect the decisions of the people. All levels and branches of government were bound by an expression of the majority will. Dorr and his supporters dismissed the idea of an appeal to Congress, the president, or the federal courts to sanction the right of the people to act. But the attitude and actions of President Tyler forced them to recognize some role for the federal authorities in the process of changing government. Faced with the possibility of intervention in favor of the charter government, the Suffragists constructed a theory that required federal defense of the decisions of local majorities. When their efforts to persuade Congress and the president failed, it was an easy leap from dependence on the political branches of government to the judiciary.

Suffragists had no choice but to develop legal arguments in defense of their theories after the treason prosecutions began in late 1842.[9] Two lines of thought were suggested, and Suffragists used them indiscriminately. One relied on the claim that treason was an exclusively national crime. The other rested on a fuller grasp of the juridical implications of the doctrine of peaceable revolution. Dorr used the former in his own trial in 1844, and Samuel Y. Atwell developed the latter in defense of Franklin Cooley, tried for treason in December 1842. Atwell held that the government of Rhode Island had been legally altered in May 1842, when the People's Constitution took effect. He offered in evidence the results of the ratification and general elections held in December 1841-January 1842 and April 1842. In addition, he cited numerous authorities to prove that American majorities could alter government at will. When Dorr read the record of the trial, he discovered that Cooley's counsel had imposed a legal gloss on the political theory incorporated in the *Nine Lawyers' Opinion* and Dorr's speech of 18 November 1841. Encouraged by the result, he doubted that Cooley could be convicted.[10]

For once he was right. The jury refused to follow the instructions of the judge, and a new trial had to be scheduled.[11] The example made a strong impression on the Suffragists. Within less than a year, the two Luther cases were initiated in federal court. Dorr and White, however, were not convinced that a case could be brought before the Supreme Court with any hope of success. Even if one could be arranged, the Court would merely determine whether the rival governments were republican in form. Undoubtedly the decision would go against the Suffragists, because the charter provided for the proper form. The Court would not bother with alleged defects.[12] Moreover, Dorr argued that theoretical considerations militated against reliance on the judiciary. There was always the possibility that a court would "decide that the People of a State *cannot* make a Constitution without permission from the government." In that event, would the people "be satisfied" with the ruling? He doubted that they would. "They would justly say, this is a Tory Court and push on for their rights." He still believed the Rhode Island question was "a People's question, properly to be settled at home." The Suffragists should not commit themselves to abide by the doubtful decision of an untrustworthy institution.[13]

Meanwhile the Algerine government discovered the means to assure convictions in the state treason trials. The alleged crimes had been committed in Providence County, but the Algerine Act of 1842 allowed trial anywhere in the state at the superior court's discretion. After offering amnesty to those who would recant, the government moved all further treason trials outside Providence County. The stratagem proved successful. Three trials occurred before Dorr's, and all three ended in convictions.[14] Two of the defendants escaped punishment by seeking nolle prosequis from the government. The third, Martin Luther of Warren, courted martyrdom. Serving as his own counsel, he informed the court that "the law under which I am indicted was null and void; in fact, a constitution had been adopted, and the law was in violation of it, and the constitution of the United States." He followed Atwell's example and offered election results in proof of his contentions. As for the acts charged, "I do not deny them. In the same situation I would do them again. I only deny that I acted in any way illegally or contrary to law."[15] Judge Durfee ruled the evidence inadmissible. This time the jury accepted the court's ruling and found the accused guilty of the crimes charged. Luther was sentenced to six months in solitary confinement at hard labor and fined $500, the minimum penalty. No doubt his intransigence influenced the decision to punish him.

From Newport Prison in early 1844, Luther wrote encouraging advice to Dorr. He explained that he had not pressed his argument because he preferred imprisonment to evasion. "I believe I can do more good in this room to the cause than I can out of it." Fear of prisons had already done enough damage. Luther thought it past time that "some of us Shook of[f] the Sin and Cowardice, and came up with you to the help of the Lord." He urged Dorr to "plead against the jurisdiction of the Court, for there is no way the Court can let themselves down so gracefully as to sustain that plea." Luther knew that Dorr intended to appeal to the Supreme Court of the United States. He offered tactical suggestions on the means to the end.[16]

Dorr was not yet convinced of the merits of the judicial strategy. After his conviction in Newport, he perfected his appeal to the Supreme Court on the treason issue. However, by the time his case reached the Court's docket, he had changed his mind. The Luther cases covered the ground more fully than his own, and they were sponsored collectively by the Rhode Island Suffragists. Thus he turned all attention to them. Describing them as involving the basic principles of American government, he searched for counsel competent to argue before the Supreme Court in December 1845. When the trial date arrived, he had already secured written authorization from Martin Luther to act as chief counsel.[17]

Martin Luther and his mother consulted other Suffragists before instituting their suits. Welcome B. Sayles, Hezekiah Willard, Charles F. Townsend, Samuel Y. Atwell, Benjamin F. Hallett (a leading Massachusetts Democratic lawyer), and a few others participated in these discussions.[18] By late 1843 the Suffragists were ready. When Justice Joseph Story convened the circuit court in Providence, the case of *Martin Luther* v. *Luther M. Borden et al.* began its slow course toward resolution.[19] Benjamin F. Hallett represented Martin Luther, while John Whipple and Richard Ward Greene, acting privately rather than as United States district attorney, spoke for the defendants. Hallett asked $5,000 damages for his client, charging that the defendants had committed trespass by invading Luther's home without leave or warrant. Defense counsel entered a four-part plea admitting that the entry occurred, but insisting that the men acting under cover of martial law had not committed legal trespass. Hallett countered that the defendants had acted at their own risk, since martial law was unknown to the American constitution. Even if it had been possible to institute martial law as the defendants claimed, Hallett contended, the charter government had possessed no authority to do so. With the issue joined, argument on the merits proceeded.

Hallett offered to prove that the People's Constitution and Government displaced the charter and the old government in May 1842. He submitted as evidence documents pertaining to the elections and the operations of the People's Government. In response, Whipple and Greene insisted that the charter had never been legally superseded until May 1843. They presented legislative journals, court records, military orders, and other materials to prove their contentions. In addition, they cited the statute establishing martial law and the specific orders addressed to Borden and the other militiamen. Hallett objected to these arguments. Both sides emphasized the constitutional questions involved, giving only secondary attention to the definition of martial law and the responsibilities of military commanders. The court had to decide between them.

Justice Story ruled that Hallett's arguments and proffered evidence were irrelevant. This had been previously arranged, with the understanding that Hallett would object. The strategy agreed to by the parties and the judges was to use a pro forma decision to construct the grounds for an appeal to the Supreme Court.[20] The issues were far too important to be left to a jury, or to be resolved by an inferior court. The first Luther case ended in a verdict of *not guilty* intended as a temporary delay. Focusing on the means of changing government in the United States, it was designed to force the Supreme Court to define the bases of legitimacy. Most Suffragists were confident that their arguments were logically and legally irrefutable. Few suspected that the Supreme Court would merely uphold the perfunctory circuit court verdict, ignoring the weighty issues.

Aaron White did warn against the perils of overconfidence. After Martin Luther's case was appealed, White predicted that "if it goes to Washington on the ground stated . . . it will injure our cause exceedingly."[21] Even if the Court sustained the People's Constitution, that would mean at most that the Algerine Constitution was equally legitimate, since the majority of Rhode Islanders had registered and voted under its terms. White thought the only proper reliance for Suffragists was on the people themselves. People changed their minds; they could be influenced to support reform. But appeal to the Supreme Court bound the Suffragists to abide by a decision, even a hostile one. Majorities should never invite that possibility. Courts lacked the competency or incentive to decide such cases fairly. White thought that "they are & always have been, the worst tribunals possible; . . . always adverse to popular rights." Anyone who read the decisions of the Supreme Court knew that "the Judges always stick by the Govt. right or wrong."[22] But White's advice fell on ears nearly deafened by precipitate shouts of victory. Dorr and the Suffragists had once again found a panacea.

Rachel Luther brought suit against the same militiamen on grounds of personal trespass.[23] Her counsel contended that the charter government had acted contrary to law in suspending the civil institutions in June 1842. The second Luther case was undoubtedly intended as a precautionary measure. Should the Supreme Court rule unfavorably on Martin Luther's case, the Suffragists could still win a major victory in a decision outlawing the use of military force to suppress political dissent. Aaron White probably deserves the credit for convincing the Suffragists to initiate the case. He urged them to secure a ruling on "whether the Power retained by the States to proclaim Martial Law is in fact a power to abrogate all law." He accused the Algerines of acting as if "Martial Law and no law were the same thing."[24] White apparently believed martial law was the law of war, and that the authority to invoke it was exclusively national under the Constitution. If the states had any military power at all, it extended only to the use of the militia to aid in the enforcement of statutory law.[25] No government or official had the authority in the United States to suspend the laws. White's analysis formed the basis for the second Luther case.

Once again Hallett argued for the Suffragists. He accepted White's arguments and refused to concede the legitimacy of martial law as used by the charter government.[26] Describing it as the law of war that accrued solely to the military in the event of necessity, Hallett denied that any legislature had the authority to invoke it. Moreover, even if martial law had existed legitimately in Providence and Chepachet because of the presence of armed troops, it could extend no farther. It was limited to the theater of hostilities occupied by the contending armies. English and American law admitted no more than that. Hallett urged the judges to instruct the jury that men who acted as the militiamen did must bear the consequences.

Justice Story stated that he thought this trial had been designed to determine whether authority under martial law "was abused." When Hallett rejected that interpretation, Story ruled abruptly that "martial law . . . declared by the State,

... extended all over the State." The term "State," in Story's usage, referred to people and territory. He denied that martial law was merely the law of the camp, and thus restricted to military situations. He agreed that military commanders must act summarily in the exigency of battle. If that entailed damage to property or abuse to citizens, the commanders could legitimately urge the necessity of the situation and claim indemnity from prosecution or suit for damages. Their government incurred responsibility for their actions. But practice during war emergencies had no direct bearing on the issues in Rachel Luther's case. The circumstances and the applicable law were very different.[27]

In Rhode Island during the summer of 1842, the General Assembly had invoked the inherent power of all governments to protect the state against violence. The situation had become "so urgent, that . . . [the] legislature judge[d] a resort to the most extraordinary means of resistance necessary, and accordingly declare[d] martial law." Once proclaimed, martial law had bound all persons and institutions within the state. "It is the same with this as with any other law—courts cannot look into the causes of its being enacted; they find it on the statute-book, and are bound to carry it out." Story regarded martial law as the emergency power of any government to deal with challenges to its authority. As such, it might be related to the authority of military commanders to resort to summary procedures, but it differed in its legal impact. Story compared the usage in Rhode Island to that in Massachusetts during Shays's Rebellion and in Pennsylvania during the Whiskey Rebellion. He found no difference worth noting among these episodes. In all three the state resorted to military force and summary procedures to preserve legitimate authority.[28]

Judging by the examples he used and by the circumstances that had existed in the summer of 1842, Justice Story went far beyond a mere restatement of applicable American law. With but one exception (Andrew Jackson's usage during the War of 1812), all earlier American resorts to military power had been limited to the Hallett definition. In Massachusetts and Pennsylvania, martial law had not been declared and troops remained subordinate to the civil officials. There was no attempt to suspend the civil institutions. In Rhode Island, regular institutions gave way before the prerogatives of military power. There was not even a pretense of maintaining the supremacy of civil authority. Story's ruling had the effect of obscuring the novelties of the usage in Rhode Island. But most important, his opinion granted legitimacy in law to acts previously regarded as outside the law. Denying the claim that martial law was merely the law of war, Story outlined a theory of emergency powers that transformed the law of war into the positive, domestic law of the United States.

Having gone so far, Story offered explanations and qualifications. Martial law could not be merely the law of war, since that would limit its operation to the field of hostilities, as Hallett contended. To accept that view would mean that rebels within any state could adopt guerrilla tactics and escape the rigors of martial law by moving about freely. "Such a doctrine could not be maintained for a moment." Surely the state had the authority to extend martial law over its entire territory to deal effectively with rebels who refused to stand and fight. Story's reasoning was at best specious, at worst disingenuous. No doubt rebels would resort to the tactics he described; but equally clear, Hallett's definition allowed martial law to extend wherever opposing armies appeared. Thus to follow Hallett's line of reasoning would have meant that martial law could never be territorially limited in any strict sense. Story preferred the certainty of control that instantaneous state-wide application provided.

But state-wide extension did not mean that military commanders or anyone else could "exercise unbridled authority." To exemplify proper usage, Story cited the only incident involving a resort to martial law in American history since 1787. In 1814 General Andrew Jackson imposed it over the city of New Orleans because of an impending British attack. No one objected to Jackson's actions until after the battle had been won and the British had retired from the area. Then complaints proliferated when the general refused to lift the arbitrary rule. Conflict between civil and military authority inevitably occurred, with the result that a federal territorial judge fined General Jackson for his indiscreet acts. Story stated the rule from the Jackson case as follows: Military officers have no "right, much less . . . [an] exclusive right, to declare martial law." Further, military officers must conduct themselves in accordance with the law at all times, or suffer the consequences. When the judge fined Jackson, he created the precedent that applied to the Rhode Island case.

Finally, Story demonstrated precisely how the Jackson precedent applied. The Rhode Island legislature had established martial law as the law of the state. All military officers had been bound to obey that law. Martial law was at most "an order for all military officers to act according to the exigency of the case." It suspended the common law of the state, and gave "summary power to the military." The soldiers owed allegiance and thus obedience to the state as all citizens did, but soldiers had also to obey the orders of their superiors. They "were not bound to inquire or to judge" whether orders were reasonable or just. The officer issuing the orders assumed the responsibility for them, and the soldiers had merely to obey. Legal liability accrued only from abuse of authority. Thus soldiers acting under cover of martial law incurred culpability only for "any wanton, malicious, mischievous act, which was wholly unnecessary to the object they had in view." Claimants must prove that "the acts were done purposely, maliciously, and designedly" in excess of authority. No other criteria applied.[29]

Story's rulings revealed his fundamental concern, as did his observation "If these principles are not correct, no one can tell what the situation of any State in this Union may be."[30] In the voice of the conservatism stirred into self-consciousness by the Dorr War, Story articulated pervasive doubts about institutional stability. Through his opinion he demonstrated how traditionalism could serve as the basis for necessary innovation to protect the accomplishments of Americans since the Revolution. In a very real sense, Story provides a model useful in the effort to understand how American constitutional thought crystallized into new form under pressure. What emerged was a legal and rational administrative approach to political problems. The new mentality is best described as institutional conservatism. Thus, Story's rulings are important not because they exerted a directive influence over American behavior, but because they reveal the ideological basis for subsequent developments.

Charged by the judge in these terms, the jury might have been expected to refuse damages. Since neither the court nor the jury could question the validity of the decision of the General Assembly to invoke martial law, only the secondary considerations of conduct remained. Using Story's criteria, it is difficult to see how any acts committed under cover of martial law could entail liability. Despite the charge, one juror held out for an award of $100 in damages.[31] He could not explain why, but he was firm. Thus Rachel Luther's case ended a mistrial. In chagrin, Justice Story resorted to fabrication to remove the case from his docket. He manufactured a division of opinion between himself and Federal District Judge John Pitman concerning the right of the jury to decide whether the facts proved the necessity for martial law in 1842.[32] With this tactic, Story sent the second Luther case to Washington to be tried simultaneously with the first.

By 1845 Dorr was convinced that the Supreme Court "will sustain the R.I. cause of popular sovereignty & self-government." Only Aaron White among the Suffragists remained dubious. Men outside the state also changed their minds about the potential of the cases from Rhode Island. The Algerines engaged Daniel Webster to act as counsel, an expensive undertaking indicating uncertainty about the outcome. Friends of the Suffragists followed Dorr's example and accepted the judicial strategy. Silas Wright, for example, who had rejected peaceable revolution and scouted the appeal to the judiciary in 1842, described the Luther cases in August 1844 as "entirely the most important . . . ever . . . submitted for decision . . . under our institutions." He advised the managers of the case to secure counsel competent to expose the sophistry of Justice Story's circuit rulings. Above all, the argument must concentrate on the issues of popular sovereignty and peaceable revolution. David Dudley Field of New York concurred. He wrote to Dorr that "the principles of your movement were the principles of our revolution." He offered his services as a lawyer if Dorr needed them. One Democratic editor caught the common mood of liberals and radicals and described the cases as the means "to settle or overthrow the whole doctrines of the Declaration of Independence." The justices of the Supreme Court had the awesome responsibility of deciding the future of the American experiment in free government.[33]

For three years the Luther cases languished because of tactical and political considerations.[34] Though galling to Dorr and the radicals, these delays provided time to perfect the brief. By late 1847 all points except those concerning martial law had been clarified. In addition, Attorney General Nathan Clifford had been secured as senior counsel. Benjamin F. Hallett and George Turner would assist. Dorr retained intellectual, if not tactical, control over the cases. He instructed Clifford and Hallett to argue the cases "on the high ground of Popular Sovereignty." They were to ignore the "minor point, that in R. Island there was no prescribed mode of proceeding to amend the government." Such trivialities were beneath notice. The Suffragists held that "constitutions and plans of government" erected no "barriers against Popular Sovereignty." Such instruments were merely "forms of expressing, protecting, & securing the Rights of the People, intended to remain in use until the People shall otherwise indicate and direct."[35] Hallett, and Clifford somewhat less enthusiastically, shared Dorr's belief that "the day of triumph will come, when the great doctrine of popular sovereignty now pending before this high tribunal . . . will be reaffirmed as the supreme law of the land."[36]

Argument opened in late January 1848. Clifford and Hallett opposed Webster and Whipple before a bench of six justices. Apparently the desire for final resolution of the controversy overcame Chief Justice Roger B. Taney's reluctance to allow constitutional decisions by less than a full Court. Illness and other causes had delayed the cases far too long already. The members of the Court, opposing counsel, the parties, and many other Americans believed that the time for decision had come. Even so, the Court withheld its judgment until the following year, probably because of disagreement and the political implications during a presidential election year. To judge by the political affiliations of the justices, Suffragists and Democrats had few worries. Taney had been Andrew Jackson's hackman during the bank controversy of the early thirties. Nelson, Wayne, Grier, and Woodbury were all strong Democrats before and after ascending the federal bench. Only McLean of Ohio exhibited Whiggish tendencies, but he usually went with the political wind in the hope of attaining the presidency.[37] If judges voted their political preferences and reflected their backgrounds, the Suffragist-Democrats had a sure victory in sight.

Counsel for both sides began their discussions with an analysis of the jurisdictional question. Hallett urged the Court to decide this controversy on its merits. Referring to earlier decisions, he agreed that in most cases the judges must take judicial notice of existing constitutions and laws. However, that rule did not apply in all instances. If the very basis of law within a state was in contention, the judges must determine where the right lay before rendering a decision. "It is not the question what was the State of Rhode Island," he reminded the Court. "The State is permanent and unchangeable. The constitution is the form of government, and may be changed in form, as well as a statute, if rightly done."[38] Justice Nelson asked Hallett how a court of law could possibly provide relief in a dispute such as this one. Courts merely applied known laws; they did not make laws, nor could they choose which to enforce. Hallett handled the query

easily by pointing out that Nelson's theory applied only when
the courts that were asked to dispense justice in such controversies held their authority by virtue of the disputed constitutions or laws. In this case no such relationships existed. Neither
the charter nor the Algerine Constitution bound the United
States Supreme Court. For that matter, the People's Constitution had no legal existence either, until recognized by the
Supreme Court. The Court must apply the federal Constitution,
specifically the self-activating republican guarantee clause, to
resolve the Rhode Island disputes. That meant, of course, that
the Court must decide in favor of the right of a majority of the
people to change their forms of government at will. The only
applicable criteria reflected the purposes of the guarantee
clause, namely, that all changes broaden popular participation
in government and respect the formal requirements of republicanism.[39]

Hallett ventured beyond those vague statements to explain
precisely what the Court must do. He held that proper judicial
procedure and jurisprudential theory required even a state court
to respect the decisions of the people, whether incorporated in
legislative acts or in referenda. He cited the 1846 decision of the
New York Supreme Court to prove that once the people ratified
a change in the existing constitution, new legal relationships
came into force. He thought the New York precedent aptly
illustrated the rule that popular ratification of a constitution
bound "'the whole community PROPRIO VIGORE.'"[40] He
reminded the Court that the charter government had possessed
no more right or authority in May 1842 to resist the implementation of the People's Constitution than "the old Congress
under the Confederation [in 1789] had . . . to hold over against
the new Congress . . . under the Constitution." In neither
instance had the established government "given antecedent authority or consent" to its own displacement. No one had ever
denied the legitimacy of the achievement in 1789. Hallett
contended that this precedent, combined with the New York
decision, made a clear case in favor of the Suffragists.

Webster's argument on jurisdiction summarized Judge Durfee's ruling in the Dorr treason trial of 1844. The perfunctory tone of the great lawyer's remarks indicated that he doubted the Court would evade the major issues by denying its own jurisdiction to hear the cases. Nonetheless, he stressed the difficulties of decision in controversies affecting the federal nature of the Union. Earlier Supreme Court opinions, particularly *Barron* v. *Baltimore* in 1833, had consistently recognized the supremacy of state governments concerning the great mass of common law rights Americans claimed.[41] Webster urged the Court to remember that the highest court in Rhode Island had already decided the issues involved in the Luther cases. All matters of local law had thereby been placed "above all objection, and after all challenge."[42] The Supreme Court should never reopen settled disputes; otherwise there would be no end to litigation, no security for rights or property. This must surely be the rule on matters of state rather than national power. Webster argued throughout as if the Supreme Court stood in relation to the People's Constitution and the charter exactly as Durfee's court had. He refused to recognize the distinction that Hallett pressed, a distinction based on the source of the Court's authority. He hoped in this way to convince the justices to dismiss the cases, but he hardly expected to win so easily.

At any rate the Court initially accepted Hallett's views and allowed argument on the merits of the cases. This willingness to entertain a ranging review of American constitutional theory characterized the behavior of all the judges who participated in the Luther litigation. For example, neither Justice Story nor Judge John Pitman had questioned the diversity of citizenship between the parties required to sustain federal jurisdiction in the first Luther case. They merely assumed that Martin Luther had established permanent residence in Massachusetts, although everyone knew that he kept his home in Warren and that he had been convicted of treason in Rhode Island. Moreover, no one bothered to state clearly the basis of federal jurisdiction in the second Luther case. In all likelihood, the Suffragists urged the exclusive nature of the war power under the Constitution. But it cannot be established definitively because neither counsel presented argument specifically on that point. This same easy waiver of jurisdictional problems by the justices of the Supreme Court implies a consensus among the parties and judges about the need for a solution to this fundamental argument over proper theory. To avoid further imbroglios such as those in Maryland, Michigan, Pennsylvania, Rhode Island, New York, and Ohio, and to halt the spread of ideas deemed dangerous to the American experiment in free government, the Supreme Court had to decide one way or the other.

Hallett's brief relied on Dorr's theoretical claims and the line of argument developed in the earlier Suffragist litigation. He requested that the Court decide whether "popular sovereignty is a living principle, or a theory, always restrained in practice by the will of the law-making body, and therefore subject and not sovereign." In detail, he stressed the absence in Rhode Island of any constitutionally or statutorily prescribed means of altering the constitution. In doing this he violated Dorr's instructions, but only in the hope of appealing to the known conservative biases of the justices. Having made that concession, he asserted that a change in government executed by the people directly was not "*rebellion*, because a new fundamental law was established, and new duties created between the people and their *agent*, the government. There was no treason, for a new oath and a new allegiance grew out of this fundamental change of law." American principles protected such an "exercise of an inherent, inalienable, fundamental right." The Court should recognize that to rule otherwise meant that "the people will turn out to be very great sovereigns, with very great powers, but without any possible *right* to exercise" them. Unless the Court confirmed the doctrine of peaceable revolution, the American people would be thrown back upon violent rebellion as the only means to change "government of their own creation."[43] Such a decision would abort the American experiment, with serious consequences for all mankind. Americans would find themselves embarked on the dreary road traveled by the peoples of Europe. At the end of the journey, only anarchy, tyranny, oppression, and civil conflagration beckoned.

Hallett realized that Webster intended to portray the Suffragists as unsuccessful revolutionaries. To controvert that argument and to characterize the unique aspects of American constitutionalism, he carefully explained the difference between the right of *revolution* and a *right* of revolution. Both were political, but the former was generic, physical, and natural, the latter specific, legal, and constitutional. Webster and the supporters of the Rhode Island Algerines erroneously conflated the two, thus obliterating the legacy of the Revolution. They held that all revolutions resembled each other and that success was the only criterion for judging their legitimacy. Hallett accused them of confusing a legal right with one dependent on "physical force." The difference between the two conceptions had to be maintained if the American republic was to endure. Hallett argued that the Revolution and the adoption of the Constitution had legitimated and constitutionalized the *right* of revolution for Americans. Juridical considerations, not force, provided the standards for judgment. Under the principle of peaceable revolution, de facto government was not automatically de jure. Might never made right. The right to govern depended on the support and consent of the people. Once the people transferred their allegiance, new governmental forms followed legally and naturally. Force had nothing to do with the process.

To clarify his charges, Hallett warned that Webster and the Algerine supporters intended to substitute governmental for popular sovereignty. Thus, the "moment they have given us the right of revolution, they send the President, at the head of all the troops of the United States, to suppress it." The effect rendered "all State institutions subservient . . . to the military power of the President." Such an arbitrary system of government would prevail for a time, but the long-term result would be to "legalize civil war and disunion." Americans simply would not tolerate encroachments on their autonomy. Abuse of the people in one state would inevitably create unrest within other states, since Americans realized that tyranny could not be territorially limited. At some future date, a federal invasion of one state would lead directly to "civil war . . . through[out] the Union." Because of these considerations, forcible revolution could never serve as the proper foundation for American liberty. "It fails, and we fall back upon the great conservative right of the people; the American doctrine of popular government, . . . that peaceable changes in government are provided as the substitute of violence and bloodshed." In closing, Hallett quoted as the proper guide for the Court James Wilson's aphorism that " 'the people possess over our constitutions control in act as well as in right.' "[44]

Hallett's analysis rested on a view of American constitutionalism widely accepted during the early national period. The exponents of this view gloried in the almost anarchic implications of popular sovereignty and peaceable revolution. Hallett's eulogy to majoritarianism reflected accurately the traditional revolutionary ideology nurtured by the spontaneity and formlessness of American conditions during the first fifty years after independence. Those who espoused this view denied absolutely that majoritarianism would sanction "anything wicked, wrong, or unjust." Moreover, majority rule did not mean that all persons within the polity could participate in government. Criminals, dependent persons, and slaves could not use majoritarian arguments to alter their subordinate status.[45] Instead they must wait for the majority of free, independent citizens to recognize the legitimacy of their claims. Popular sovereignty, while superficially anarchic, nevertheless presumed the maintenance of proper standards for juridical and societal arrangements. In effect, it meant that the beliefs of the majority gave form to the laws and defined social relationships. There was no denial of governmental authority. Rather, the advocates of popular sovereignty affirmed the power of government to carry out the desires of the majority. Indeed majoritarians far surpassed their

opponents in their assertions of the power available to government. But they insisted that government could act only in
accordance with the will of the majority.

This willingness to use government to accomplish ends acceptable to the majority, but not necessarily reflective of the
interests of established groups, raised grave doubts in the minds
of many Americans. Useful to all when no establishment existed, the idea became suspect once the society matured. Although the Suffragists never intended to challenge existing
property rights and social arrangements, their theories carried
the threat that something like that could occur. Far too much
was at stake to acquiesce in the continuance of principles so
potentially dangerous to stability and permanence. Hallett's
arguments revealed the latent radicalism of Suffragist theory
and elicited a response designed to convince Americans that the
revolutionary age had passed. The new imperatives required the
defense of all that had been achieved. Otherwise mindless
change threatened to subvert what now came to be identified as
the American way of life.

Webster and Whipple presented an elaborate refutation of
Hallett's conceptual analysis of American constitutionalism.
Whipple denied that peaceable revolution had any place in the
body of American law. "The boasted power of majorities can
only show itself under the law, and not against the law, in any
government of laws. It can only act upon the days and places
appointed by law."[46] No one, aside from the misguided Suffragists, had ever argued that the federal Constitution could be
amended at the mere whim of transient majorities. "What then
becomes of this vaunted doctrine of popular sovereignty, acting
by majorities?" It existed merely as the right of the qualified
citizens to participate in government under the terms laid down
in constitutions and laws. Whipple contended that "no resistance to the law is countenanced, unless in case of oppression
irremedial otherwise." As Hallett charged, Whipple recognized
only the moral right of violent revolution. At the same time, he

stressed obligation of government to preserve inviolate all existing constitutions and laws. Success constituted the only criterion for justifying a resort to the right of *revolution*.

Webster extended Whipple's argument by tracing American
ideas and institutions to their English origins. He held that
Americans had always espoused a "peculiar conservatism."
They had changed their governments only "where the form"
conflicted with the popular attributes established during the
Revolution. They had never allowed themselves to be misled by
visionary speculation so long as the substance of free government prevailed. Webster denied that Americans had ever
claimed more than the physical power to destroy a government
that became abusive. Even then, they had waited patiently until
all avenues of possible redress short of war had been tried. As
everyone knew who had thought seriously about government
and studied American history, "The Constitution does not
proceed on the *ground* of revolution; it does not proceed on
any *right* of revolution;—but it goes on the idea that within and
under the Constitution, no new Constitution can be established
without the authority of the existing government."[47] Any
other view failed to take into account the conservative traditions in the United States. For Webster, as for Whipple and the
Rhode Island Algerines, revolution referred exclusively to an
appeal to heaven for redress when no earthly judge existed.
Short of such an extreme, people must abide the law as announced by the established government.

In a ranging review of constitutional practice in the United
States, Webster argued that the very purpose of constitutions
militated against Hallett's contentions. The American system
predicated lawful change as conditions required, not a whirl-
wind induced by excessive attention to fads and vagaries. The
best judge of the need for change was the legislature, consisting
as it did of agents representative of all groups within the
society. From 1787 to 1840 Americans had relied on legally
convoked constitutional conventions to solve whatever problems arose. No one before the Suffragists had ever suggested

that people could assemble and alter government at will. If that were the rule, why erect procedures for amendment and qualifications for participation in government? He agreed that sovereignty was "with the people; but they cannot exercise it in masses or *per capita;* they can only exercise it by their representatives." So long as the people elected their governors, no one could deny the popular basis for government in the United States. Suffrage, after all, was "every man's part in the exercise of sovereign power; to have a voice in it, if he has the proper qualifications. . . . Suffrage is the delegation of the power of an individual to some agent." It could only be exercised in accordance with law so as to prevent fraud and assure representativeness. The lawful exercise of political power was the essence of the American constitutional system.

Webster defined republicanism to mean the right of the citizens to elect their governments and the corresponding duty to obey the law until new elections were held. The will of the people should never be confused with that of the popular majority, since the latter changed according to the fancies of the moment. To be known, the popular will had to be registered and measured according to standards previously set by law. Men could not be allowed to gather and count themselves to decide questions of the utmost importance to the entire society. If they could, chaos rather than stability would become the American way. He believed that all Americans preferred security and certainty to the anarchic evils of Suffragist theory. The Court, as the embodiment of law, should exert its authority in support of that preference.

As for the republican guarantee clause, Webster held that it looked primarily to forms. In addition, the domestic violence section of that clause obligated Congress and the president to respect the decisions of existing state governments. Arguing that the clause had to be interpreted in its entirety, Webster concluded that the federal government must support established governments that satisfied the formal requirements. The Constitution and Enforcement Acts adopted by Congress left no recourse. Even if three-fourths of a state's population opposed the existing political establishment, the federal government was obliged to compel compliance with proper principles. The foremost prerequisite for change was the consent of government. Webster quoted the Enforcement Act of 1795 to underscore his argument: "And in case of an insurrection in any State, against the government thereof," the president was charged to order out the militia and to provide assistance upon demand.[48] Under these rules, President Tyler could "not possibly have decided otherwise" in 1842. That ended the argument in Webster's view.

Despite his misgivings about the Luther cases and his obvious desire to convince the Court that it should stay out of the controversy, Webster predicted a great deal of good would flow from a proper decision on the merits. The comic denouement of the grandiose plans of the Suffragists would dispel popular illusions about the nature of government in the United States. Webster's peroration eulogized the "long-seeing" framers of the Constitution who had erected an edifice on the basis of law. The tumultuous passions of majorities, threatening to undermine the social and political order established after the Revolution, could be curbed and controlled by timely action. If the pertinent law was carefully explained and if governmental officials applied it hereafter without compromise or excess, "free government" might continue forever. With these words, Webster articulated the concerns of those Americans who no longer trusted their own judgment on matters of constitutional significance. Free government had come to mean institutional protection against the unpredictable acts of political factions. Judicial activism promised to achieve what political coercion could not—the legitimacy of an imposed consensus on government and society.

Almost as if in afterthought, both counsel presented arguments on the meaning and scope of martial law. Hallett and Clifford followed the reasoning suggested by Dorr, that "martial law is in fact a suspension of all law and a substitution, for a time, of

the military vis major."[49] Dorr also denied its legitimacy under
the Constitution. He instructed Clifford to argue that by resorting to it, the charter government became a "military despotism." Both Suffragist lawyers based their remarks on the claim
that martial law meant military law in the United States and as
such never applied to civilians.[50] They agreed that military
officers could proclaim it during emergencies, but they held
that it never existed unless armed forces took the field for
battle. Thus the deliberate act of the charter government suspending the civil institutions was null and void. Damages should
be awarded to the Luthers, even if the Court refused to recognize the doctrines of peaceable revolution and popular sovereignty. At the very least, Americans should be assured of the
supremacy of the civil authorities at all times. Otherwise, "the
will of the people is dependent on the *military;* and . . . whatever government they set up, or is set up under . . . [military]
auspices, is valid and rightful; . . . [then] might is the criterion of
right, the principle of the Despotisms of the old world."[51] Hallett
and Clifford doubted that the Supreme Court would sanction
such a drastic departure from the Anglo-American legal tradition.

Webster contented himself with a brief citation of Story's
circuit opinion and a statement urging the necessity of summary
power in government. He misconstrued Story's rulings to define
martial law as "the law of the camp," or "the law of war, a
resort to military authority in cases where the civil law is not
sufficient." The only limit to the power "is to be found in the
nature and character of the exigency."[52] In those few words,
Webster provided a definition of prerogative martial law at odds
with the traditional, common law understandings.[53] The institutional bias of the argument was blatant, but it flowed logically from the entire Webster brief and the total response to the
Suffragist theoretical challenge. The Court had to choose between two integrated systems of constitutional thought. Few
Americans realized fully the importance of the choice, not only
for a proper understanding of the law, but for the conditions of
American life and the continuance of the old republic.

With the arguments complete, Dorr waited impatiently for news of the decision. Urged by his friends to come on to Washington, he refused, just as he had refused earlier to argue the cases before the Supreme Court. Deprived of his rights as a citizen by his conviction for treason, he played the role of martyr, respecting the terms of his unjust punishment. By February 1848, however, he became concerned about the delay in Washington. He urged Hallett and Clifford to provide Democratic editors with material to combat the Whig propaganda. Recent developments were mildly encouraging. Webster's brief had initially received wide support for "announcing, in the clearest and most decisive terms, the true theory of American government." But even Whigs were having second thoughts. They realized that "if *government* can do all that Mr. Webster ascribes to it, they . . . are hanging by a single thread; and Mr. Webster, if he have not already deservedly pocketed his subscription fee of $1000, may prepare to submit to a discount upon his full claim for services."[54]

Hallett's letter arrived shortly thereafter to sustain Dorr's lift in spirit. He had done everything possible to correct mistaken impressions in the capital. Webster and Whipple had tried hard to ridicule Dorr and the Suffragists, but they had failed. Most people recognized the fallacies in their arguments. On the whole, Hallett took pride in the forensic efforts of the Suffragists' counsel. He noted that Webster admitted that "we got the question of the People's Constitution fairly before" the Court. "Now what the Court will do is surmise."[55]

Hallett's optimistic appraisal of the Luther hearings and Dorr's myopic faith in the power of right obscured what was actually at stake. The judicial strategy depended for its efficacy on a judiciary responsive to the desires of the majority of Americans. By 1849, when decision was finally rendered, conditions had changed so much that the principles adduced by Hallett, Dorr, Clifford, and other Suffragist theorists had lost whatever power they had exerted earlier on the American mind. New concerns had surfaced, stimulated by the fixation of Americans on the consummation of their continental destiny and the preservation of a mythologized way of life.[56] If the Supreme Court decided on the basis of majority sentiment—that is, consensus—the Suffragists would unquestionably lose.

More important, the managers of the Luther litigation seemed unaware that even a favorable decision might have the effect of reducing the discretion in political action traditionally assigned to the people. If they were aware of that possibility, as Dorr had been earlier, they weighed it against the benefits expected from the establishment of a legal right to change government. But their balance sheet failed to account for another contingency. A decision by the Court sustaining the Suffragists could relegate the paramount right of the people to change government to a technical status equivalent to that of other procedural guarantees, such as the right to a hearing. If so, procedural considerations being equal, what would remain of the "inalienable" right?[57] On the other hand, to have accepted the urgings of Webster and Whipple would have produced the same result. Undoubtedly the Suffragists and their friends preferred to try once and for all to eliminate the threat to popular sovereignty they perceived in the forcible suppression of the Rhode Island reform movement. If they won, institutional prerogatives became irrelevant—it seemed worth the risk.

In a profound sense, the appeal to the Supreme Court manifested a sure grasp of the meaning of constitutionalism. Since the founding period, when James Wilson had postulated a synthesis of politicism and institutionalism, Americans had been struggling to articulate the principles which combined protection of rights with security against tyranny.[58] The Suffragists came as close to the Wilsonian synthesis as any group before them. In addition, their arguments offered assurances that the effort was worthwhile. Although they lacked the insight, energy, and ideological perspective, not to mention the favorable conditions, necessary to success, they nonetheless deserve remembrance as men who devoted themselves to the preservation of American republican ideals.

THE SUPREME COURT

Dorrism had been pronounced a "miserable stain."

Argument ended on the Luther cases in February 1848, but the Court delayed decision for nearly a year. Speculation about the outcome titillated the public mind. A *New York Tribune* correspondent reported that "Dorrism had been pronounced a 'miserable stain' by the Supreme Court . . . composed of eight Loco-Foco and only one Whig." Chief Justice Roger B. Taney, "the friend and disciple of Jackson, is to be the Executor." No one knew whether there would be a dissent, although rumor had it that three of the justices "were in favor of sustaining Dorrism."[1] According to this prediction, the Suffragists would lose because their friends on the high bench would desert them.

Benjamin F. Hallett, junior counsel for the Suffragists, advised Dorr even before the hearings ended that hope was fading fast. Most informed persons thought the Court would evade the substantive issues. Far too few people across the country recognized the need to defend "popular sovereignty." Conditions had changed so much in recent years that "it is considered rather disreputable by the people for any one to stand up on that side against the Aristocracy." He took pride that he had been able to "make the 'Dorr rebellion' and 'Dorr case' (as they sneeringly called it when I began), respectable."[2] While the majority of Americans withheld their active support, they at least sympathized with the great cause of democracy.

Sympathy, however, was not enough. Hallett thought the Court would hold that the Luther cases involved "a political &

local question" not amenable to judicial resolution. Failing that, the justices would probably refuse to "go behind the existing Govt & the decision of the State Courts." Either way, the Suffragists would lose. Hallett felt reasonably certain that at least one justice, Levi Woodbury, Democrat from New Hampshire, "will meet the issue fully." The other five remained as inscrutable as the chief justice himself, whose "mysterious mind . . . none can penetrate till he speaks out." In any case, "We cannot expect a decision until the close of the term, if then."[3]

Conflicting accounts such as these kept Dorr's hopes alive. The longer the delay, the more opportunity for public sentiment to sway the judges. Clifford saw no way that the Court could evade all the issues, referring specifically to martial law.[4] Hallett urged Dorr to prepare a "book on Popular Sovereignty," to become a "manual" for the people. The chance of a favorable decision depended on the success of the Suffragist-Democrats in an educational campaign forcing the justices to take into account the beliefs of the American majority. The problems associated with such an effort were intensified because 1848 was an important election year. Dorr thought the Court might "prefer to continue the case till political affairs shall have resumed their usual tranquility in Dec. next."[5] If so, Hallett and Clifford should hold out for postponement and reargument. They must take all necessary precautions to avert a compromise decision. Dorr suggested a timely reminder to the justices of the benefits of feigned illness to secure a delay. Undaunted, the Rhode Islander wanted a decision bearing directly on all the issues. At the same time he wanted a strategy designed to erase all doubts about the venerable principles of American constitutionalism.

Dorr's tactics and suggestions had little to do with the year's delay. Actually the Court withheld judgment for a number of reasons. The chief justice, who intended to deliver the majority opinion, was ill for a time during the spring. But more important, everyone realized the potential of the decision during an election year. Undoubtedly the justices preferred a calmer atmosphere for the discussion of such explosive issues. Finally, while the chief justice never wavered, he found it necessary to convince some of his associates whose second thoughts revealed questions about the implications of governmental sovereignty.[6] No one really knew how the decision would go until summer, and then it remained a closely guarded secret. Nonetheless, people more or less consciously realized that the Court must decide "whether the people have the right themselves to alter or abolish the governments under which they existed."[7]

Dorr received inside information concerning the decision in early March. Edmund Burke wrote that Woodbury had stated that the outcome "will be adverse to the people." All the details had yet to be arranged, but at least Woodbury would dissent. The New Hampshire jurist "will take the ground that the US Government has no right to interfere in the political discusions [sic] of the people of a State, and that a State Government has no right to declare martial law."[8] Burke regretted the obstructionism of the majority, and he believed the decision proved the untrustworthiness of courts as the defenders of civil liberty. In hindsight, he thought that Dorr had erred in refusing to argue the cases himself. Had he appeared before the high court, the result might have been different.

But Dorr clung to his belief that the justices would have to reaffirm the principle of popular sovereignty. How could it turn out otherwise? The American people would never accept a court decision telling them that government controlled them rather than the reverse. In a letter written on 12 April 1848, he explained the theory sustaining his optimism.

The visible and continually acting powers of a State are those derived from the prescriptions of a Constitution; while the constituent and preeminent power of ultimate Sovereignty is latent and invisible, and held in reserve for the great occasions, which rarely occur, when it becomes necessary to lay anew the foundations of the political State. Hence the People are apt to forget the true origin of political power; as they are accustomed to see no other than that exercised by government, or by themselves, under prescribed and definite rules. It becomes all-important, therefore, that the true doctrine of original and imprescriptable Sovereignty should be kept distinctly in the view of each generation of our countrymen; and that the anti-republican and detestable Sophism of Sovereignty in the government, which is now revived among us, by monarchists in disguise should be thoroughly confuted, and held up to general reprobation.[9]

If men of principle fulfilled their obligations, the Court would have no choice but to respect the will of the people.

Dorr convinced himself during the summer that the public had been properly educated and that the Court would respond. Reflecting on the revolutionary activity in Europe during that year, he explained that the Court would not dare to oppose the prevailing political currents. "What becomes of Webster's injurious Toryism and of the faltering Court, in the midst of the grand resurrection of Popular Sovereignty now going on all over the civilized world!" The most significant aspect of Dorr's reasoning was the obvious return to politicism from the constitutionalism he had espoused in 1845. Whereas he had argued for three years that the Court had the juridical authority and responsibility to affirm popular sovereignty, now he began to argue that the aroused people would force the Court to decide properly. "A decision against the Sovereignty of the People in December next will subject the Court to general derision, and have the much needed effect of putting an end to their life *tenure* of office."[10] With the judges threatening apostasy, Dorr reverted to his earlier position that brooked no impediment to majority rule. Incorrigible in his faith, he anticipated a rising of the people in support of the principles of popular sovereignty and peaceable revolution. Despite the frustrations of the past, he somehow believed that Americans would respond. Less than a week later, he tried once again to commit the Democratic National Convention to "our common cause."[11]

In May Burke sent news that shattered whatever illusions Dorr retained about the merits of the judicial strategy. Reporting on a confidential conversation, Burke informed Dorr that only Woodbury would be "sound on all points" in the case. The judge believed as firmly as Dorr himself in the principle of popular sovereignty. But the majority would hold as predicted. "Therefore they do not go back to inquire how a constitution originated; and in the R.I. Case they leave that great and main question . . . untouched." Only the use of martial law would figure in the decision, and the state would be sustained in all respects. Woodbury's dissent would concentrate on that aspect of the ruling. Burke believed that the decision was acceptable, since it left the main points for resolution by the people themselves in their political actions. He cautioned Dorr that "these, however, are intimations not to be known or present to the public."[1 2]

Nothing changed between May 1848 and January 1849. The opinions came forth just as Burke predicted. But much happened in the larger political sphere. The Democrats splintered in the election of 1848, reflecting disagreements over patronage, the war to expand the American empire, and the principal concern in the Luther cases.[1 3] The major issue in the Democratic campaign was Lewis Cass's version of popular sovereignty. He defined it so vaguely and ambiguously that it meant all things to all persons. He intended in this way to hold together the South-West alliance that guaranteed Democratic supremacy. But two portentous developments spoiled Cass's strategy. First, southerners rejected rhetorical flourishes and voted instead for a military hero who happened also to be a southerner and a slaveholder. Second, a new party emerged, composed of erstwhile Liberty men, Conscience Whigs, and Equal Rights Democrats, led by the redoubtable Martin Van Buren.[1 4] Through this upheaval, Dorr steadfastly urged popular sovereignty as the only principle capable of unifying all sections of the country. He refused to abandon the Democratic party, despite his dissatisfaction with its candidates. He urged all dissidents to return to the fold and thus force the party and its leaders to live up to stated principles.[1 5] Even before the Court announced the decision on the Luther cases, Dorr had returned to politicism and direct action majoritarianism as the guides to American government. In a sense, his regression can be explained as the result of renewed awareness that a people unwilling to help themselves cannot depend on institutions for succor. Ironically, he had helped to create the situation in which institutionalism prevailed. He had now to discover the means to control the institutions.

Taney's opinion on the first Luther case served for both, although he appended a short note pertaining exclusively to the second. The chief justice obviously thought they depended on the same principles for resolution. After giving five pages to review the background, he used nine of tersely written prose to decide the disputes. He considered it irrelevant that the first Luther case had never actually been tried on circuit.[16] As he said, "Much of the argument on the part of the plaintiff turned upon political rights and political questions, upon which the Court has been urged to express an opinion. We decline doing so."[17] This brief yet remarkably complex statement disposed of the Suffragists' contentions, Dorr's subtleties, and Hallett's eloquence without deigning to consider them seriously. Courts simply had no jurisdiction over political questions.

Yet the remainder of the decision belied the ruling. In fact the opinion seemed deliberately calculated to obscure, even to deny, the significance of the Luther cases and to belittle the sponsors. No doubt the alleged right of the people to alter government must be seen as basically a political right, perhaps the highest. For over seventy-five years Americans had conducted their political affairs as if that right laid the base for constitutional government.[18] Acting out their "distinctive revolutionary tradition," they insisted on popular control of government.[19] It might almost appear that the United States had no governmental establishment, so firmly did the citizens hold to the right to change at will.[20] To be sure, arguments had proliferated about the legitimacy of the changes required by altered conditions and demanded by majorities acting with little concern for formal technicalities or the attitudes of established regimes. The advocates of institutional stability had fought hard against the political majoritarians to hold and fix the evolution of constitutional doctrine. To the institutionalists, change seemed often for no purpose at all, but in every contest until 1842 the majoritarians won. Perhaps more significant, not until 1842 did an established regime use military force to maintain itself against a movement for change. Taney's decision shrouded the departure from earlier practice.

In a most profound way, Taney's opinion settled the political dispute by opting for one side. The Suffragists had argued that majorities had the incontestable right to change government. Chief Justice Taney accepted that proposition, but qualified it rigidly. Majorities could change government, but only if they had the physical power to prevail. The right of revolution was a natural and physical right, not a constitutional and legal one. Those who discussed it as a legal right simply misunderstood the principles and practices of popular government. The chief justice, supported by a majority of his colleagues, ruled in effect that might indeed made right, particularly under the American constitutional system. In the final analysis, no other definition would suffice.

Taney noted initially that a decision favoring the Luthers would invalidate the acts of the charter government between the establishment of the People's Government and the ratification of the Algerine Constitution. For six months, if the Suffragists were right, tyranny had prevailed in Rhode Island. The chief justice mentioned this possibility to underscore the need for careful deliberation. Then he turned directly to a discussion of the merits on the request for judgment. Observing that no one questioned the legitimacy of the current Rhode Island government, he explained that the Supreme Court was not impugning the competency of Judge Durfee's court to rule on the legitimacy of the Suffragist movement. Rather the soundness and cogency of the state court's verdict of treason was at issue.[21] These comments were necessary to lay the proper foundation for a review of the issues and to demonstrate the essentially political nature of the controversy.

"No one, we believe, has ever doubted the proposition, that, according to the institutions of this country, the sovereignty in every State resides in the people of the State, and that they may alter and change their form of government at their pleasure." But the validity of a decision to do so could neither be established nor defended in a court of law. "It is the province of a court to expound the law, not to make it. And certainly it is no part of the judicial functions . . . to prescribe the qualifications of voters . . . nor has it the right to determine what political privileges the citizens of a State are entitled to, unless there is an established constitution or law to govern its decision." Taney recognized only those rights specifically enumerated in constitutions or statutes. In this ruling he repudiated the natural rights ideology prevalent in the United States since the Revolution. In its place, he supported the doctrine that governmental prerogatives took precedence over claims of individual rights.

To sustain this view Taney expounded the republican guarantee clause and the Enforcement Acts. The constitutional clause imposed on Congress the obligation to protect the states as political units, just as the Enforcement Acts indicated. The guarantee had no specific or implicit reference to individual rights. Hence the courts had no function to perform in its implementation. The admission and continuance of a state's chosen representatives in Congress constituted official notice to the country of "the proper constitutional authority . . . of the government" and its "republican character." A decision by Congress to admit the representatives from a state "is binding on every other department of government, and could not be questioned in a judicial tribunal." In all respects, the guarantee in Article IV, Section 4 was political, and thus not appropriate for judicial enforcement.

Despite his disclaimer of jurisdiction over the merits, Taney recognized the cogency of the demand for republican government. He admitted that "a military government, established as the permanent government of the State, would not be a republican government." Moreover, if military government was permanently attempted, "it would be the duty of Congress to overthrow it." Nothing of the sort had occurred in Rhode Island, however. Hence the Court would not presume to say that the president or Congress had erred in judgment. But Taney's opinion implied, almost stated, that if Congress approved a military government, the Court would remind the congressmen of their obligations under the Constitution. This part of the Luther opinion reveals that the Court decided the cases as much on the merits as on technical constitutional rules concerning the separation of powers doctrine.

Returning to the major premise, Taney reiterated that the guarantee clause vested no concrete right in individuals. This had to be so, because the people of the states differed radically in their political ideas and preferences. If Congress acquiesced in the form of a state government or tacitly accepted the means used to change an existent government, no objections were allowable. Of course, dissidents always retained the right to agitate for change within their own states, but they must confine their activities to responsible political methods. "It rested with Congress . . . to determine upon the means proper to be adopted to fulfill this guarantee."[22] Congress had done so by adopting the Enforcement Acts delegating discretionary authority to the president to act when the states requested assistance. In the event of disputes such as that in Rhode Island, "the President must, of necessity, decide which is the government, and which party is unlawfully arrayed against it, before he can perform the duty imposed upon him by the acts of Congress." If courts assumed the power to review decisions by the president, "the guarantee . . . is . . . of anarchy, and not of order." More important in functional terms, since the courts had no review authority while a conflict raged within a state, they "cannot, when peace is restored, punish as offences and crimes the acts which [they were] . . . bound to recognize, as lawful" when executed. It made no difference whether the president actually ordered out the troops of the nation to implement his decision. Merely to decide was "as effectual as if the militia had been assembled under his orders."

As for the claim that the charter government had made illegal use of martial law, Taney chided plaintiff's counsel for loose definitions. He denied that the usage in Rhode Island could be compared to that in England under the Tudor and Stuart monarchs. Royal absolutism had no relationship to republican authority. But there were some similarities. The power to defend themselves against insurrection accrued to "the States of this Union as to any other government." That power was "essential to the preservation of order and free institutions." In 1842 the legitimate state government adopted temporary measures "to meet the peril in which . . . [it] was placed by the armed resistance to its authority." No one could impugn such a decision by a legitimate government. As the chief justice remarked, "If the government of Rhode Island deemed the armed resistance so formidable, and so ramified throughout the State, as to require use of its military force and the declaration of martial law, we see no ground upon which this court can question its authority." The government's discretion must be respected, or government could not exist. Once the decision had been made, "it was a state of war; and the established government resorted to the rights and usages of war to maintain itself, and to overcome unlawful opposition." While the declared emergency lasted, military force remained the criterion of law. Military commanders had unlimited and unlimitable authority to seek out, arrest, and even to execute those persons believed on "reasonable grounds" to have "engaged in the insurrection." Of course, this authority extended only to measures necessary to the defense of government and society. But the chief justice failed utterly to identify the boundaries.

In fact, there were no boundaries. Since only the state could identify emergencies, only the state could define the measures necessary to deal with them. Taney held that no one could challenge a decision made by a legitimate state government on questions such as these. But he also stated that military commanders responsible for the administration of martial law would "undoubtedly be answerable" for any "injury wilfully done to person or property," or for measures designed "for the purposes of oppression." He meant in this way to insure that military officers remain subordinate to civil officials. So long as the officers adhered to the charges and instructions given by the civil authorities, there could be no check on their authority. If they resorted to looting, willful murder, or calculated usurpation, suits would lie against them. Even with all this, however, Taney's ruling ignored the major problem. For he merely assumed that the civil authorities would resort to violent measures only for legitimate purposes. If they acted for illegitimate purposes, their authority was nonetheless unchecked. The Rhode Island case was classic in this respect. The charter government deliberately provoked violent resistance from the Suffragists after President Tyler provided the absolute assurances of assistance. Chief Justice Taney's ruling condoned forcible suppression of political dissent. The usual limits on governmental prerogatives had been stretched beyond recognition.[23]

In closing, Taney criticized Justice Story's circuit rulings because of technical errors. Story had allowed counsel for the defendants and the state to submit evidence proving that the charter was not superseded until May 1843. Taney regarded that evidence as irrelevant and unnecessary. Its admission violated proper rules of procedure. All courts, including federal circuit courts, must "know the constitution and laws" of the states in which they functioned. Thus Story should have ruled at the outset that the charter government had been the only legitimate political entity in Rhode Island during the summer of 1842. Had he done so, all the secondary issues would have been avoided. However, his failure did not affect the ultimate resolution of the case. The justice had committed a mere harmless error, since he had been "bound to recognize" the charter government anyway.

The chief justice's opinion contained a ringing statement of institutionalism. The accent throughout rested on the imperative need for governmental authority and prerogatives to preserve stability, order, and liberty. Except with regard to the possible establishment of permanent military government, he rejected the Suffragist arguments. The states had almost absolute discretion over the extent of civil and political liberty within their boundaries. On the point of military government, he suggested that Congress had a "constitutional duty" to control the states. But even there, his major preoccupation with law and order prevailed. That martial law had been deliberately invoked, suspending the usual constitutional rights and guarantees, elicited only a few soothing remarks about the sovereign power of existing governments to decide the needs of the people. Actually Taney's opinion said much more about the prerogatives of state governments than about martial law or the rights of American citizens. Moreover, he failed to provide any standards by which to judge the legitimacy of a resort to arbitrary power by an existing regime. Civil liberty took second place to an institutional concern for stability and order.

Justice Woodbury alone dissented from the chief justice's opinion; but he confined most of his remarks to the proper definition of martial law, since he was in nearly complete agreement with Taney on the other issues. He explained that he wrote his dissent primarily to demonstrate that the views he had entertained before ascending the bench in 1845 had not changed, but that his altered situation imposed new demands. He had supported the Suffragists and defended Dorr while serving as a United States senator. As a political officer of government, he had responsibly taken a position and held to it. But since the issues involved in the Dorr War were political, he had no right as a judge to express even an opinion on them. "The adjustment of these questions belongs to the people and their political representatives, either in the State or general government." The resolution of such questions depended more on "inclination,—or prejudice or compromise," than "on strict legal principles." Movements to settle them sometimes "succeed or are defeated by public policy alone, or mere naked power, rather than intrinsic right."[24] Because Americans of various areas, occupations, and situations entertained such a range of political ideas, one definitive philosophy could never suffice. Woodbury preferred the pluralism of the past.

On the other hand, judges "for their guides, have fixed constitutions and laws, given to them by others and not provided by themselves."[25] If judges assumed the power to decide political questions, "all political privileges and rights would, in a dispute among the people, depend on our decision finally. We would possess the power to decide against as well as for them, and under a prejudiced or arbitrary judiciary the public liberties and popular privileges might thus be much perverted, if not entirely prostrated." According to proper legal principles, "our power begins after theirs ends. . . . We speak what is the law, *jus dicere*, we speak or construe what is the constitution, after both are made, but we make or revise, or control neither." Otherwise an erroneous decision would inevitably produce "revolution, while a wrong decision by a political forum can often be peaceably corrected by new elections or instructions in a single month." Courts checked the other departments of government, but they could not control the people. To provide the courts with the authority to review decisions of the people would erect a political monstrosity "more dangerous, in theory at least, than the worst elective oligarchy in the worst of times."

Despite his concurrence in the chief justice's ruling, Woodbury's analysis proceeded from a quite distinct perspective. Taney had agreed with Webster, that governmental institutions exercised the sovereign power within the society. Woodbury argued from a politicist position, holding that the people remained sovereign and could change government at will if they had the physical power. As Dorr and the Suffragists had done, Woodbury reviewed American history to show that the popular will had always prevailed since the Revolution. No formalities had been allowed to interfere with the progressive realization of republicanism. However, he held that the right of the people to change their government was merely a political privilege. If an established government resisted, and if it had the preponderance of force, those agitating and acting in favor of change "will often be punished as rebellious or treasonable." Woodbury saw no alternative. <u>All that republicanism and civil liberty required was that the defeated groups retain the freedom to strive for stronger parties capable of winning at some future date.</u> A free people had only their own moral and physical power to sustain them against either tyranny or anarchy. If they wanted a change in government, they must attempt it for themselves, assuming all the corresponding risks.

Woodbury defined popular sovereignty as the inalienable right of any people to decide for themselves the nature of their institutions. No person or institution could force them to decide. Nor could their refusal to decide be used to subvert an established government in a court of law. American principles presumed the active participation of the citizenry in politics and government. If the presumption proved unfounded, courts had no authority to change it. Those who wanted it corrected must convince the people of the need. If they succeeded, new conditions would follow accordingly. Once a governmental edifice had been erected, the rule of law bound courts and citizens alike. In Woodbury's analysis, courts had merely to acquiesce in any changes approved by the people and the political branches of government. He regretted but accepted the hard fact that established governments were sovereign so long as their monopoly of power endured. He seemed fully oblivious to the consequence of his theory, that might after all made right.

Having gone this far with the majority opinion, Woodbury registered vehement opposition to the ruling on martial law.[26] He agreed that established governments possessed the authority to compel compliance with the law. But he denied that they could suspend the laws ostensibly to maintain respect for them. After a review of Anglo-American legal history, he held that prerogative martial law, like that used in Rhode Island, had been illegal and unconstitutional since at least 1688. If the term martial law meant anything at all, it referred to the common law of public self-defense. He denied that it was synonymous with military law, since "nothing is better settled than that military law applies only to the military." The only possible definition was based on the responsibility of government to use force to repel force. Military might could be invoked to enforce the laws when the civil institutions failed. But there must be conclusive evidence that the courts could not function before the government could resort to summary procedure. Even then, the troops must be used solely to aid the civil agencies, not to supplant them.

Any other view of martial law "would go in practice to render the whole country . . . a *camp*, and the administration of government a campaign." Never before 1842 had either the federal or state governments laid claim to this power. When emergencies had arisen, the military commanders had assumed both the power and the responsibility to act as circumstances required. If they violated the law, they sought indemnity from "a grateful country." To speak of martial law as used in Rhode Island conjured images of Latin American dictatorships. Precedents clearly showed that such arbitrary power had been "forbidden for nearly two centuries" in "every country which makes any claim to political or civil liberty." To sanction its resurrection, as the chief justice had done, was to expose every citizen "to be hung up by a military despot at the next lamppost, under the sentence of some drumhead court-martial." Woodbury doubted that Americans would ever accept so loose a definition entailing such dire possibilities.

By these definitions and rules, Woodbury concluded that mistrials had occurred on circuit. He was not certain whether the plaintiffs could prove their claims for damages, or whether the defendants had the better side of the disputes. But he was certain that the constitutional authority to wage war was exclusively national. Hence, the government of Rhode Island had no "rights of war . . . which could justify so extreme a measure as martial law over the whole State as incident to them." Since the act declaring martial law had been unconstitutional, and since Story had failed to strike it down, neither trial had been legitimate. He warned that to allow the circuit rulings to stand "will open the door in future domestic dissentions . . . to a series of butchery, rapine, confiscation, plunder, conflagration, and cruelty, unparalleled in the worst contests in history between mere dynastics for supreme power." The only course of action open to the Supreme Court was to remand the cases for retrial under proper principles.

Woodbury's dissenting opinion very nearly reached the constitutional position asserted by Dorr, Hallett, and the Suffragists. The justice went so far as to postulate a constitutional duty of the federal judiciary to preserve civil liberty. Although he found no basis for his decision in the republican guarantee clause, he obviously concurred with the chief justice's contention that permanent military government violated the constitutional requirement. Yet he rejected the Suffragist argument that the guarantee clause provided substantial guidelines for state political practice. In doing so, he ignored the distinction that Hallett had drawn between cases on the federal and state levels involving the doctrine of political questions. In part he accepted the distinction, as his analysis of martial law revealed. It seems highly probable that he brushed aside this line of argument because he sincerely feared the impact of judicial rationalism under a consolidated national government. When the majority of the justices decided in favor of governmental sovereignty, Woodbury reacted as Dorr had by affirming politicist majoritarianism. He thought the only defense for American liberty lay in the preservation of popular sovereignty.

On comparison, Woodbury's opinion was far more conservative than Taney's. The dissenter noted time and again that the chief justice introduced new doctrine by sanctioning the measures instituted by the charter government to suppress the Suffragists. Taney's primary concern was for institutional prerogatives, while Woodbury hoped to maintain the autonomy of

Americans. Within the context of his own presuppositions and the rising concern in the country for stability and permanence, Woodbury had no choice but to settle for a repudiation of arbitrary power like that exerted in Rhode Island in 1842. Nonetheless, even he missed the irony in telling Americans they had the right to change their government unless the government objected.

Contemporary reaction to the Luther decision revealed a wide diversity of opinion. In January 1849 Dorr published an interpretive commentary reflecting his complete withdrawal from Wilsonian constitutionalism. He agreed wholeheartedly with Justice Woodbury. "So far . . . from deciding the Rhode Island Question against the claims of the people . . . , the Court [held] . . . that they did not go far enough; that they did not take the necessary measures to make their government a reality, a fact such as the Court can regard." If anything, the decision actually impugned "our halfway friends, . . . who desired an organization and then insisted that nothing should be done under it, and that the whole object should be referred to the Courts of Law."[27] Dorr, too, missed the irony in a decision purporting to accept Suffragist theory but refusing them redress. As Dorr concluded, the Suffragists deservedly lost their bid to change the government of Rhode Island because they failed to ground popular sovereignty on its necessary base of superior force. After all had been done and said, peaceable revolution meant violent revolution unless the government acquiesced; there was no *right* of revolution distinct from the right of *revolution*.

Henry B. Anthony offered curious corroboration of Dorr's conclusions. "We admit that the question whether the majority of the people of a State . . . have the right in their primary capacity and without reference to the existing laws, to change their . . . government, has not been decided." Actually it had never been before the Court. "It has been decided," he added, "without the intention of the Court, that . . . a few demagogues, taking the name of the people and assuming to act for them, [cannot] make a constitution and adopt and verify it by their own authority. . . . and it has been . . . decided that when the same men take a few rusty muskets and steal a few cannon and throw up a mud fort, and talk very big and run away at the first sight of a hostile bayonet, the government is not thereby revolutionized."[28]

Those decisions had been made by the state government during the summer of 1842. The Supreme Court confirmed them in the Luther cases. Anthony concluded that no one would ever again confuse majority rule with revolution. The former "derives its authority from the law, the other from the overthrow of the law." A majority acting outside lawful procedures was nothing but a mob. In principle, mob action resembled "violence at the polls." In contrast, government based on majority rule required positive proof of a *"legal majority."*[29] Revolution depended solely on superior force; right was irrelevant. Dorr had absurdly attempted to merge these two conceptions. In doing so, he vitiated both. The Court had clarified the issues in its decision. Henceforth all Americans would know that their governmental system ran on the basis of established law.

Aaron White, Dorr's confidant during the years of struggle, offered an apt appraisal of the significance of the Dorr War and the Luther decision. In 1842 he had urged Suffragists and their friends to work to prevent the Rhode Island "Precedent" from becoming law. He had described the events of 1842 as revolutionary, "in precisely the same way in which Revolutions in all former Republics have been accomplished. That is to say by an usurpation of power on the part of those into whose hands power has been entrusted. Since the 25⁻⁻ of June 1842 R.I. has ceased to be a Republic."[30] Initially hopeful that good men everywhere would unite in defense of republicanism, White eventually concluded that nothing would be done. Americans passively accepted rather than actively resisted the transformation of their political system from republicanism to despotism.

As he observed Dorr's futile struggle to vindicate traditional ideals, White changed his interpretation of the crisis of 1842. Indications of an altered perspective appeared in his letters as early as June 1842. Even before the declaration of martial law, he had suggested that the governmental acts might be used as precedents for purposes quite other than the law and order men had in mind. "When President [James] Birney [the abolitionist] takes the throne, we will cram Emancipating Constitutions down the throats of the Southern nabobs by the same rule. For if President Tyler under pretence of suppressing domestic violence can interfere in behalf of a minority of a minority to guarantee an Aristocratic Constitution, a fortiori, may President Birney interfere to guarantee a Republican Constitution, recognizing the equal Rights of all men."[31] Only the will to act was needed.

By 1849 White had either forgiven or come to understand the necessity behind President Tyler's actions. In addition, he argued that the Suffragists had won a pragmatic victory in 1842, albeit at high cost. After all, the franchise had been broadened, and government had become more representative. He had consistently opposed the judicial strategy because he expected a hostile decision. The outcome "has been that which I have always anticipated, viz an avoidance of the main question." Still, it was not as bad as it could have been. He concurred with Dorr's analysis. Far from justifying the claims of the law and order men, the Court actually sustained "your principle of . . . 'popular Sovereignty.' Your view of what would have been the result of successful force in behalf of the People's Constitution is certainly correct & no one can say that you did not do your part to make force successful."[32] The Luther decision confirmed either a politicist or an institutional view of American government. White obviously believed that Americans would soon use it to achieve desired objectives, but in a real way, the decision disallowed the development of the Wilsonian alternative that White and the Suffragists had invoked in 1842.

In the years since 1849 historians have continued the argument between Dorr and Anthony. Some have opted for White's views as well. The standard view until recently has been that the Luther decision falls logically into the line of precedents beginning in the 1790s that denied jurisdiction to courts over political questions.[33] Yet ambiguity pervades the commentaries of most historians. For while they insist that the political questions doctrine required the Court to withhold its hand, at the same time they argue that the decision reflected a desire to avoid imposing a legal straitjacket on the discretion of legislatures and popular majorities. It certainly appears that Woodbury had that objective in mind. But to hold that the majority opinion rested on the same ideological base goes too far. Michael Conron noted this discrepancy in his observation that Taney's opinion served fundamentally to "guarantee civil order." As Conron concluded, the Court actually decided the cases on their merits while disclaiming the power to do so. "An abrogation of positive action had the effect of positive action." Taney and his four supporters acted as the "American counterparts of the Italian *Podesta*, the French crown jurists, and English judges from the time of Henry II to that of Blackstone."[34] Disguising "political activism" in the form of "judicial rationalism," the Taney Court substituted centralized executive power for local autonomy. The effect was to transform an atomistic, not to say semifeudal, society into a unitary state.

For all his incisiveness, Conron missed the larger significance of Taney's opinion. The chief justice resolved the cases by domesticating and emasculating popular sovereignty. Under Taney's legal scalpel, the principle lost its potential to stimulate responsible political action within an autonomous constituency. In institutional form, it required behavior channeled according to formally stipulated means and procedures. Conron erred when he denied that Taney shared the convictions of Calhoun and Causin.[35] All three men viewed the republican guarantee clause as an instrument for the defense of state institutions. The federal government had the obligation under the directives of

Article IV, Section 4 to use military force to protect what existed against subversion. By guaranteeing civil order despite the cogency of complaints about the lack of representativeness in established regimes, the Taney Court legitimated an intensifying urge to view dissent as treasonable. To prevent it, the national government must lend its strength to that of state governments under challenge. What had been a guarantee of form became under this exegesis an assurance of the status quo.

In addition, Conron went too far in his insistence that Taney contributed directly and consciously to the establishment of the unitary state. Actually Taney, Calhoun, Causin, and other conservative Americans hoped through slight innovations to channel and thus to moderate the demands for change. The intent was to shore up the federal government so that it could maintain a nearly static society. So long as it acted only to maintain, to preserve, and to protect previously erected structural arrangements, no limits on its powers could be found. These men did not hope to halt all change, merely to control it. But they failed to appreciate the double-edged character of the power they helped to call into existence. In their hands, the power served its intended purpose. But what would happen when political control shifted? Then the conservatives would learn, as had the Suffragists before them, that power to protect institutions can also be used to destroy them.

Other historians have questioned Conron's argument. Recently William Wiecek has written that Taney erred only in placing all guarantee clause cases under the rubric of political questions. The Luther cases were rightly decided because only the domestic violence section of the guarantee clause was at issue.[36] Proper relationships among the departments of the federal government coerce the Court to acquiesce in a decision made by the president and tacitly confirmed by Congress. However, Wiecek argued, courts can properly adjudicate cases concerned exclusively with republican form under the first section of the guarantee clause. Thus the Taney Court should have distinguished the Luther cases from others that might arise by emphasizing that the president's discretionary actions had closed off other options. Wiecek thought that this approach would leave the way open for litigation of controversies involving the substance of republicanism.

Application of Wiecek's theory to cases akin to those arising in the Dorr War produces the same results that Taney and Woodbury obtained. Under Wiecek's analysis, as with Taney's and Woodbury's, the Suffragists could have won in 1842 only by mobilizing a force more powerful than that of the state and nation combined. Nothing of the sort was possible. Had the Court confined itself to the republican guarantee, ignoring the domestic violence section, it would have sustained illusory rights while sanctioning forcible abrogation of them. In fact, Taney and Woodbury did that. As Hallett, Dorr, and the Suffragists insisted, the only possible theory that preserves rights as the focus of concern requires an interpretation of Article IV, Section 4 in its entirety. The federal government has the constitutional obligation to insure that state governments reflect the aspirations of their constituencies by promoting the widest possible participation in government, and by respecting the equal rights of all citizens. Governmental establishments failing those tests must be changed, either by direct popular action or by mandate from some department of the federal government. To allow nonrepresentative regimes to invoke federal power in their defense against their own constituencies flies in the face of any possible definition of republican government. But it does assure stability, order, and measured change.

Decision in the Luther cases marked a dramatic turning point in the evolution of American social and constitutional ideals. Both Woodbury and Taney used language in their opinions indicating that they feared a decision by the Court on the issues would unrealistically constrict the public space for political action. As already demonstrated, Woodbury's apprehension was more than rhetorical. However, the chief justice defined public space in terms of state prerogatives, undoubtedly because he realized that states with anachronistic institutions would resist standard-ization. But the long-range impact of the Luther decision was to frustrate the intentions of both men. On the one hand, major-itarianism stood no chance until some external force could be invoked to loosen the grip of entrenched minorities. Thus Woodbury could not even guarantee to majorities who lacked physical power the right to agitate and organize for better times. On the other, states could defend their institutions against internal attack so long as the federal government stood ready to aid them. But when local institutions came under attack by a national majority in control of the federal govern-ment, state resistance would become rebellion. In either case, institutionalism prevailed. The only difference lay in the groups deciding which institutions must be protected and preserved. The Luther decision confirmed that conclusion.

The justices relied on the venerable doctrine of political questions to decide the cases. But the final ruling reflected political beliefs and ideals rather than any great concern for technical precision. Equally obvious, the popular side in the controversy suffered a severe defeat. Statements in either opin-ion concerning majority rule were qualified by the contra-dictory insistence on proper forms and procedures. In the last analysis, the Court recognized only the Lockean origins of American constitutionalism, denying the creativeness of the founding generation. Lockeanism was politicism, emphasizing *revolution* rather than the *right* itself. The pronouncement on political questions provided legitimacy for the institutional anal-ysis of American government. Reduced to its fundamental ele-ment, the doctrine of political questions is governmental sover-eignty dressed in legal terminology. It holds that existent gov-ernmental institutions have discretionary powers to decide what is or is not acceptable behavior. So the Taney Court used it in 1849.

In this context, the Wilsonian theory of constitutional gov-ernment seemed hopelessly anachronistic. Dorr and the Suffrag-ists continued to urge its acceptance, but even they no longer understood it.[37] On the one hand, the demands and felt necessities of an ordered society grounded upon the rule of law overwhelmingly balanced the scales in favor of institutionalism against either Jeffersonian politicism or Wilsonian constitutionalism. On the other, the defeated reformers and ideologues saw their only hope in the restoration of simple majoritarianism. No one much bothered with a constitutionalism based on the legal right of the people to alter their governments at will. Something vital had gone out of American ideology.

Epilogue

THE "PRECEDENT OF 1842"

The builder of the family's glory knows what it cost him to do the work, and he keeps the qualities that created his glory and made it last. The son who comes after him had personal contact with his father and thus learned those things from him. However, he is inferior to him in this respect, inasmuch as a person who learns things through study is inferior to a person who knows them from practical application. The third generation must be content with imitation and, in particular, with reliance upon tradition. This member is inferior to him of the second generation, inasmuch as a person who relies upon tradition is inferior to a person who exercises independent judgment. The fourth generation, then, is inferior to the preceding ones in every respect. Its member has lost the qualities that preserved the edifice of its glory. . . . He imagines that the edifice was not built through application and effort. He thinks that it was something due his people from the very beginning by virtue of the mere fact of their descent, and not something that resulted from group (effort) and (individual) qualities.

Ibn Khaldun, *The Muqaddimah* (1381)

On the surface, politics changed little for Rhode Islanders after 1842. The same groups ruled the state, although men and parties realigned themselves in the wake of the Dorr War. Dorr's challenge had shown that while Americans wanted their rights they were uncertain of their ground and refused to use violent means to get them. With the established groups holding firmly to the reins of power, protected by the federal government under the precedents of 1842 and 1849, not much could be done to change matters. So long as the dominant groups applied the lessons of the Whig campaign of 1840 and the suppression of the Suffragists in 1842 to justify their claims to power on the basis of consent given in the past, the demands of anxious reformers failed to excite the electorate. Politics had apparently been routinized into an administrative process.

Aaron White noted the beginnings of change. "No man regrets more than I do the establishment of a military Despotism in R.I. but there it is and what is worse the People of the State are every day becoming more and more familiarized with and reconciled to it. You and I and others have done all that we could to sustain the fundamental principle of popular sovereignty in R.I. but we have not succeeded. There was not virtue enough in our materials, or if virtue there was not strength."[1] In fact, not until well after the Civil War did some persistent reformers spark another "fire" in the hope of winning popular control of government.[2] The Dorr War left Rhode Islanders chary of further instruction in constitutional law when the "modern teachers . . . have rec$\underline{d}$ their text books . . . in the shape of . . . cartridges."[3]

Nonetheless, the struggle to exonerate Dorr continued for nine years after his release from prison in 1845. The amnesty that freed him did not restore his political and civil rights. It was six years before the General Assembly lifted the disabilities imposed by the conviction for treason.[4] Still a relatively young man and deeply interested in politics, he remained in the background and played the role of martyr and elder statesman. When offered a federal patronage position he indignantly refused. "See here, seventeen months of imprisonment in a low damp cell, for a conscientious discharge of my duty . . . paid by an appointment to an office? No! Never will I so demean myself. . . . I [would] rather stay at home with my mother."[5]

Principle alone, however, did not fully explain his refusal. In the late 1840s his always fragile health gave way completely. With his death imminent, Dorr's friends stirred in a last effort to remove the marks against his reputation and the stain from the escutcheon of the old republic. During the January 1854 session of the legislature, a coalition of Equal Rights Democrats and Conscience Whigs introduced a bill to expunge from the state judicial records all mention of Dorr's trial and conviction.[6] In February the legislation passed by a better than two-to-one margin. Dorr's friends reordered history through an exercise of legislative sovereignty to prove their fidelity to the principles of the republic and their respect for the man who symbolized it. Pleased by the tribute, he seemed oblivious to the implications of the act.[7]

Other groups protested this last Suffragist outrage on proper principles of government. Consequently a vigorous minority pushed a resolution through the General Assembly in April 1854 requesting a ruling from the state supreme court on the validity of the Dorr legislation. With unconscious irony, the court held the expungement unconstitutional on the grounds that the legislature had usurped judicial authority to order it. As the judges concluded, "The union of all the powers of government in the same hands is but the definition of despotism."[8] The doctrine of political questions and the principle of the separation of powers served once again as the means to achieve a desired end. The court that had convicted Dorr for treason against the charter in 1844 ruled ten years later that the charter had authorized a despotic, nonrepublican, and un-American form of government. The Suffragist theory had finally been vindicated. But any who derived comfort ignored the impact of the court's action. For much as the Luther ruling had done in 1849, the Dorr decision mocked Suffragist principles. Courts, not people, would define republicanism. The major concerns would be procedural nicety and defense of prerogatives. Whether the decision meant more than that remained to be seen.

Dorr died that same year on 27 December, at the age of forty-nine.[9] During the preceding summer the Congress with the Kansas-Nebraska Act had extended popular sovereignty to the remaining territories of the United States.[10] To a man grown old and enfeebled in the service of the "good old cause," the savor of triumph must have seemed sweet. He had no forewarning of the trauma Americans would suffer over the next few years in a convulsive effort to throw off the cherished principle and replace it with its converse, the theory of governmental sovereignty.[11] Had he glimpsed the future, he would undoubtedly have urged Americans, as he had Rhode Islanders a decade earlier, to hold to popular sovereignty. Any other principle of government was beneath the dignity of a free people. Either they retained their freedom and power to act or they submitted to political servitude in return for the promise of security. But the American people and their leaders opted for the latter, and the Luther decision served as the blueprint for the creation of a nation from the components of the Union. After some hesitation, President Abraham Lincoln and the Radical Republicans became the architect and craftsmen who designed and engineered the remodeling. Dorr's early death spared him this denouement.

The public response to the Dorr War revealed the changes in attitude among Americans since the founding generation. As R. W. B. Lewis has remarked, "The American mind had been . . . jolted at some point between the waning of the Colonial age and the second quarter of the nineteenth century; and it had, as a consequence, become aware of the temporal order and of the distinctions within it of past and present."[12] Besieged by new pressures caused by changing conditions which broke their earlier "deep, organic communion with actual concrete history," Americans were forced to create a new ideological justification for society and government.[13] Central to this restructuring of the symbols of authority was the emergence of a new historical consciousness.[14]

As they lost contact with the founding period, Americans came increasingly to identify the natural order of things by reference to existing institutions and social arrangements. To compensate for the loss of the certainty and security that the myth of the founding had provided, they sanctified the artifacts they had created over time in the belief that the past lingered in the present in the existing institutional structure. Invoking an "institutionalized antiquity" of tradition and familiar arrangements, Americans discovered a new source of certainty and identity in a world that changed so rapidly that few could grasp what was happening.[15] Nourished earlier by the environmental hypothesis of a perfect creation into which life had thrust them and their ancestors, they found it difficult to explain or to halt the perceived degeneration into corruption and disorder. After an initial effort to reform the environment, they arrived by the 1840s at the conclusion that their culture and institutions must also be nearly perfect, as the natural products of the perfect environment.[16] When that happened, the urge to reorder history, to deny its inexorable impetus toward change, lost its power. The desire for a return to the founding, fed by a static and cyclical view of history in which time was the measure of degeneration, no longer moved Americans to action. Instead they accepted what existed as proof of the natural order of things decreed by Nature and Nature's God for the new American nation. Of course, that profound alteration of perspective transformed history from the record of past evils to be avoided into a theodicy justifying the acts of Nature and God.[17] No longer conceivable as mere record, history became process as well. As record it had been manipulable; as process it had simply to be accepted.

The Rhode Island incident proved the unsuitability of the traditional revolutionary ideology that Americans had imbibed since the founding of the republic.[18] Mythic in character, metaphysical in function, that ideology finally collapsed under the strains of its own ambiguities. The Rhode Islanders had not been allowed to alter their government as they saw fit, because of the risks of such indeterminate action to the historic achievements of Americans. Instead, change came in 1843 at the benevolence of constituted authorities. Perhaps change had always happened that way, but great numbers of Americans had believed otherwise. Logically the new dispensation meant that whatever government bestowed it could withdraw. Historically it meant that government had become the rational administration of immanent policies and programs instead of the creative process it had been earlier.[19] In practical terms, the Wilsonian concepts of popular sovereignty and peaceable revolution were found wanting. Required to choose between the formlessness of the semimythical founding period, a time already shrouded in the veil of passing years, and the familiar structure of the historic present, Americans opted for the comforting way of life they knew. The choice was rationalized in Websterian imagery.[20] "American government [and society] was a generic growth from English institutions, and it established sovereignty in the permanent constitutional order of the state."[21] Of course, by the late 1840s "state" no longer referred to the particularist wholes making up the voluntary union, but to the new imperial edifice stretching from the Atlantic to the Pacific. The determinism of the past imposed order on the contingencies of the existential present.

Americans had finally learned that history is the realm of freedom within the realm of necessity. To deny history as the Suffragists had tried to do merely insured that it would exact a harsh toll. This recognition of the determinate as well as the contingent in the human condition made existence less dynamic and much more predictable. As a result, the American self-image lost much of its emphasis on the unique. "America now took her place among the nations of the world. Americans were merely men. The land had come of age, and age was time and tragedy and the end."[22] But as in all history and historic visions, the end was ambiguous; it was also a beginning.[23]

In the wake of the Rhode Island debates of 1842 to 1849, the nation became the scene of a similar struggle over the rights of individuals versus the imperatives of government. The details differ, but the parallels are clear. To show that the logic of the Luther decision applied to more than state concerns, the Supreme Court in 1857 considered popular sovereignty in another context. With Chief Justice Taney again serving as spokesman, the Court ruled that federal power could not be used to destroy existing institutions, specifically the institution of human slavery.[24] The resolution of *Dred Scott* v. *Sandford*, the case that Taney selected as the occasion for his pronouncement denying the power of Congress to abolish slavery in the territories, followed logically from the institutional thrust of the Luther decision eight years earlier. In neither instance did the Supreme Court act from a pure regard for the doctrine of political questions, although the later decision more blatantly displayed judicial activism. In both instances the majority of the justices expressed their apprehensions about the permanence and stability of American social and political institutions.

Taney's Dred Scott decision, like his earlier Luther decision, placed state security and prerogatives above all other considerations. He virtually ordered that American history come to a full stop and that society remain static.[25] Although he argued that practices and arrangements traced to the founding period had special protection under the Constitution, changeable only if the Constitution was altered, Chief Justice Taney based his interpretation on his perception of and support for contemporary arrangements. The Dred Scott decision was an attempt to imprison Americans within an institutional structure idealized in the present but projected into the past.[26] Equally important, it asserted the function of the Court to serve as the bulwark of conservative defense against change.

Taney's 1857 decision collided full force with the new theodicy. Unwittingly he had helped prepare the way for this result in his earlier Luther opinion. In 1849 he had ruled that all governments must have the power to protect the institutions Americans created. In 1857 he invoked this power to protect the states and their institutions against attack by a rising national majority opposed to the perpetuation and expansion of one particular institution, human slavery. Believing that what existed was both natural and beneficial, inclined to define the good society by reference to new cultural forms gradually being shaped by historical experience, the new majority idealized the emerging social order in the North and West that was based on the concepts of free labor and free men. Ironically, Taney's earlier Luther ruling had both manifested and reinforced the new attitudes responsible for the rejection of his Dred Scott opinion.[27] Too many Americans no longer believed in a static and timeless order of things. Thrust into the nineteenth century and its miasma of change, they had come to expect and to welcome qualitative alterations in the way of life. They recognized, if only dimly, the importance of Taney's attempt to protect the present by controlling the past. They knew from recent experience that history happened to them as to all historical peoples, and that change came whether wanted or not. The new theodicy taught that change was always for the better. Having converted to this new ideology, these Americans led their contemporaries (a majority of southerners excepted) in the defense of the historical progress of the nation in 1861.[28]

Taney's Dred Scott decision and the national reaction to it were consequences of the attitudinal shifts revealed by the Dorr War and the Luther decision. Another development of equal importance was the easy acceptance of the new theory of emergency powers Taney had announced in *Luther* v. *Borden*.[29] Basing his decision in 1849 on concern for the prerogatives of state governments, he soon discovered that a doctrine on the make brooks no restraints. Within ten years his theory had been broadened and applied to an analysis of the powers available to all "states," using the term generically rather than in its special American meaning. In 1861 President Lincoln and his supporters used this reasoning to justify the measures taken to resist southern secession. Taney struggled to correct what he saw as misconceptions, but to no avail. By 1861 he was reduced to accusing Lincoln and the Republicans of treason against the Union because of their innovations. Time had confirmed the cogency of Woodbury's dissent in 1849.

After 1857 no one much bothered with popular sovereignty. In its institutionalized form, it was hardly worth bothering with.[30] Some radicals continued to profess loyalty to it as the fundamental principle of American government, but politicians cynically exploited it as a mere vote-getting symbol.[31] Most people probably shared Aaron White's earlier conclusion. Rather than trust the integrity and virtue of the American people to hold the nation on course, new waves of reformers won their objectives by securing control of national power and using it to force the correction of perceived abuses within the society. Coercion, not voluntary compliance and accommodation, became the basis for American government. When that happened, the old republic metamorphosed into something new and different.

The years after 1842 witnessed this rapid decline of the doctrine of popular sovereignty as an ideological imperative. Military suppression of the Suffragists was a symptom of decay; the Luther decision confirmed it; Taney's ruling in *Dred Scott v. Sandford* nearly finished the doctrine; but Lincoln and the Republicans executed the coup de grâce when they led the nation in successful resistance to southern secession. Southerners had actually thought and acted more in terms of state than popular sovereignty, as had Calhoun, Tyler, and Taney. However, most people overlooked the difference and associated the venerable doctrine with the southerners' vicious treason against the hypostatized Union.[32] The graveyards that dot the southern landscape today mark the collective burial ground for popular sovereignty.[33]

Peaceable revolution, the corollary of popular sovereignty,

suffered a similar eclipse. In 1857 James Buchanan, an early defender of the idea, defined it in institutional terms and thus deprived it of practical meaning.[34] Americans had learned from the Dorr War and the Luther decision that there was no difference between the right of *revolution* and the *right* of revolution. Only southerners acted as if the Dorr War had not occurred, and they paid a high price for their temerity. By 1865 everyone recognized that the right of the people to control their governments depended equally upon their ability to mobilize an effective fighting force and upon the acquiescence of established governments. To confirm that conclusion and to explain the historical relationships entailed, the Supreme Court ruled in 1869 that the United States consisted of an "indestructible" union of "indestructible" states.[35] As one scholar has remarked, the nation emerged from the crucible of war fully conscious of itself, determined to develop its resources and to pursue its historic destiny.[36]

These developments laid bare the ideological ramifications of the national reaction to the Dorr War and the Supreme Court decision in *Luther* v. *Borden*. This is not to say that the earlier events caused the later ones in any rigid, deterministic way. Rather, both manifested developmental patterns influenced by ideological and environmental changes. As the old voluntary union of semiautonomous states gave way before the standardizing tendencies of the centralized, industrial nation, juridical rationalism displaced the earlier political theory based on popular sovereignty and peaceable revolution. In a circular and dialectical way, reality and ideality impelled the process toward the emergence of a different America. When the microcosm became the macrocosm, the response to challenge was predictable. Protection for state institutions was easily transformed into protection for national institutions, once the perspective had changed. By 1861 conditions were such in the United States that Americans were forced to create a new ideology to explain reality. The simple republicanism of the first hundred years would no longer suffice.

The crisis of 1861 was, as one scholar has recently argued, a "crisis in law and order."[37] In this respect, it resembled the earlier one in Rhode Island. The response patterns were equally similar, with the Rhode Island incident providing the precedents for action.[38] Americans rushed to the defense of those institutions that had assured order and decency throughout the national period. No doubt, both northerners and southerners saw themselves as the defenders of the American way. But in another sense, the victors had stood at Armageddon to guarantee the historic destiny of the American nation. In doing so, probably without realizing what was happening, they had answered with their arms the query posed by the Suffragists and southerners about the validity of traditional ideals.

In the years after 1865 (with beginnings much earlier), a new American ideology took shape. In form it differed little from the old, the usual pattern when ideals change. People cannot shed their ideologies as easily and completely as snakes molt their skins. An end of ideology is at once a demise and a new borning.[39] The cathartic experience of symbolic death and rebirth disguises the changes that occur as old ideologies receive new meaning that makes sense out of altered conditions by providing new perspectives. In another sense, the end of an ideology refers to the restructuring of its internal components giving the whole new substance while the form remains the same.[40] The Civil War forced Americans into this process of restructuring their old symbols. Out of it came an ideology more in tune with the expectations of inevitable and unending progress into a future that rushed down on them so rapidly as to shatter their awareness of continuity. The extended crisis of the middle period of American history was punctuated by the various moments in this process. The Dorr War of 1842 marked the collapse of belief; the Civil War became at once the crucible of death and the womb of rebirth; and the late nineteenth century provided the time and impetus for reconstructing the symbols of authority.

After the Civil War Americans no longer had a revolutionary

tradition.[41] The loss of millions of lives and dollars in the struggle to erase it from the American mind cannot be overlooked. Still, forcible repression of ideas carries only so far. Americans more nearly outgrew their older ideology or traded it for one promising security, stability, and progress than surrendered it on threat of violent repression. They came to prefer order, stability, and institutionalized liberty assured by the advent of juridical rationalism to excessive worry about the conditions of freedom.[42] The paradox of the Dorr War (as Aaron White pointed out in 1842) and of the Civil War is that both contributed to this denouement despite the intentions of the participants.[43]

Fred Somkin has speculated that somewhere in the years between 1815 and 1862 "a great American body lies buried."[44] Unappreciated and unmourned, the old republic died giving birth to the republican empire. Use of metaphorical language does not mean that one abstraction replaced another. Rather the intent is to characterize what changed as Americans altered their images of themselves and their society. Undoubtedly most did not recognize the future as it enveloped them. Unquestionably most continued to believe that nothing of substance had changed. But the reality of historical evolution exacted its usual price of destroying the old to make way for the new. Should the gravesite be sought by curious visitors, a search through the period between 1842 and 1849 will lead to those clues that establish its precise location.

NOTES

Prologue

1. Louis Hartz, *The Liberal Tradition in America* (New York: Harcourt, Brace & World, 1955), chap. 1.

2. Louis Hartz, "The Rise of the Democratic Idea," in *Advance of Democracy*, ed. J. R. Pole (New York: Harper & Row, 1967), p. 24.

3. Richard Hofstadter, *The Progressive Historians: Turner, Beard, Parrington* (New York: Alfred A. Knopf, 1969), p. 453.

4. See: George M. Dennison, "The Dorr War and the Triumph of Institutionalism" (Paper delivered at the Organization of American Historians' Convention, Chicago, April 1973); George M. Dennison, "American Constitutionalism and the Idea of Revolution" (Paper delivered at the Pacific Coast Branch of the American Society for Legal History Convention, Los Angeles, November 1974); Gordon Wood, *The Creation of the American Republic: 1776-1787* (Chapel Hill: University of North Carolina Press, 1969); and Paul K. Conkin, *Self-Evident Truths: Being a Discourse on the Origins and Development of the First Principles of American Government—Popular Sovereignty, Natural Rights, and Balance & Separation of Powers* (Bloomington, Ind.: Indiana University Press, 1974), for analyses of the origins of the ideology. See also Robert G. McCloskey, ed., *The Works of James Wilson*, 2 vols. (Cambridge: Harvard University Press, Belknap Press, 1969), 2:770-71, for a statement of the key idea.

5. See: Marvin E. Gettleman, *"Political Opposition and Radicalism in the Dorr Rebellion"* (Paper delivered at the Organization of American Historians' Convention, Philadelphia, April 1969); and Jacques Ellul, *The Technological Society*, tr. John Wilkinson (New York: Random House, 1964), chap. 1, for similarities between the American and Roman views on this point.

6. Fred Somkin, *Unquiet Eagle: Memory and Desire in the Idea of American Freedom, 1815-1860* (Ithaca, N.Y.: Cornell University Press, 1967), p. 4.

7. George M. Dennison, "Martial Law: The Development of a Theory of Emergency Powers, 1776-1861," *American Journal of Legal History* 18, no. 1 (January 1974): 52-79.

8. For useful surveys, see: Arthur May Mowry, *The Dorr War; or, The Constitutional Struggle in Rhode Island* (1901; reprint ed., New York: Chelsea House, 1970); George M. Dennison, "The Constitutional Issues of the Dorr War: A Study in the Evolution of American Constitutionalism, 1776-1849" (Ph.D. diss., University of Washington, 1967), chaps. 4-7; and William M. Wiecek, *The Republican Guarantee Clause of the U.S. Constitution* (Ithaca, N.Y.: Cornell University Press, 1972), chap. 3.

9. Aaron White, Jr., to Dorr, 1 September 1842, vol. 5 of the Dorr Correspondence: Personal and Political Letters Written to Thomas W. Dorr, with Copies of His Answers to His Correspondents Arranged in Chronological Order, Covering the Years 1820-1854, John Hay Library, Brown University, Providence, R.I. (hereafter cited as DC).

10. Richard Hofstadter, *The Paranoid Style in American Politics and Other Essays* (New York: Random House, 1967), chap. 1; and Karl Mannheim, *Ideology and Utopia: An Introduction to the Sociology of Knowledge* (1936; reprint ed., New York: Harcourt, Brace & World, 1968), pp. 97-101, 156-60, 276-77.

11. See Robert E. Shalhope, "Toward a Republican Consensus: The Emergence of an Understanding of Republicanism in American Historiography," *William and Mary Quarterly*, 3d ser. 29, no. 1 (January 1972): 49-80.

12. Edward A. Shils and Henry A. Finch, eds., *Max Weber on the Methodology of the Social Sciences* (Glencoe, Ill.: Free Press, 1949), pp. 52-54, 89ff., 147-48, 160-88.

13. George M. Dennison, "*The Idea of a Party System:* A Critique," *Rocky Mountain Social Science Journal* 9, no. 3 (April 1972): 31-43.

14. Aaron White, Jr., to Dorr, 1 September 1842, DC, vol. 5.

15. *Martin Luther* v. *Luther M. Borden et al.*, 7 *Howard* 1 ff. (1849).

Chapter 1

1. Martin Luther to Dorr, 28 March 1844; and (for the characterization of Mrs. Luther) Lydia Dorr to Dorr, 22 April 1844, DC, vol. 8. See also Dan King, *The Life and Times of Thomas Wilson Dorr, with Outlines of the Political History of Rhode Island* (Boston: Dan King, 1859), p. 183.

2. It was referred to as the charter government because it was based on the old royal charter of 1663.

3. Events reconstructed from testimony in: *Martin Luther* v. *Luther M. Borden et al.* and *Rachel Luther* v. *Luther M. Borden et al.*, 7 *Howard* 1 ff. (1849); *House Reports*, 28th Cong., 1st Sess. (1843-44), series no. 447, vol. 3, doc. nos. 546 and 581, pp. 357-76 and 157-67 (hereafter cited as *House Reports*, ser. 447, vol. 3, proper doc. no.); "Supreme Court, U.S., No. 6, December Term 1848, Luther v. Borden et al." National Archives Microfilm (housed in University of Washington Law School Library, Seattle) of RG (Record Group) 267: Appellate Case no. 2419 (Transcript of Record, Mandate, etc.)(hereafter cited as *Luther* v. *Borden*, RG 267: Appellate Case no. 2419); "Records of the United States Circuit Court for the District of Rhode Island (Record Group 21), *Martin Luther* v. *Luther M. Borden* and *Rachel Luther* v. *Luther M. Borden*," Microfilm (in author's possession) of Case Files, Minutes and Dockets, and "Final Records," Archives Branch, Federal Records Center, Waltham, Massachusetts (hereafter cited as *Luther* v. *Borden*, R.I. Circuit, "Records of Circuit Court"); and *Providence Daily Journal*, 17-19 April 1844.

4. Still the standard account, Arthur May Mowry, *The Dorr War; or, The Constitutional Struggle in Rhode Island* (1901; reprint ed., New York: Chelsea House, 1970), chaps. 1-4.

5. *Rhode Island Acts . . .* (various eds., Providence and Newport: By Order of the General Assembly, 1724-1800). See also Chilton Williamson, *American Suffrage: From Property to Democracy, 1760-1860* (Princeton, N.J.: Princeton University Press, 1960), pp. 58, 178-79, 243.

6. Jacob Frieze, *A Concise History of the Efforts to Obtain an Extension of the Suffrage in Rhode Island; from the Year 1811 to 1842; and the Dorr War, 1842,* 3d ed. (Providence, R.I.: Thomas S. Hammond, 1912), pp. 16, 145-46; and Peter J. Coleman, *The Transformation of Rhode Island: 1790-1860* (Providence, R.I.: Brown University Press, 1963), p. 262. Coleman is an excellent source of information on economic and political change in Rhode Island.

7. *Public Laws of the State of Rhode Island* (Providence: Order of the General Assembly, 1798), pp. 146-50, 180-88, with the provisions remaining unchanged until after 1842.

8. *House Reports,* ser. 447, vol. 3, no. 546, pp. 249-50, 274-76, on events of 1820-1821.

9. Marvin E. Gettleman and Noel P. Conlon, eds., "Responses to the Rhode Island Workingmen's Reform Agitation of 1833," *Rhode Island History* 28, no. 4 (October 1969): 75-94.

10. For comparison, consult Loren Baritz, *City on a Hill: A History of Ideas and Myths in America* (New York, London, and Sydney: John Wiley & Sons, 1964), chap. 5, on Emerson. On Dorr, see George M. Dennison, "Thomas Wilson Dorr: Counsel of Record in Luther v. Borden," *Saint Louis University Law Journal* 15, no. 3 (Spring 1971): 398-428; and C. Peter Magrath, "Optimistic Democrat: Thomas W. Dorr and the Case of Luther vs. Borden," *Rhode Island History* 29, no. 4 (October 1970): 94-112.

· 11. Charles Tabor Congdon, *Reminiscences of a Journalist* (Boston: James R. Osgood & Co., 1880), pp. 108-9.

12. See: Mary Ann Newton, "Rebellion in Rhode Island" (Master's thesis, Columbia University, 1947), pp. 43-44, 46, 122-24, 146-47, 189; and Mrs. F. H. (W.) Green (MacDougal), *Might and Right: By a Rhode Islander,* 2d ed. (Providence, R.I.: A. H. Stillwell, 1844), pp. 325 ff.

13. Dorr to William B. Adams, 7 March 1831, DC, vol. 1.

14. Dorr's draft of a letter to George Bancroft, 25 November 1835, DC, vol. 1.

15. Dorr to William B. Adams, 28 May 1832, DC, vol. 1. See also Chilion Williamson, "The Disenchantment of Thomas Wilson Dorr," *Rhode Island History* 17, no. 4 (October 1958): 97-108, esp. 100-101; and G. J. Fox to Dorr, 12 October 1832, DC, vol. 1.

16. *An Address to the People of Rhode-Island, from the Convention Assembled at Providence, on the 22d Day of February and Again on the 12th Day of March, 1834, to Promote the Establishment of a State Constitution* (Providence, R.I.: Cranston & Hammond, 1834). This was signed by others, but written by Dorr.

17. Dorr to Christopher Robinson, 2 April 1834, and Charles Randall to Dorr, 11 August 1834, DC, vol. 1.

18. Various letters of 1834, esp. Randall to Dorr, 11 August and 22 October 1834, DC, vol. 1.

19. Gettleman and Conlon, "Responses," pp. 84-87.

20. Frieze, *Concise History,* pp. 24-28; Green, *Might and Right,* p. 70; Mowry, *Dorr War,* pp. 43-45; and various letters, 1834-1835, DC, vol. 1.

21. Welcome Arnold Greene, *The Providence Plantations for Two Hundred and Fifty Years: An Historical Review of the Foundation, Rise, and Progress of the City of Providence . . . and the Other Towns of the State . . .* (Providence, R.I.: J. A. & R. A. Reid, 1886), p. 79.

22. Philip A. Grant, Jr., "Party Chaos Embroils Rhode Island," *Rhode*

Island History 26-27, nos. 4 and 1 (October 1967 and January 1968): 113-25, 24-33.

23. Charles Randall to Dorr, 18 August 1835; and J. A. Brown to Dorr, 12 November 1835, DC, vol. 1.

24. Charles B. Peckham to Dorr, 11 March 1836, DC, vol. 1.

25. This can be seen especially clearly in Charles Tilley to Dorr, 1 June 1837, DC, vol. 2.

26. William Peckham to Dorr, 31 May 1837, DC, vol. 2; and Grani, "Party Chaos."

27. Bryon Diman to Dorr, 2 January 1837, marginalia, DC, vol. 2.

28. George Curtis to Dorr, 17 August 1837, DC, vol. 2; and the broadside, Aristides [Dorr], *Political Frauds Exposed; or, A Narrative of the Proceedings of "The Junio in Providence," concerning the Senatorial Question, from 1833 to 1838* (n.p., 1838), dealing with the election of 1837-1838.

29. "Private Daily Note Book for 1845-1850 of Thomas W. Dorr," entry for ? January 1848, Dorr Manuscripts, John Hay Library, Brown University Library, Providence, R.I. (hereafter cited as DM). This is a separate collection from the Dorr Correspondence (cited as DC).

30. Ibid., entry for 26 July 1848.

31. Charles Randall to Dorr, 15 August 1837, DC, vol. 2.

32. William M. Chace to Dorr, 18 July 1837; and Dorr to William M. Chace, 25 July 1837, DC, vol. 2.

33. Dorr to Dan King, 18 and 23 August 1837, DC, vol. 2.

34. Philip B. Stiness to Dorr, 8 November 1838, marginalia, DC, vol. 2.

35. E. R. Potter, Jr., to Dorr, 19 August 1839, and other letters of 1839, including one addressed to President Martin Van Buren, signed by Dorr and Dutee J. Pearce, a Democratic congressman, DC, vol. 2.

36. Dorr to James G. Birney, 26 December 1837, and Dorr to J. C. Ames, 7 June 1838, DC, vol. 2.

37. Dorr to Edmund Quincy, 29 September 1838, DC, vol. 2. Newton, "Rebellion in Rhode Island," p. 46, among others, argues erroneously that Dorr repudiated his antislavery stance.

38. Dorr to John L. O'Sullivan, ? January 1838 and 18 November 1840, DC, vol. 2.

39. "Private Daily Note Book for 1845-1850 of Thomas W. Dorr," entry for ? January 1848, DM; and Dorr to John L. O'Sullivan, ? January 1838 and 18 November 1840, DC, vol. 2.

40. Dorr to William Boyce et al., of Philadelphia, 2 January 1843, DC, vol. 5.

41. Dorr to William Simons, 26 September 1842, DC, vol. 5; see also draft of undelivered letter from Dorr to Theodore Sedgwick, the younger, condemning Sedgwick as "a pretender to democracy," 24 February 1844, DC, vol. 8.

42. Magrath, "Optimistic Democrat," p. 112.

43. Dorr to Franklin Cooley, Samuel Wales, and F. L. Beckford, 1 February 1843, DC, vol. 6. See also: Dorr to William M. Chace, 25 July 1835, DC, vol. 2; Aaron White, Jr., to Dorr, 28 November and 30 December 1842, DC, vol. 5; Dorr to Aaron White, Jr., 27 April 1843, DC, vol. 7. Also "Private Daily Note Book for 1845-1850 for Thomas W. Dorr," entries for ? January and 26 July 1848, DM; and "Autobiographical Sketch," Dorr to John L. O'Sullivan, 1 August 1845, DM.

44. See Dennison, "Dorr War and the Triumph of Institutionalism."

45. Remarks of John C. Calhoun, 2-3 January 1837, *Congressional Globe*, 24th Cong., 2d Sess., "Appendix," pp. 64-89; John Tyler to James Lyon, 29 December 1838, Tyler Papers (microfilm), Manuscripts Division, Library of Congress.

46. *Providence Daily Journal*, 2 October 1841.

47. See: Kurt B. Meyer, *Economic Development and Population Growth in Rhode Island* (Providence, R.I.: Brown University Press, 1953), pp. 19-20, 25-26, 31, 41-42; Coleman, *Transformation*, pp. 90-98, 120-24, 135-36, 185, 219-21, 225-29, 236-37, 256-59; William M. Wiecek, *The Republican Guarantee Clause of the U.S. Constitution* (Ithaca, N.Y.: Cornell University Press, 1972), pp. 86-89; and Dennison, "Constitutional Issues," chap. 4.

48. *House Reports*, ser. 447, vol. 3, no. 546, pp. 377-401. The report is mentioned in Congdon, *Reminiscences*, p. 105, and Abraham Payne, *Reminiscences of the Rhode Island Bar* (Providence, R.I.: Tibbits & Preston, 1885), pp. 48-49. It figured in reform literature as a great abuse.

49. William Peckham to Dorr, 3 February 1837, DC, vol. 2.

50. Mitford Mathews, *A Dictionary of Americanisms on Historical Principles* (Chicago: University of Chicago Press, 1956), p. 389. For usage of the term to apply to Whigs in Rhode Island, C. W. Woodbury to Dorr, 26 June 1840, DC, vol. 3.

51. Congdon, *Reminiscences*, pp. 78, 104-6.

52. Ibid., pp. 106-7. Actually the association was founded in early 1840, but deliberately remained quiescent until after the election, as see Green, *Might and Right*, pp. 70-72. The *New Age* remained in existence as a weekly until April 1843, although the publishers and title changed periodically, and it also had a daily counterpart. I refer exclusively to the weekly, which included the materials from the daily, and cite *New Age* as the title throughout.

Chapter 2

1. Remarks of James Buchanan, 2-3 January 1837, *Congressional Globe*, 24th Cong., 2d Sess., "Appendix," pp. 64-89. The context is discussed in George M. Dennison, "An Empire of Liberty: Congressional Attitudes toward Popular Sovereignty in the Territories, 1787-1867" (Paper delivered at the Rocky Mountain Social Science Association Convention, El Paso, April, 1974).

2. William Peckham to Dorr, 3 February 1837, DC, vol. 2.

3. On the circular, see: John Bach McMaster, *A History of the United States from the Revolution to the Civil War*, 2d ed., 8 vols. (New York: D. Appleton & Co., 1896-1913), 7:167; Edward Field, ed., *State of Rhode Island and Providence Plantations at the End of the Century: A History*, 3 vols. (Boston and Syracuse: Mason Publishing Co., 1902), 3:661; and Arthur May Mowry, *The Dorr War; or, The Constitutional Struggle in Rhode Island* (1901; reprint ed., New York: Chelsea House, 1970), p. 48.

4. Chilton Williamson, "Rhode Island Suffrage since the Dorr War," *New England Quarterly* 28, no. 3 (March 1955): 34-50.

5. Dorr to William Simons, 27 February 1843, DC, vol. 6. See also Robert L. Ciaburi, "The Dorr Rebellion in Rhode Island: The Moderate Phase," *Rhode Island History* 26, no. 3 (July 1967): 73-87.

6. For quotations from the charter, see Mrs. F. H. (W.) Green (MacDougal), *Might and Right: By a Rhode Islander*, 2d ed. (Providence, R.I.: A. H. Stillwell,

1844), pp. 70-75. Joseph Sabin, ed., *Dictionary of Books relating to America*, 29 vols. (1868-1936; reprint ed., Amsterdam: N. Israel, 1962), 18:185, attributes the charter to Jacob Frieze.

7. See: Green, *Might and Right*, pp. 76-78; Mowry, *Dorr War*, pp. 46-48; and *New Age*, November 1840-April 1841.

8. See: *New Age*, April-June 1841; *Providence Daily Journal*, February-May 1841; and Green, *Might and Right*, pp. 80-86, 90-91.

9. As quoted in Field, *History*, 1:336.

10. *New Age*, 19 February 1841.

11. On the "counterrevolutionary" tradition in American history, see Roland Van Zandt, *The Metaphysical Foundation of American History* (The Hague: Mouton & Co., 1959), pp. 45-50. I understand the counterrevolution tradition as a disguise for revolution, thus making the latter more palatable.

12. *New Age*, 12 February 1841. See also Green, *Might and Right*, p. 78, and Mowry, *Dorr War*, p. 59.

13. *New Age*, 14 May 1841. See also *Providence Daily Journal*, 11 May 1841, and Mowry, *Dorr War*, pp. 63-71.

14. Ciaburi, "Moderate Phase," pp. 73-87; and C. Peter Magrath, "Optimistic Democrat: Thomas W. Dorr and the Case of Luther vs. Borden," *Rhode Island History* 29, no. 4 (October 1970): 94-112.

15. Kirk Thompson, "Constitutional Theory and Political Action," *Journal of Politics* 31, no. 3 (August 1969): 655-81.

16. *New Age*, 19 March 1841; *Providence Daily Journal*, 11-12 June 1841; and Mowry, *Dorr War*, pp. 35-37.

17. *New Age*, 19 March 1841.

18. *New Age*, 12 and 19 March 1841.

19. Ciaburi, "Moderate Phase," pp. 73-87.

20. On Atwell generally, see Abraham Payne, *Reminiscences of the Rhode Island Bar* (Providence, R.I.: Tibbits & Preston, 1885), pp. 97-102; on his report, *Providence Daily Journal*, 26-27 June 1841.

21. *New Age*, 1-30 June 1841, esp. 3 and 25 June 1841.

22. *New Age*, 2, 9, and 23 July 1841; and *Providence Daily Journal*, 7 July 1841.

23. *New Age*, 23 July 1841.

24. Ibid. See also *House Reports*, ser. 447, vol. 3, no. 546, pp. 269-71.

25. *New Age*, 6 August 1841. See also issue for 30 July 1841.

26. The judgment was made by a critic of the movement, as see Henry C. Dorr to Dorr, 17 June 1841, DC, vol. 3.

27. Henry C. Dorr to Dorr, 25 October 1841, DC, vol. 3.

28. *New Age*, 27 August and 3 September 1841; *Providence Daily Journal*, 28 August 1841. See also Mowry, *Dorr War*, p. 95, for the vote. Westerly, East Greenwich, and West Greenwich did not elect delegates to the People's Convention. Mowry found that five out of eight People's delegates were qualified freemen.

29. Dorr to Jesse Calder, 4 May 1841, DC, vol. 3. See also Jesse Calder to Dorr, 3 May 1841, and Wyllys Ames to Dorr, 4 January 1841, marginalia, DC, vol. 3; *New Age*, 3 September 1841; and Charles Tabor Congdon, *Reminiscences of a Journalist* (Boston: James R. Osgood & Co., 1880), pp. 108-9.

30. Henry C. Dorr to Dorr, 17 June 1841; and John L. O'Sullivan to Dorr, 9 August 1841, DC, vol. 3.

31. Philip B. Stiness to Dorr, 8 November 1838, marginalia, DC, vol. 2.

32. See Parley M. Mathewson, Chairman of the Citizens of the Second Ward

of Providence, to Dorr, 11 August 1841, DC, vol. 3, for a request that Dorr stand as a candidate.

33. On the incident, see *Providence Daily Journal*, 30 August 1841. On the Suffragist position, see *New Age*, 13 and 20 August 1841. See also *Providence Daily Journal*, 8 February 1841, on a new statute adopted by the General Assembly exempting from taxation and militia duty blacks who were not permitted to vote.

34. On Goddard, see Walter C. Bronson, *The History of Brown University: 1764-1914* (Providence, R.I.: Brown University Press, 1914), pp. 229, 253, 254-57. For Congdon's exposure of Goddard and the first "Town Born" letter, *New Age*, 10 September 1841; succeeding letters from Goddard appeared in *Providence Daily Journal*, September-November 1841.

35. For the debates, *Providence Daily Journal*, 5, 7, 9, 10, and 11 October 1841; and *New Age*, 8 and 22 October 1841.

36. *Providence Daily Journal*, 9 October 1841. For a convenient copy of the People's Constitution, see Mowry, *Dorr War*, pp. 322-46.

37. Frederick Douglass, *Life and Times of Frederick Douglass: His Early Life as a Slave, His Escape from Bondage, and His Complete History*, rev. ed. (1892; reprint ed., New York: Collier Books, 1962), pp. 220-21.

38. *Providence Daily Journal*, 9-11 and 27 October 1841. One man voted against the constitution because of the provisions affecting the judiciary.

39. Henry C. Dorr to Dorr, 25 October 1841, DC, vol. 3.

40. A. H. Everett to editor of *New Age*, 8 November; and Dorr, Samuel H. Wales, and John A. Brown to John Quincy Adams, 22 October 1841, DC, vol. 3.

41. Adams's response in Green, *Might and Right*, p. 68.

42. *New Age*, 29 October 1841.

43. See William M. Wiecek, *The Republican Guarantee Clause of the U.S. Constitution* (Ithaca, N.Y.: Cornell University Press, 1972), chaps. 3-4.

44. *New Age*, 29 October 1841.

45. For coverage, *New Age*, 12 and 26 November 1841. For comment, Congdon, *Reminiscences*, pp. 104-5.

46. *New Age*, 19 November and 10 December 1841.

47. *New Age*, 5, 12, and 19 November 1841. For an attack on the Suffragists by William L. Garrison, see *New Age*, 12 November 1841.

48. *New Age Extra*, 18 November 1841.

49. On the colonial proxy system, see George M. Dennison, "Constitutional Issues of the Dorr War: A Study in the Evolution of American Constitutionalism, 1776-1849" (Ph.D. diss., University of Washington, 1967), p. 133.

50. Dorr's speech is in *New Age*, 25 December 1841. The analysis in the following paragraphs draws upon this source.

51. *New Age*, December 1841-May 1842, on these groupings.

52. See generally Mowry, *Dorr War*, pp. 88-93; and Marvin E. Gettleman, "Political Opposition and Radicalism in the Dorr Rebellion" (Paper delivered at the Organization of American Historians' Convention, Philadelphia, April, 1969).

53. *New Age*, 14 January 1842; Jacob Frieze, *Facts for the People; Containing a Comparison and Exposition of the Votes on Occasions Relating to the Free Suffrage Movements* (Providence, R.I.: Knowles & Vose, 1842), pp. 3-9; William G. Goddard, *An Address to the People of Rhode-Island, Delivered in Newport, on Wednesday, May 3, 1843, in the Presence of the General Assembly, on the Occasion of the Change in the Civil Government of Rhode-Island,*

by the Adoption of the Constitution, Which Superceded the Charter of 1663
(Providence, R.I.: Knowles & Vose, 1843), note E, pp. 56-57; Welcome Arnold
Greene, *The Providence Plantations for Two Hundred and Fifty Years: An
Historical Review of the Foundation, Rise, and Progress of the City of Provi-
dence . . . and the Other Towns of the State . . .* (Providence, R.I.: J. A. & R.
A. Reid, 1886), p. 81; and Mowry, *Dorr War,* pp. 115-17, who alone denied a
"clear majority" for the constitution.

54. *New Age,* 14 January 1842.

55. Letter from "Fifth Ward," *Providence Daily Journal,* 28 February 1842.

56. Congdon, *Reminiscences,* pp. 108-9.

57. See: George M. Dennison, "The Dorr War and the Triumph of Institutionalism" (Paper delivered at the Organization of American Historians' Convention, Chicago, April 1973); and George M. Dennison, "American Constitutionalism and the Idea of Revolution" (Paper delivered at the Pacific Coast
Branch of the American Society for Legal History Convention, Los Angeles,
November 1974).

58. Henry C. Dorr to Dorr, ? January 1842, DC, vol. 3.

59. *New Age,* 14 January 1842.

60. *Providence Daily Journal,* 22 January 1842.

61. On the Michigan incident cited as precedent, see Dennison, "Empire of
Liberty."

62. *Providence Daily Journal,* 24 January 1842.

63. Henry C. Dorr to Dorr, ? January 1842, DC, vol. 3.

64. On Pitman and men who agreed with him, see William M. Wiecek,
"Popular Sovereignty in the Dorr War: Conservative Counterblast," *Rhode
Island History* 32, no. 2 (May 1973): 34-51.

65. John Pitman, *To the Members of the General Assembly of Rhode Island*
(Providence, R.I.: n.p., 1842), pp. 9-11, 18-19, 21-22, 24, for the quotations in
the text.

66. Ibid., p. 10.

67. Ibid., pp. 15, 18-19.

68. Ibid., pp. 21-22, 24.

Chapter 3

1. *Providence Daily Journal,* 29 January 1842; Arthur May Mowry, *The
Dorr War; or, The Constitutional Struggle in Rhode Island* (1901; reprint ed.,
New York: Chelsea House, 1970), p. 119.

2. On the process generally, see Theodore Lowi, *The Politics of Disorder*
(New York: Basic Books, 1971), chap. 2.

3. James C. Davies, "Toward a Theory of Revolution," *American Sociological Review* 27, no. 1 (February 1962): 11.

4. *New Age,* 18 February 1842; Jacob Frieze, *A Concise History of the
Efforts to Obtain an Extension of the Suffrage in Rhode Island; From the Year
1811 to 1842; and the Dorr War, 1842,* 3d ed. (Providence, R.I.: Thomas S.
Hammond, 1912), pp. 118-29; Mowry, *Dorr War,* pp. 100-106.

5. *New Age,* 21 February and 5 March 1842. *Providence Daily Journal,*
February and March 1842.

6. *Providence Daily Journal,* 9 October 1841.

7. *Providence Daily Journal,* 28 February 1842; *House Reports,* ser. 447,
vol. 3, no. 546, pp. 660-68; *Executive Documents* (U.S. House of Representatives), 28th Cong., 1st Sess. (1843-44), series no. 443, vol. 5, document no.

225, pp. 16-17 (hereafter cited *Executive Documents*, ser. 443, vol. 5, no. 225); Dutee J. Pearce to Dorr, 6 March 1842, DC, vol. 4; Abraham Payne, *Reminiscences of the Rhode Island Bar* (Providence, R.I.: Tibbits & Preston, 1885), p. 226; Mowry, *Dorr War*, p. 123; and Noah J. Arnold, "The History of Suffrage in Rhode Island," *Narragansett Historical Register* 6, no. 3 (July 1888): 317-19.

8. Payne, *Reminiscences*, p. 226.

9. Ibid., p. 102. See also E. R. Potter to Dorr, 31 December 1841, DC, vol. 3, for another expression of early Democratic support for the Suffragists.

10. Marvin E. Gettleman, "Political Opposition and Radicalism in the Dorr Rebellion" (Paper delivered at the Organization of American Historians' Convention, Philadelphia, April 1969).

11. See, for the same view, Mary Ann Newton, "Rebellion in Rhode Island" (Master's thesis, Columbia University, 1947), pp. 76, 188-89.

12. *Providence Daily Journal*, 3 March 1842. On the treason issue, see George M. Dennison, "Thomas Wilson Dorr: Counsel of Record in Luther v. Borden," *Saint Louis University Law Journal* 15, no. 3 (Spring 1971): 398-428.

13. *New Age*, 4 March 1842.

14. For the lecture, see *House Reports*, ser. 447, vol. 3, no. 546, pp. 706-17. On Durfee, "Life and Writings of Chief Justice Durfee," *The American Review*, n.s. 1, no. 5 (May 1848): 471-83. For comment, see: Mowry, *Dorr War*, p. 130; Payne, *Reminiscences*, pp. 274-77; *New Age*, 1 March 1842; *Providence Daily Journal*, 3, 4, and 5 March 1842; and Mrs. F. H. (W.) Green (MacDougal), *Might and Right: By a Rhode Islander*, 2d ed. (Providence, R.I.: A. H. Stillwell, 1844), p. 211.

15. On these forms of analysis, see George M. Dennison, "The Dorr War and the Triumph of Institutionalism" (Paper delivered at the Organization of American Historians' Convention, Chicago, April 1973).

16. Joshua B. Rathbun to Dorr, 4 March 1842, DC, vol. 4. See also Dutee J. Pearce to Dorr, 6 March 1842, DC, vol. 4; and Newton, "Rebellion in Rhode Island," p. 76.

17. Joshua B. Rathbun to Dorr, 4 March 1842, DC, vol. 4. See also *House Reports*, ser. 447, vol. 3, no. 546, pp. 270-80.

18. *Nine Lawyers' Opinion*, tract no. 11 in *Rhode Island Historical Tracts*, ed. Sidney S. Rider (Providence: S. S. Rider, 1880), pp. 65-92. It was signed by Dorr, Atwell, Joseph K. Angell, Thomas F. Carpenter, David Daniels, Levi C. Eaton, John P. Knowles, Pearce, and Aaron White, Jr., all lawyers of some repute in Rhode Island. The analysis in the text relies on and quotes from this source. On the *Opinion*, see Payne, *Reminiscences*, pp. 274-77.

19. For discussion of Wilson's theory, see George M. Dennison, "American Constitutionalism and the Idea of Revolution" (Paper delivered at the Pacific Coast Branch of the American Society for Legal History Convention, Los Angeles, November 1974).

20. For the votes and an analysis, see: Jacob Frieze, *Facts for the People, Containing a Comparison and Exposition of the Votes on Occasions Relating to the Free Suffrage Movements* (Providence, R.I.: Knowles & Vose, 1842); *Documents Relating to the Affairs of Rhode Island* ([Providence]: Order of the General Assembly, 1842); *New Age*, 25 March and 2 April 1842. Mowry, *Dorr War*, pp. 128-38, noted that aside from Providence County only Kent County rejected the constitution.

21. *Report of the Committee on the Action of the General Assembly on the*

Subject of the Constitution, (n.p.: Order of the General Assembly, 1842). See also Green, *Might and Right*, pp. 173-74.

22. *New Age*, 2 April 1842.

23. Green, *Might and Right*, pp. 176-84.

24. *New Age*, 9 April 1842. Congdon meant to conjure up images of North African tyranny with this usage, which became widespread.

25. On this legislation, see: *Report of the Committee*, p. 11; *Providence Daily Journal*, 2 and 4 April 1842; Green, *Might and Right*, pp. 177-80; Frieze, *Concise History*, pp. 70-71, 136-38; *New Age*, 2 April 1842; "Private Daily Note Book for 1845-1850 of Thomas W. Dorr," entry for 13 October 1848, DM; and Aaron White, Jr., to Dorr, 30 April 1843, DC, vol. 7.

26. Mowry, *Dorr War*, pp. 134-38.

27. Sullivan Dorr to Dorr, 8 April 1842; and Dorr to Aaron White, Jr., 4 April 1842, DC, vol. 4.

28. *Documents Relating to Rhode Island*, the report of the commission; *Providence Daily Journal*, 4 April 1842; and *New Age*, 9 April 1842.

29. As quoted from a memorandum drawn by Elisha R. Potter, Jr., of an interview with President John Tyler in William M. Wiecek, "Popular Sovereignty in the Dorr War: Conservative Counterblast," *Rhode Island History* 32, no. 2 (May 1973): 47.

30. Green, *Might and Right*, pp. 220-21.

31. For the Suffragist claim, see: Dr. John A. Brown to Dorr, 10 April 1842, DC, vol. 4; *New Age*, 16 April 1842; and Green, *Might and Right*, pp. 220-21. For the government claim, see: *Documents Relating to Rhode Island; Executive Documents*, ser. 443, vol. 5, no. 225; and *New York Tribune*, 14-15 April 1842.

32. Concerning this interpretation, see: *House Reports*, ser. 447, vol. 3, no. 546, pp. 278-79; and Silas Wright, Jr., to Dorr, 25 April 1842, DC, vol. 4.

33. Dorr to Levi Woodbury, 13 April 1842, DC, vol. 4.

34. See Robert L. Ciaburi, "The Dorr Rebellion in Rhode Island: The Moderate Phase," *Rhode Island History* 26, no. 3 (July 1967): 81, for the quotation from a letter to Levi Woodbury from Dorr (not found in DC).

35. Various of these letters (all in DC) are excerpted and printed in John Bell Rae, "Democrats and the Dorr Rebellion," *New England Quarterly* 9, no. 3 (September 1936): 476-82. See also Dorr to Aaron White, Jr., 19 April 1842, DC, vol. 4.

36. Silas Wright, Jr., to Dorr, 25 April 1842, DC, vol. 4.

37. Ibid.

38. On this point, see William M. Wiecek, *The Republican Guarantee Clause of the U.S. Constitution* (Ithaca, N.Y.: Cornell University Press, 1972), pp. 78-86.

39. Unless otherwise noted, all quotations from Dorr to William Allen, 14 April 1842, DC, vol. 4.

40. As quoted in Ciaburi, "Moderate Phase," p. 81, from a letter from Dorr to Levi Woodbury (not in DC).

41. Louis Lapham to Dorr, 16 April 1842, DC, vol. 4.

42. Dorr to William Allen, 14 April 1842, DC, vol. 4.

43. Ariel Ballou to Dorr, 19 April 1842, DC, vol. 4.

44. Allan Smiffen to Dorr, 20 April 1842, DC, vol. 4.

45. Separate elections were held by the Suffragists and the government three days apart.

46. *Providence Daily Journal*, 18 April 1842. See also unsigned letter to

Suffragist State Committee, 2 April 1842, DC, vol. 4. I have concluded that Atwell wrote the letter because of the position taken by its author. Referring to the Algerine Act, the author said: "This tyranical & accursed Law renders it impossible to organise the govt, to elect even the officers who are the instruments of organization."

47. *New Age*, 16 and 23 April 1842; *Providence Daily Journal*, 16-20 April 1842. See also Mowry, *Dorr War*, pp. 135-37.

48. *Providence Daily Journal*, 26, 27, and 28 April 1842; *New Age*, 23 and 30 April 1842.

49. *Providence Daily Journal*, 5 May 1842; *New Age*, 7 May 1842.

50. Mowry, *Dorr War*, chap. 13; *New Age*, 7 and 14 May 1842; and *Providence Daily Journal*, 5-15 May 1842. Pearce, Anthony, and Dorr were among those to be arrested.

51. Green, *Might and Right*, pp. 235-38; and Joseph S. Pitman, ed., *Report of the Trial of Thomas Wilson Dorr, for Treason against the State of Rhode Island, containing the Arguments of Counsel, and the Charge of Chief Justice Durfee* (Boston: Tappan & Dennett, 1844), pp. 24-26, 96-100.

52. "Journals" of both houses of the People's Government, *House Reports*, ser. 447, vol. 3, no. 546, pp. 447-69, 667. *New Age*, 26 March-23 April 1842, reports numerous resolutions adopted by local chapters of the association pledging support for a People's Government "unless otherwise ordered by the government of this nation." See Charles Tabor Congdon, *Reminiscences of a Journalist* (Boston: James R. Osgood & Co., 1880), pp. 109-10, for caustic comment on these doings.

53. John S. Harris to Dorr, 9 May 1842, DC, vol. 4.

54. Dr. John A. Brown to Dorr, 5 May 1842, marginalia; John S. Harris to Dorr, 9 May 1842; John S. Harris to Dorr, 9 (p.m.) May 1842; Walter S. Burges to Dorr, 9 May 1842; and John S. Harris to Dorr, 11 May 1842, DC, vol. 4.

55. Dorr to Bradford Allen, 8 May 1842, DC, vol. 4.

56. Newton, "Rebellion in Rhode Island," pp. 100-110, and Mowry, *Dorr War*, chap. 14, have convinced most scholars that Dorr went to Washington seeking more than federal neutrality: he asked for active assistance but came away frustrated. I disagree, because of the evidence offered in the text.

57. Dorr to Walter S. Burges, 12 May 1842, DC, vol. 4. Also see Mrs. Catharine R. Williams, "Recollections of the Life and Conversation of Thomas W. Dorr," pp. 3-6, DM, a manuscript memoir of the events of 1842.

58. Dorr to Aaron White, Jr., 12 May 1842, DC, vol. 4.

59. Dorr to Walter S. Burges, 12 May 1842, DC, vol. 4. For an earlier assurance of aid from private groups in New York, see *New Age*, 23 April 1842. On the same subject see: Louis Lapham to Dorr, 16 April 1842; and Allan Smiffen to Dorr, 20 April 1842, DC, vol. 4.

60. Dorr to Aaron White, Jr., 12 May 1842, DC, vol. 4.

61. Dorr's activities in New York received wide notice. On the secret meeting, see: Mowry, *Dorr War*, pp. 191-96; Newton, "Rebellion in Rhode Island," pp. 109-10; Green, *Might and Right*, pp. 258-59; various letters concerning the meeting in *New Age*, 28 May and 4 June 1842; and Dorr to Aaron White, Jr., 12 May 1842, DC, vol. 4, wherein Dorr rejected any compromise.

62. *New Age*, 28 May and 4 June 1842; *Providence Daily Journal*, 17 May 1842.

63. Aaron White, Jr., to Dorr, 13 and 15 May 1842, DC, vol. 4.

64. Orestes A. Brownson to Dorr, 14 May 1842, DC, vol. 4, urging: "All we

are afraid of here is, that the Suffrage Party will not be firm." Subsequently Brownson denied that he had ever communicated with Dorr.

65. Quotations taken from Dorr to Governor John Fairfield of Maine, 17 May 1842, in *New Age*, 4 June 1842; and Dorr to Governor Chauncy F. Cleveland of Connecticut, 13 May 1842, DC, vol. 4. On the plans for defense of right, see: Dorr to people of Rhode Island, 21 and 26 May 1842, in *New Age*, 4 June 1842; John L. O'Sullivan to Dorr, 14 and 18 May 1842; and Edmund Burke to Dorr, 17 May 1842, DC, vol. 4; Pitman, *Trial of Dorr*, pp. 96-100; and *House Reports*, ser. 447, vol. 3, no. 546, pp. 679-80.

66. Dennison, "American Constitutionalism and the Idea of Revolution."

Chapter 4

1. Quotations from Dorr's proclamation in *House Reports*, ser. 447, vol. 3, no. 546, pp. 679-80. See also: Mrs. F. H. (W.) Green (MacDougal), *Might and Right: By a Rhode Islander*, 2d ed. (Providence, R.I.: A. H. Stillwell, 1844), pp. 241-42; *New Age*, 21 May 1842; and *Providence Daily Journal*, 17 May 1842.

2. *Providence Daily Journal*, 19 and 26 May 1842; *New Age*, 28 May and 4 June 1842; Green, *Might and Right*, pp. 241-42; Arthur May Mowry, *The Dorr War; or, The Constitutional Struggle in Rhode Island* (1901; reprint ed., New York: Chelsea House, 1970), chap. 15; and Joseph S. Pitman, ed., *Report of the Trial of Thomas Wilson Dorr, for Treason against the State of Rhode Island, containing the Arguments of Counsel, and the Charge of Chief Justice Durfee* (Boston: Tappan & Dennett, 1844), pp. 26-42, 96-100.

3. *Providence Daily Journal*, 17 May 1842; Mowry, *Dorr War*, pp. 181-96.

4. Charles Tabor Congdon, *Reminiscences of a Journalist* (Boston: James R. Osgood & Co., 1880), pp. 110-11; and Welcome Arnold Greene, *The Providence Plantations for Two Hundred and Fifty Years: An Historical Review of the Foundation, Rise, and Progress of the City of Providence . . . and the Other Towns of the State . . .* (Providence: J. A. & R. A. Reid, 1886), p. 83, on the guns.

5. Dorr to Henry D'Wolf, 19 May 1842, DC, vol. 4.

6. Ibid., marginalia (D'Wolf returned the letter the same day); and Dorr to L. Sprague, 6 June 1842, DC, vol. 4.

7. *New Age*, 28 May and 4 June 1842; and Mowry, *Dorr War*, pp. 181-96.

8. Aaron White, Jr., to Dorr, 25 May 1842, DC, vol. 4. See also Aaron White, Jr., to Dorr, 29 May 1842; Dorr to Aaron White, Jr., 27 May 1842; William Mitchell to Dorr, 21 May 1842; John S. Harris to Dorr, 30 May 1842; David Parmenter to Dorr, 30 May 1842; and anonymous to Dorr, 1 June 1842, DC, vol. 4.

9. On the indictments, see: *House Reports*, ser. 447, vol. 3, no. 546, pp. 792-95; *New Age*, 4 June 1842; and Aaron White, Jr., to Dorr, 3 and 5 June 1842, DC, vol. 4.

10. All quotations from *New Age*, 28 May, 4 and 11 June 1842. See also: David Parmenter to Dorr, 30 May 1842; and John S. Harris to Dorr, 2 June 1842, DC, vol. 4.

11. Dorr to Aaron White, Jr., 27 May 1842; and Edmund Burke to Dorr, 19 May 1842, DC, vol. 4.

12. John L. O'Sullivan to Dorr, 18 May 1842, DC, vol. 4.

13. Dorr to Aaron White, Jr., 27 May 1842, DC, vol. 4.

14. Dorr to Aaron White, Jr., 1 June 1842, DC, vol. 4.

15. On his possible arrest, see: *New Age*, 4 and 11 June 1842; Mowry, *Dorr War*, p. 238; *Executive Documents*, ser. 443, vol. 5, no. 225, p. 33; and Dorr to Aaron White, Jr., 27 May and 1 June 1842, DC, vol. 4.

16. Edmund Burke to Dorr, 17 May 1842, DC, vol. 4.

17. For a discussion of this phenomenon, see Theodore Lowi, *The Politics of Disorder* (New York: Basic Books, 1971), pp. 53-61; and William Kornhauser, *The Politics of Mass Society* (New York: The Free Press, 1959), pp. 227-38.

18. Aaron White, Jr., to Dorr, 1 September 1842, DC, vol. 5.

19. For various letters, see *Executive Documents*, ser. 443, vol. 5, no. 225; for a discussion, see William M. Wiecek, "Popular Sovereignty in the Dorr War: Conservative Counterblast," *Rhode Island History* 32, no. 2 (May 1973): 34-51.

20. *House Reports*, ser. 447, vol. 3, no. 546, pp. 695-705; *Executive Documents*, ser. 443, vol. 5, no. 225, pp. 54-59; and Mowry, *Dorr War*, p. 146.

21. For discussion, see Wiecek, "Conservative Counterblast," p. 42.

22. Aaron White, Jr., to Dorr, 3 June 1842, DC, vol. 4. See also Aaron White, Jr., to Dorr, 5 June 1842, DC, vol. 4.

23. Dorr to Aaron White, Jr., 27 May 1842, DC, vol. 4; and Dorr to Edmund Burke, 26 February 1844, vol. 1 of Edmund Burke Papers, Manuscripts Division, Library of Congress (hereafter cited as Burke Papers).

24. Benjamin Colwell, *A Letter to the Hon. Samuel W. King, Late Governor of the State of Rhode Island; With an Appendix*, 2d ed. (Providence, R.I.: n.p., June 1842), pp. 21-30.

25. William Goodell, *The Rights and Wrongs of Rhode Island: Comprising Views of Liberty and Law, of Religion and Rights, as Exhibited in the Recent and Existing Difficulties in that State* (1842; microcard ed., Louisville, Ky.: Lost Cause Press, 1965), p. 77.

26. Aaron White, Jr., to Dorr, 3, 12, 18, and 26 June 1842, DC, vol. 4; *New Age*, June 1842; *Providence Daily Journal*, June 1842.

27. Aaron White, Jr., to Dorr, 3 June 1842, DC, vol. 4.

28. Mowry, *Dorr War*, pp. 206-9.

29. L. Sprague to Dorr, 15 June 1842; Burrington Anthony to Dorr, 17 June 1842, and marginalia; Dorr to Brigadier General L. Sprague, 6 June 1842, DC, vol. 4.

30. *New Age*, 25 June 1842.

31. On the situation in general, see: Greene, *Providence Plantations*, pp. 84-85; Mowry, *Dorr War*, pp. 206 ff.; Green, *Might and Right*, pp. 264 ff.; David Parmenter to Dorr, 17 June 1842; and John S. Harris to Dorr, 12 June 1842, DC, vol. 4; and *Providence Daily Journal*, 15-25 June 1842.

32. *Washington Globe*, 9 May 1842. For a discussion of the legal background, see George M. Dennison, "Martial Law: The Development of a Theory of Emergency Powers, 1776-1861," *American Journal of Legal History* 18, no. 1 (January 1974): 52-79.

33. Mowry, *Dorr War*, pp. 206 ff., has been the standard, accepted account.

34. *Providence Daily Journal*, 25 June 1842.

35. Broadside signed by Burges et al., 25 June 1842, DC, vol. 4.

36. Dorr to Walter S. Burges, 27 (a.m.) June 1842, DC, vol. 4.

37. Dorr to Walter S. Burges, 27 (p.m.) June 1842, DC, vol. 4.

38. "Private Daily Note Book for 1845-1850 of Thomas W. Dorr," entry for ? March 1849, DM. Mowry, *Dorr War*, 206-22, raised the estimate and stressed the importance of outsiders. Most studies have followed Mowry.

39. On Acote's Hill, see: *New Age*, 21 October 1842; *House Reports*, ser.

447, vol. 3, no. 546, pp. 307-10, 731-65; Green, *Might and Right*, pp. 271-87; *Executive Documents*, ser. 443, vol. 5, no. 225, pp. 48-59; Pitman, *Trial of Dorr*, pp. 35-59, 97-100; Mowry, *Dorr War*, pp. 216-18; and Dorr to Edmund Burke, 26 February 1844, Burke Papers, vol. 1. On Dorr's escape, Eleanor W. Talbot Smith, "Thomas W. Dorr's Escape," *Rhode Island Historical Society Collections* 25, no. 3 (October 1932): 107-8.

40. *Executive Documents*, ser. 443, vol. 5, no. 225, pp. 36-48; *House Reports*, ser. 447, vol. 3, no. 546, pp. 684-705.

41. On this incident, see: *House Reports*, ser. 447, vol. 3, no. 546, pp. 292-307; John S. Harris to Dorr, 29 September 1842, DC, vol. 5; Dan King, *The Life and Times of Thomas Wilson Dorr, with Outlines of the Political History of Rhode Island* (Boston: Dan King, 1859), p. 174; Mowry, *Dorr War*, pp. 207-22; and Arthur B. Darling, *Political Change in Massachusetts, 1824-1848: A Study of Liberal Movements in Politics* (New Haven, Conn.: Yale University Press; London: Oxford University Press, 1925), pp. 288-89.

42. On this topic, see: *House Reports*, ser. 447, vol. 3, no. 546, pp. 307-53; Elias Smith to Dorr, 15 August 1842; Seth Luther to Walter S. Burges, 19 August 1842; John A. Brown to Dorr, 2 September 1842; John S. Harris to Dorr, 2 September 1842; David Parmenter to Dorr, 18 August 1842; Ausin Bugbee to Dorr, 10 August 1842, DC, vol. 4; and William Miller to Dorr, 11 December 1842, DC, vol. 5. Also see Louis Hartz, "Seth Luther: Working Class Rebel," *New England Quarterly* 13, no. 3 (September 1940): 401-18, claiming that Luther was convicted of treason, for which I can find no proof. See also Mowry, *Dorr War*, p. 238; and the sermons listed in Mowry's bibliography (by Francis Wayland, Mark Tucker, Francis Vinton, Edward W. Peet, and Archibald Kenyon) for an appreciation of how the conservative majority viewed the situation.

43. See *House Reports*, ser. 447, vol. 3, no. 546, pp. 307-10; Ausin Bugbee to Dorr, 10 August 1842, and John A. Brown to Dorr, 2 September 1842, DC, vol. 4; and William Miller to Dorr, 11 December 1842, DC, vol. 5.

44. For daily reports, see *Providence Daily Journal*, 2 July to 8 August 1842. On the situation and details, see: *House Reports*, ser. 447, vol. 3, no. 546, pp. 307-52; Elisha Dyer, "Reminiscences of Rhode Island in 1842 as Connected with the Dorr Rebellion," *Narragansett Historical Register* 6, no. 2 (April 1888): 145-97; Mowry, *Dorr War*, p. 228; and Mahlon H. Hellerich, "The Luther Cases in the Lower Courts," *Rhode Island History* 11, no. 2 (April 1952): 33-45.

45. *Providence Daily Journal*, 1, 7 July, and 8 August 1842.

46. *Providence Daily Journal*, 7 July 1842.

47. *Providence Daily Journal*, 26 July 1842. See also *House Reports*, ser. 447, vol. 3, no. 546, pp. 771-816. The Algerine Act allowed trial outside the county where the alleged crime had been committed if the superior court thought it necessary.

48. *Providence Daily Journal*, 31 August 1842.

49. *Providence Daily Journal*, 12 September-12 October 1842; *New Age*, 9 September-11 November 1842; Mowry, *Dorr War*, pp. 367 ff.; Dorr to William Simons, 23 August 1842, DC, vol. 4; and *Executive Documents*, ser. 443, vol. 5, no. 225, pp. 161-64.

50. On the election, see *New Age*, 25 November 1842. By a vote of about 3 to 1 of a total of 4,000, blacks were enfranchised.

51. On this point, see: Mowry, *Dorr War*, p. 287; *New Age*, 4 and 25

November, 2, 9, 16, and 23 December 1842; Dorr to William Simons, 12 December 1842; and John S. Harris to Dorr, 1 December 1842, DC, vol. 5; and *House Reports*, ser. 447, vol. 3, no. 546, pp. 665-66.

52. On the development of this strategy, see: *New Age*, 2, 16, and 23 December 1842; Dorr to William Simons, 29 December 1842, DC, vol. 5; and B. F. Albro to Dorr, 28 January 1843; Franklin Cooley et al. to Dorr, 28 January 1843; F. L. Beckford to Dorr, 29 January 1843; Samuel Low to Dorr, 29 January 1843; Dorr to Franklin Cooley et al., 1 February 1843; Dorr to F. L. Beckford, 6 February 1843; William H. Smith to Dorr, 16 March 1843; and Aaron White, Jr., to Dorr, 20 March 1843, DC, vol. 6.

53. Dorr to Franklin Cooley et al., 1 February 1843, DC, vol. 6.

54. Dorr to William Simons, 29 December 1842, DC, vol. 5.

55. For Dorr's thinking on the last point, see: John S. Harris to Dorr, 29 September 1842; Dorr to David Parmenter, 21 October 1842; and Dorr to William Simons, 18 October, 11 and 12 November 1842, DC, vol. 5.

56. See: Dorr to William Simons, 4 and 26 September 1842, DC, vol. 5; B. F. Albro to Dorr, 28 January 1843; Dorr to William Simons, 7 January 1843, DC, vol. 6; and *New Age*, 23 and 30 December 1842.

57. Chilton Williamson, "Rhode Island Suffrage since the Dorr War," *New England Quarterly* 28, no. 3 (March 1955): 34-40. See also: *New Age*, 10 February 1843; Dorr to Franklin Cooley et al., 1 February 1843, DC, vol. 6; Franklin Pierce to Dorr, 1 April 1843; F. L. Beckford to Dorr, 21 April 1843; and Dorr to Aaron White, Jr., 27 April 1843, DC, vol. 7.

58. *New Age*, 14 April 1843.

59. Dorr to Walter S. Burges, 12 April 1843, DC, vol. 7.

60. Dorr to Aaron White, Jr., 27 April 1843, DC, vol. 7.

61. Aaron White, Jr., to Dorr, 30 December 1842, DC, vol. 5. See also Aaron White, Jr., to Dorr, 17 April 1843, DC, vol. 7.

62. Aaron White, Jr., to Dorr, 28 November 1842, DC, vol. 5.

63. Dorr to Walter S. Burges, 12 April 1843, DC, vol. 7.

64. Dorr to Walter S. Burges, 31 May and 12 April 1843, DC, vol. 7.

65. On this position, see: George M. Dennison, "American Constitutionalism and the Idea of Revolution" (Paper delivered at the Pacific Coast Branch of the American Society for Legal History Convention, Los Angeles, November 1974); and George M. Dennison, "The Dorr War and the Triumph of Institutionalism" (Paper delivered at the Organization of American Historians' Convention, Chicago, April 1973).

66. James Manchester to Dorr, 21 April 1843, DC, vol. 7.

67. Aaron White, Jr., to Dorr, 30 April 1843, DC, vol. 7.

68. Dorr to Walter S. Burges, 31 May 1843; Dorr to Matthew Harding, 12 February 1844, DC, vol. 7.

69. Aaron White, Jr., to Dorr, 10 June 1843, DC, vol. 7.

70. On his health, see: Dorr to Walter S. Burges, 31 May and 28 July 1843; Dorr to Ida Rupell, 29 August 1843; Welcome B. Sayles to Dorr, 16 October 1843; and Dorr to Saul B. Scott, 20 October 1843, DC, vol. 7.

71. On his determination to return, see: Aaron White, Jr., to Dorr, 10 June 1843, marginalia, DC, vol. 7. See also: Dorr to Saul B. Scott, 20 October 1843, and Dorr to Matthew Harding, 12 February 1844, DC, vol. 7; and Mowry, *Dorr War*, pp. 240-42.

72. Dorr to Matthew Harding, 12 February 1844, DC, vol. 7. See also: Mowry, *Dorr War*, pp. 242-54; Green, *Might and Right*, pp. 316-17; Greene,

Providence Plantations, p. 85. Chilton Williamson, "The Disenchantment of Thomas Wilson Dorr," *Rhode Island History* 17, no. 4 (October 1958): 97-108, stresses the theme of disillusionment, unproved but based on Aaron White, Jr., to Dorr, 8 June 1844, marginalia, DC, vol. 8. Evidence to the contrary appears elsewhere in the letters as indicated in the discussion in the text. Finally, see Mrs. Catharine R. Williams, "Recollections of the Life and Conversation of Thomas W. Dorr," pp. 23-29, DM.

73. On the offers, see: Dorr to Walter S. Burges, 18 and 25 March, 11 April, and 16 June 1844; Edmund Burke to Dorr, 4 February 1844; David Dudley Field to Dorr, 16 March 1844; and Aaron White, Jr., to Dorr, 13 January 1844, DC, vol. 8. See also John L. O'Sullivan to Dorr, 16 November 1843, DC, vol. 7.

74. See Pitman, *Trial of Dorr*, for coverage of the proceedings; see also *House Reports*, ser. 447, vol. 3, no. 546, pp. 865-1047, for George Turner's account of the trial. Mowry, *Dorr War*, chap. 19, covers the trial, as does Green, *Might and Right*, pp. 318-22, 332-37.

75. Pitman, *Trial of Dorr*, pp. 121-31, for Durfee's charge quoted in the text. On the treason issue, see Joseph Story, "Charge to the Grand Jury—Treason," 30 *Federal Cases*, no. 18, 275 (June 1842), pp. 1046-47; George M. Dennison, "Thomas Wilson Dorr: Counsel of Record in Luther v. Borden," *Saint Louis University Law Journal* 15, no. 3 (Spring 1971): 412-15; and Silas Wright, Jr., to Dorr, 7 February 1844, DC, vol. 8.

76. For critical review of the decision, see: John S. Schuchman, "The Political Background of the Political-Question Doctrine: The Judges and the Dorr War," *American Journal of Legal History* 16, no. 2 (April 1972): 111-25; and Michael A. Conron, "Law, Politics, and Chief Justice Taney: A Reinterpretation of the Luther v. Borden Decision," *American Journal of Legal History* 11, no. 4 (October 1967): 377-88.

77. *Baker* v. *Carr*, 369 *U.S.* 186 ff. (1962).

78. The Algerine Act allowed the superior court to change the venue when this was deemed necessary for an impartial trial. On the question, see: Green, *Might and Right*, pp. 317-22; *House Reports*, ser. 447, vol. 3, no. 546, pp. 1000-1047; Dorr to Walter S. Burges, 16 May 1844; and Edmund Burke to Dorr, 10 June 1844, DC, vol. 8.

79. All quotations from Green, *Might and Right*, pp. 333-37. See also Dorr to Walter S. Burges, 8 May 1844, DC, vol. 8.

80. On Dorr's imprisonment and the political struggle to release him, see: "Prison Documents," a collection of letters, newspaper excerpts, and the like, for June 1844 to July 1845, DM; and Williams, "Recollections of Dorr," pp. 29 ff., DM.

81. Dennison, "Counsel of Record," pp. 415-18.

82. Hellerich, "Luther Cases," pp. 33-45. See also *Luther* v. *Borden*, R.I. Circuit, "Records of Circuit Court," concerning the Luther cases in the federal circuit court in Rhode Island (microfilm in author's possession; records in Federal Records Center, Waltham, Massachusetts).

83. Dennison, "Counsel of Record," p. 418.

84. King, *Life of Dorr*, p. 271; Greene, *Providence Plantations*, p. 370; Mowry, *Dorr War*, pp. 255-59; "Liberation Society Documents, 1844-1845," DM; Williams, "Recollections of Dorr," pp. 29 ff., DM; Green, *Might and Right*, p. 345; assorted newspaper articles in Burke Papers, vol. 1; and Dorr to Walter S. Burges, 31 May 1844, DC, vol. 8.

85. Aaron White, Jr., to Dorr, 1 September 1842, DC, vol. 5.

86. Aaron White, Jr., to Dorr, 19 February 1844, DC, vol. 8.

87. Aaron White, Jr., to Dorr, 1 September 1842, DC, vol. 5. See also: Aaron White, Jr., to Dorr, 17 and 30 April 1843, DC, vol. 7.

Chapter 5

1. Charles Francis Adams, ed., *Memoirs of John Quincy Adams, comprising Portions of His Diary from 1795 to 1848*, 12 vols. (Philadelphia: J. B. Lippincott & Co., 1874-1877), 11:160.

2. "The Rhode Island Affair," *Democratic Review*, n.s. 10, no. 48 (June 1842): 602-7. See also "Mr. Camp's Democracy," ibid., no. 44 (February 1842): 122-28; "The Rhode Island Question," ibid., n.s. 11, no. 49 (July 1842): 70-83; and John L. O'Sullivan to Dorr, 1, 2, and 8 July 1842, DC, vol. 4.

3. For discussion of total ideological divisions, see Karl Mannheim, *Ideology and Utopia: An Introduction to the Sociology of Knowledge* (1936; reprint ed., New York: Harcourt, Brace & World, 1968), pp. 49-51.

4. *Ibid.*, pp. 105-8. See also Daniel Boorstin, *The Decline of American Radicalism* (New York: Random House, 1970), chap. 4, on the theory of an "indwelling law."

5. *Washington Globe*, 9 May 1842, is a typical example of Democratic newspapers; *New York Tribune*, 24 May 1842, of Whig sheets.

6. *Galveston Weekly News*, 15 November 1845. My thanks to Professor David McComb for bringing this reference to my attention.

7. *New York Tribune*, 24 May 1842. On Greeley, see Glyndon G. Van Deusen, *Horace Greeley: Nineteenth Century Crusader* (1953; reprint ed., New York: Hill & Wang, 1964), pp. 74-75.

8. *Madisonian*, 16 April, 20 May, and 23 May 1842.

9. On this point, see: *Liberator*, July-September 1842, for Garrison's distrust of the Suffragists. See Aaron White, Jr., to Dorr, 5 June 1842; and Elias Smith to Dorr, 15 August 1842, DC, vol. 4, for denials of Suffragist association with abolitionists.

10. Lexington speech of 9 June 1842, in Calvin Colton, ed., *Works of Henry Clay: Comprising His Life, Correspondence and Speeches*, 7th ed., 6 vols. (1934; reprint ed., New York: Appleton-Century-Crofts, 1963), 6:359-84.

11. *Providence Daily Journal*, 6 July 1842; Adams, *Memoirs*, 11:270; for background, see 11:257-58, 267-69.

12. All quotations are from John Quincy Adams, *The Social Compact, Exemplified in the Constitution of the Commonwealth of Massachusetts, with Remarks on the Theories of Divine Right of Hobbes and of Filmer, and the Counter Theories of Sidney, Locke, Montesquieu, and Rousseau, concerning the Origin and Nature of Government: A Lecture Delivered before the Franklin Lyceum, at Providence, R.I., November 25, 1842* (Providence, R.I.: Knowles & Vose, 1842), pp. 3, 6-7, 8-9, 18-19, 31-32. On the publication of the lecture, see Adams, *Memoirs*, 11:276.

13. John Pitman, *A Reply to the Letter of the Honorable Marcus Morton, Late Governor of Massachusetts, on the Rhode Island Question* (Providence, R.I.: Knowles & Vose, 1842), p. 32; Story to John Pitman, 10 February and 1 April 1842, in William W. Story, ed., *Life and Letters of Joseph Story* (Boston: Charles C. Little & James Brown, 1851), 2:416-19. See also John Pitman to Story, 26 January and 4 May 1842, Joseph Story Papers, Manuscripts Division, Clements Library, University of Michigan, Ann Arbor. My thanks to Professor William Wiecek for calling my attention to this reference.

14. Aaron White, Jr., to Dorr, 1 September 1842, DC, vol. 5.

15. Aaron White, Jr., to Dorr, 30 March 1844, DC, vol. 8. See also Aaron White, Jr., to Dorr, 3 June 1842, DC, vol. 4.

16. Aaron White, Jr., to Dorr, 30 March 1844, DC, vol. 8; Aaron White, Jr., to Dorr, 1 September 1842, DC, vol. 5.

17. William Goodell, *The Rights and Wrongs of Rhode Island: Comprising Views of Liberty and Law, of Religion and Rights, as Exhibited in the Recent and Existing Difficulties in that State* (1842; microcard ed., Louisville, Ky.: Lost Cause Press, 1965), pp. 3, 50.

18. Dorr to Walter S. Burges, 12 May 1842, DC, vol. 4; and Dorr to William Simons, 27 February 1843, DC, vol. 6.

19. See Mrs. Catharine R. Williams, "Recollections of the Life and Conversation of Thomas W. Dorr," pp. 4-5, DM.

20. Proceedings of 10 April 1844, *Congressional Globe*, 28th Cong., 1st Sess., pp. 522-23; and *Executive Documents*, ser. 443, vol. 5, no. 225, pp. 1-4.

21. On this precedent, see: *Executive Documents* (U.S. House of Representatives), 25th Cong., 3d Sess. (1838-39), series no. 345, vol. 2, document no. 28, pp. 1-33; Proceedings of 17 and 19 December 1838, *Congressional Globe*, 25th Cong., 3d Sess., pp. 36-39, 47-48; and Silas Wright, Jr., to Dorr, 25 April 1842, DC, vol. 4.

22. For an alternate view, see William M. Wiecek, *The Republican Guarantee Clause of the U.S. Constitution* (Ithaca, N.Y.: Cornell University Press, 1972), chap. 4; Charles O. Lerche, Jr., "The Dorr War and the Federal Constitution," *Rhode Island History* 9, no. 1 (January 1950): 1-10; and Joel Prentiss Bishop, *Commentaries on the Criminal Law*, 6th ed. (Boston: Little, Brown, and Co., 1877), 1:28, note 1.

23. On these events, see: Herbert A. Donovan, *The Barnburners: A Study of the Internal Movements of the Political History of New York State and of the Resulting Changes in Political Affiliation: 1830-1852* (New York: New York University Press, 1925), pp. 68-71; Jabez D. Hammond, *Political History of the State of New York* (Syracuse, N.Y. and New York: L. W. Hall and S. A. Barnes and Co., 1852), chaps. 18 and 21; and *New York Tribune*, 7 January, 2 February, 9 and 28 March, 17, 20, and 24 April 1846.

24. *New York Tribune*, 17 April 1846.

25. On the Ohio incidents, see: *Providence Daily Journal*, 6 January 1849; *Washington Globe*, August 1848-February 1849, for running commentary; and "Private Daily Note Book for 1845-1850 of Thomas Wilson Dorr," entry under "Political Matters, etc.," "Book III," circa 1849, DM.

26. See *Martin Luther* v. *Luther M. Borden et al.*, 7 *Howard* 1 ff. (1849).

27. *Providence Daily Journal*, 6 January 1849.

28. On this conception, see Roland Van Zandt, *The Metaphysical Foundation of American History* (The Hague: Mouton & Co., 1959), chaps. 2, 6-7.

29. See George M. Dennison, "The Dorr War and the Triumph of Institutionalism" (Paper delivered at the Organization of American Historians' Convention, Chicago, April 1973).

30. See George M. Dennison, "Martial Law: The Development of a Theory of Emergency Powers, 1776-1861," *American Journal of Legal History* 18, no. 1 (January 1974): 52-79.

31. See George M. Dennison, "An Empire of Liberty: Congressional Attitudes toward Popular Sovereignty in the Territories, 1787-1867" (Paper delivered at the Rocky Mountain Social Science Association Convention, El Paso, April 1974).

Chapter 6

1. See George M. Dennison, *"The Idea of a Party System*: A Critique," *Rocky Mountain Social Science Journal* 9, no. 3 (April 1972): 31-43.

2. See Richard McCormick, *The Second American Party System* (Chapel Hill: University of North Carolina Press, 1966), p. 355.

3. On the "release of creative energy" principle, see J. Willard Hurst, *Law and the Conditions of Freedom in the Nineteenth Century United States* (Madison: University of Wisconsin Press, 1956).

4. See George M. Dennison, "An Empire of Liberty: Congressional Attitudes toward Popular Sovereignty in the Territories, 1787-1867" (Paper delivered at the Rocky Mountain Social Science Association Convention, El Paso, April 1974); and Lee Benson, *Toward the Scientific Study of History: Selected Essays* (Philadelphia: J. B. Lippincott Co., 1972), chap. 8.

5. See George M. Dennison, "The Dorr War and the Triumph of Institutionalism" (Paper delivered at the Organization of American Historians' Convention, Chicago, April 1973).

6. See Karl Mannheim, *Ideology and Utopia: An Introduction to the Sociology of Knowledge* (1936; reprint ed., New York: Harcourt, Brace & World, 1968), pp. 105-8; and Carl G. Gustavson, *The Institutional Drive* ([Athens]: Ohio University Press, 1966), chap. 6.

7. Aaron White, Jr., to Dorr, 13 January 1844, DC, vol. 8.

8. Aaron White, Jr., to Dorr, 1 September 1842, DC, vol. 5.

9. See William M. Wiecek, *The Republican Guarantee Clause of the U.S. Constitution* (Ithaca, N.Y.: Cornell University Press, 1972), chaps. 1-4.

10. Dorr to William Simons, 29 December 1842, DC, vol. 5.

11. See: *House Reports*, ser. 447, vol. 3, no. 546, pp. 1048-68; *Madisonian*, 4 May 1842; Edmund Burke to Dorr, 17 May 1842, DC, vol. 4; and Arthur May Mowry, *The Dorr War; or, The Constitutional Struggle in Rhode Island* (1901; reprint ed., New York: Chelsea House, 1970), pp. 195-96.

12. For convenient access to most of these letters, see John Bell Rae, "Democrats and the Dorr Rebellion," *New England Quarterly* 9, no. 3 (September 1936): 476-82.

13. Levi Woodbury to Dorr, 15 April 1842, as quoted in Rae, "Democrats and Dorr," pp. 476-77.

14. Silas Wright to Dorr, 25 April 1842, DC, vol. 4.

15. Edmund Burke to Dorr, 8 and 17 May 1842, DC, vol. 4.

16. See Ariel Ballou to Dorr, 19 April 1842, DC, vol. 4.

17. Draft of the Memorial, 1 February 1844, DC, vol. 8. See also: Edmund Burke to Dorr, 4 February 1844; and Dorr to Walter S. Burges, 8 April 1844, DC, vol. 8; Dorr to Edmund Burke, 26 February 1844, Burke Papers, vol. 1; *Executive Documents* (U.S. House of Representatives), 28th Cong., 1st Sess. (1843-44), series no. 442, vol. 4, document no. 136, and series no. 443, vol. 5, documents nos. 232 and 233; and Mowry, *Dorr War*, p. 273.

18. For the debate, see Proceedings of 19 February 1844 ff., and 2 January 1845 ff., *Congressional Globe*, 28th Cong., 1st and 2d Sess., pp. 302 ff., and 81-370.

19. Edmund Burke to Dorr, 4 February, 7 and 13 April 1844, DC, vol. 8. See also Walter S. Burges to Dorr, 5 and 7 April 1844, DC, vol. 8.

20. Remarks of Henry Y. Cranston, 7 and 8 March 1844, *Congressional Globe*, 28th Cong., 1st Sess., pp. 365-68.

21. Proceedings of 21 and 23 March 1844, *Congressional Globe*, 28th Cong., 1st Sess., pp. 428-29, 436.

22. Dorr to Edmund Burke, 26 February 1844, Burke Papers, vol. 1. See also John S. Harris to Dorr, 8 April 1844, DC, vol. 8.

23. On the records, see: Aaron White, Jr., to Dorr, 1 September 1842, DC, vol. 5; and Aaron White, Jr., to Dorr, 9 February 1844, DC, vol. 8.

24. "Journal," *House Reports*, ser. 447, vol. 3, no. 546, pp. 87-92.

25. Agents were Walter S. Burges, George Turner, Benjamin Franklin Hallett, and Jesse S. Tourtellot, Suffragists all. Testimony could not be taken in Rhode Island because of the hostility to the committee's work.

26. Edmund Burke to Dorr, 7 April and 4 February 1844, DC, vol. 8.

27. Edmund Burke to Dorr, 7 April 1844, DC, vol. 8.

28. See *House Reports*, ser. 447, vol. 3, no. 546, pp. 93-101 for a schedule of more than 240 documents; ibid., no. 581, pp. 39-40 for a schedule of more than 40 documents. Also see Edmund Burke to Dorr, 13 April 1844, DC, vol. 8.

29. See Charles Francis Adams, ed., *Memoirs of John Quincy Adams, comprising Portions of His Diary from 1795 to 1848*, 12 vols. (Philadelphia: J. B. Lippincott & Co., 1874-1877), 12:47-48; and Edmund Burke to Dorr, 3 May and 4 June 1844, DC, vol. 8.

30. For the resolutions, see *House Reports*, ser. 447, vol. 3, no. 546, p. 86. See also Proceedings of 2 January 1845 ff., *Congressional Globe*, 28th Cong., 2d Sess., pp. 81 ff., esp. "Appendix," p. 260.

31. Remarks of Lucius Q. C. Elmer, 2 January and 28 February 1845, *Congressional Globe*, 28th Cong., 2d Sess., pp. 81-82; see also *Congressional Globe*, 28th Cong., 2d Sess., "Appendix," pp. 260-62.

32. Remarks of Henry Williams, 1 March 1845, *Congressional Globe*, 28th Cong., 2d Sess., p. 370.

33. See Aaron White, Jr., to Dorr, 30 April and 3 December 1843, DC, vol. 7.

34. See: Dorr to William Simons, 7 February 1843, DC, vol. 6; and Timothy Haskins to Dorr, 21 January 1844, DC, vol. 8.

35. On the resolutions, see Hezekiah Willard to Dorr, 11 May 1844, and Dorr to Walter S. Burges, 23 May 1844, DC, vol. 8.

36. Seth Luther to Dorr, 20 September 1845, DC, vol. 9.

37. Dorr to Colonel Samuel Medary, 17 May 1848, DC, vol. 12.

38. See Dennison, "Empire of Liberty"; Chaplain W. Morrison, *Democratic Politics and Sectionalism: The Wilmot Proviso Controversy* (Chapel Hill: University of North Carolina Press, 1967); and Roy Franklin Nichols, *The Disruption of American Democracy* (New York: Macmillan Co., 1948), pt. 1.

39. Roland Van Zandt, *The Metaphysical Foundation of American History* (The Hague: Mouton & Co., 1959), p. 45.

40. On the "Adamic" consciousness, see R. W. B. Lewis, *The American Adam: Innocence, Tragedy, and Tradition in the Nineteenth Century* (Chicago: University of Chicago Press, 1955), "Prologue," chaps. 1-2, and "Epilogue"; and on the change in the idea of progress, Dennison, "The Dorr War and the Triumph of Institutionalism," pp. 9-11.

41. On this attitude, see Daniel Boorstin, *The Decline of American Radicalism* (New York: Random House, 1970), chap. 4.

42. See Van Zandt, *Metaphysical Foundation*, pp. 102-3.

43. George M. Dennison, "Thomas Wilson Dorr: Counsel of Record

Luther v. Borden," *Saint Louis University Law Journal* 15, no. 3 (Spring 1971): 417-28.

Chapter 7

1. For the Wilsonian conception, see "Speech of James Wilson, 26 November 1787," in Jonathan Elliot, comp., *The Debates in the Several State Conventions, on the Adoption of the Federal Constitution, as Recommended by the General Convention at Philadelphia, in 1787*, 2d ed., 5 vols. (Philadelphia: J. B. Lippincott, 1881), 2:443; and George M. Dennison, "American Constitutionalism and the Idea of Revolution" (Paper delivered at the Pacific Coast Branch of the American Society for Legal History Convention, Los Angeles, November 1974). For Hamilton's conception, see "Federalist, No. 78," in Edward Meade Earle, ed., *The Federalist*, Modern Library (New York, n.d.), pp. 506-9.

2. See Richard E. Ellis, *The Jeffersonian Crisis: Courts and Politics in the Young Republic* (New York: Oxford University Press, 1971), chaps. 1 and 6.

3. See M. J. C. Vile, *Constitutionalism and the Separation of Powers* (Oxford: Clarendon Press, 1967), pp. 37-95, 104-5, 119 ff.

4. See Donald Morgan, *Congress and the Constitution: A Study of Responsibility* (Cambridge: Harvard University Press, Belknap Press, 1966), chaps. 1 through 7.

5. See: Alpheus T. Mason, *The Supreme Court from Taft to Warren* (New York: W. W. Norton & Co., 1958), chaps. 1 and 4; and Charles Warren, *The Supreme Court in United States History*, rev. ed., 2 vols. (Boston: Little, Brown and Co., 1926), vols. 1-2.

6. See George M. Dennison, "The Dorr War and the Triumph of Institutionalism" (Paper delivered at the Organization of American Historians' Convention, Chicago, April 1973).

7. See William M. Wiecek, *The Republican Guarantee Clause of the U.S. Constitution* (Ithaca, N.Y.: Cornell University Press, 1972), chaps. 3-4.

8. See: *William Marbury* v. *James Madison*, 1 *Cranch* 137 ff. (1803); *Susan Decatur* v. *James K. Paulding*, 14 *Peters* 497-523, 599-613 (1840); Charles Gordon Post, Jr., *The Supreme Court and Political Questions*, Johns Hopkins Studies in Historical and Political Science, vol. 14, no. 4 (Baltimore, 1936) pp. 410-542; Melville Fuller Westin, "Political Questions," *Harvard Law Review* 38, no. 3 (January 1925):296-333; John J. Gibbons, "The Interdependence of Legitimacy: An Introduction to the Meaning of Separation of Powers," *Seton Hall Law Review* 5, no. 3 (Spring 1974):435-88; and Alexander M. Bickel, *The Least Dangerous Branch: The Supreme Court at the Bar of Politics* (Indianapolis, Ind.: Bobbs-Merrill Co., 1962), pp. 183-98.

9. On the initial prosecutions, see *New Age*, 4 November, 2, 9, 16, and 23 December 1842; *House Reports*, ser. 447, vol. 3, no. 546, pp. 665-66; and John S. Harris to Dorr, 1 December 1842, DC, vol. 5.

10. Dorr to William Simons, 12 December 1842, DC, vol. 5.

11. *New Age*, 16 December 1842.

12. Dorr to David Parmenter, 21 October 1842, DC, vol. 5. See also Aaron White, Jr., to Dorr, 30 April 1843, DC, vol. 7.

13. Dorr to William Simons, 18 October 1842, DC, vol. 5. For similar sentiments, Dorr to William Simons, 11 and 12 November 1842, DC, vol. 5.

14. On these trials, see: *House Reports*, ser. 447, vol. 3, no. 546, pp. 806-10

(8 March 1844); and "Prison Documents," DM, for petitions for amnesty from two of the men convicted under the Algerine Act.

15. See *House Reports*, ser. 447, vol. 3, no. 546, pp. 802-4 (12 March 1844).

16. Martin Luther to Dorr, 28 March 1844, DC, vol. 8.

17. These developments are discussed in George M. Dennison, "Thomas Wilson Dorr: Counsel of Record in Luther v. Borden," *Saint Louis University Law Journal* 15, no. 3(Spring 1971):398-428. See also: *ex parte Dorr*, 3 *Howard* 103 ff. (1845); "Microcopy No. 215; Minutes of the Supreme Court of the United States," National Archives Microfilm, roll 3 (vols. H-L; 8 January 1838 to 24 January 1848), vol. K, pp. 4946-51, 4979-80 (11 and 27 December 1844); and "Microcopy No. 216: Dockets of the Supreme Court of the United States," National Archives Microfilm, roll 2 (vols. E-H; 23 September 1834 to 6 August 1860), vol. F, p. 2674 (23 January 1845 to 5 December 1849, relating to the case of *Thomas Wilson Dorr* v. *State of Rhode Island*, never decided).

18. On the cases, see: *Providence Daily Journal*, 16 November 1843 and succeeding issues; *House Reports*, ser. 447, vol. 3, no. 546, pp. 357-58; "Private Daily Note Book for 1845-1850 of Thomas W. Dorr," entry for ? August 1848, DM; Silas Wright, Jr., to Edmund Burke, 8 August 1844, Burke Papers, vol. 1; Aaron White, Jr., to Dorr, 22 April 1851, marginalia, DC, vol. 13; Charles F. Townsend to Dorr, 18 October 1851, DC, vol. 13; and *Luther* v. *Borden*, R.I. Circuit, "Records of Circuit Court," Dockets and Minutes, November Term 1842 through June Term 1849 (microfilm in author's possession, records in Federal Records Center, Waltham, Massachusetts).

19. 7 *Howard* 1 ff. (1849). See also: *House Reports*, ser. 447, vol. 3, no. 546, pp. 363-75; *Luther* v. *Borden*, R.I. Circuit, "Records of Circuit Court"; and *Providence Daily Journal*, 16 November 1843 and succeeding issues.

20. *Providence Daily Journal*, 22 November 1843; Benjamin F. Hallett, *The Right of the People to Establish Forms of Government. Mr. Hallett's Argument in the Rhode Island Causes, before the Supreme Court of the United States, January . . . 1848. No. 14. Martin Luther vs. Luther M. Borden and Others. No. 77. Rachel Luther vs. The Same* (Boston: Beals & Greene, 1848), pp. 6-7; Mahlon H. Hellerich, "The Luther Cases in the Lower Courts," *Rhode Island History* 11, no. 2(April 1952):42-43; *Martin Luther* v. *Luther M. Borden et al.*, 7 *Howard* 3-19 (1849); *Luther* v. *Borden*, RG 267: Appellate Case no. 2419, National Archives Microfilm, pp. 143-47; and "Dockets of the Supreme Court," National Archives Microfilm, roll 2, vol. F, p. 2560 (1 May 1844 to 19 June 1849).

21. Aaron White, Jr., to Dorr, 9 February 1844, DC, vol. 8.

22. Aaron White, Jr., to Dorr, 30 April 1843, DC, vol. 7.

23. On this case, see: *House Reports*, ser. 447, vol. 3, no. 581, p. 157; *Providence Daily Journal*, 17-19 April 1844; *Luther* v. *Borden*, R.I. Circuit, "Records of Circuit Court," Dockets and Minutes, November Term 1842 and November Term 1843.

24. Aaron White, Jr., to Dorr, 9 February 1844, DC, vol. 8. See also Aaron White, Jr., to Dorr, 14 March 1844, DC, vol. 8.

25. For discussion, see George M. Dennison, "Martial Law: The Development of a Theory of Emergency Powers, 1776-1861," *American Journal of Legal History* 18, no. 1(January 1974):52-79.

26. *Luther* v. *Borden*, R.I. Circuit, "Records of Circuit Court," Minutes of 17-19 April 1844; *Providence Daily Journal*, 17-19 April 1844; and Abraham

Payne, *Reminiscences of the Rhode Island Bar* (Providence, R.I.: Tibbits & Preston, 1885), pp. 36-37.

27. All quotations are taken from *House Reports*, ser. 447, vol. 3, no. 581, pp. 158-65.

28. Ibid.

29. Ibid.

30. Ibid.

31. *Providence Daily Journal*, 19 April 1844.

32. *Luther* v. *Borden*, R.I. Circuit, "Records of Circuit Court," Dockets, Minutes, and Case File for November Term 1844, June Term 1845, and November Term 1845. Justice Levi Woodbury, Story's successor, finally certified the case for review. On the defects in the case, see Benjamin F. Hallett to Dorr, 18 December 1847, DC, vol. 11.

33. Dorr to Edmund Burke, 1 December 1845, Burke Papers, vol. 2; Silas Wright, Jr., to Edmund Burke, 8 August 1844, Burke Papers, vol. 1; D. D. Field to Dorr, 16 March 1844, DC, vol. 8; and Warren, *Supreme Court*, 2:187.

34. See Dennison, "Counsel of Record," pp. 417-24.

35. Dorr to Nathan Clifford, 24 January 1848, DC, vol. 12.

36. As quoted from a Hallett editorial of 1845 in Warren, *Supreme Court*, 2:187-88.

37. For characterizations, see Warren, *Supreme Court*, 2:201-5.

38. Except as specifically noted, all quotations are from Hallett, *Right of the People*, pp. 4-5, 9-12, 22-26, 29-31, 60-61. On this brief, see Benjamin F. Hallett to Dorr, 21 January and 11 February 1848, DC, vol. 12.

39. For relevant opinions, see: *Charlotte Dye Owings, and Francis T. D. Owings* v. *James F. Hull*, 9 *Peters* 607 ff. (1835); *John Swift* v. *George W. Tyson*, 16 *Peters* 1 ff. (1842); and the modern case of *Baker* v. *Carr*, 369 *U.S.* 186 ff. (1962).

40. Hallett quoted Joseph Story, *Commentaries on the Constitution of the United States: With a Preliminary Review of the Colonies and the States, before the Adoption of the Constitution*, 2d ed. (Boston: Little and Brown, 1851), 1:336-37. Hallett, of course, used the 1833 edition, unchanged as far as this quotation is concerned.

41. Webster cited *John Barron* v. *Baltimore*, 7 *Peters* 243 ff. (1833).

42. Daniel Webster, "The Rhode Island Government," in *Works of Daniel Webster*, 5th ed., 6 vols. (reprint ed., Boston: Little, Brown and Co., 1853), 6:217-42, at 217-19, 235-36, 241-42.

43. All quotations from Hallett, *Right of the People*, pp. 7, 9-11, 31-32, 51-54.

44. For the quoted phrase, see Robert G. McCloskey, ed., *The Works of James Wilson*, 2 vols. (Cambridge: Harvard University Press, Belknap Press, 1967), 2:770, a Wilson remark of 1787.

45. On this point, see Hallett, *Right of the People*, pp. 61-62, and Dorr to Nathan Clifford, 24 January 1848, DC, vol. 12.

46. For Whipple's argument, *Luther* v. *Borden*, 7 *Howard* 27-29 (1849).

47. All quotations, unless otherwise noted, from Webster, "Rhode Island Government," pp. 219-22, 223-27, 230-31, 236-37, 240.

48. Webster quoted the Act of 28 February 1795, for which see Richard Peters et al., eds., *Public Statutes at Large of the United States of America*, 17 vols. (Boston: Charles C. Little and James Brown, 1846-1874), 1:424-25.

49. Dorr to Nathan Clifford, 10 December 1847, DC, vol. 11. See also:

Nathan Clifford to Dorr, 3 December 1847, DC, vol. 11; Nathan Clifford to Dorr, 12 February 1848, DC, vol. 12; George Turner to Dorr, 12 December 1847, DC, vol. 11; and Dorr to William Simons, 23 August 1842, DC, vol. 4.

50. See: Hallett, *Right of the People*, pp. 65-70; and *Luther* v. *Borden*, 7 *Howard* 34 (1849). The Nathan Clifford Papers, Maine Historical Society Archives, Portland, Maine, contain nothing of relevance for this case. Clifford's argument has been reconstructed from the comments in Nathan Clifford to Dorr, 3 December 1847, George Turner to Dorr, 12 December 1847, and Dorr to Nathan Clifford, 10 December 1847, DC, vol. 11. For background, see Dennison, "Martial Law," pp. 52-79.

51. Dorr to Franklin Cooley et al., 1 February 1843, DC, vol. 6.

52. Webster, "Rhode Island Government," pp. 240-41.

53. On this development, see Dennison, "Martial Law," pp. 52-79.

54. Dorr to Benjamin F. Hallett, 8 February 1848, DC, vol. 12.

55. Benjamin F. Hallett to Dorr, 11 February 1848, DC, vol. 12.

56. See: Dennison, "Triumph of Institutionalism" and his "An Empire of Liberty: Congressional Attitudes toward Popular Sovereignty in the Territories, 1787-1867" (Paper delivered at the Rocky Mountain Social Science Association Convention, El Paso, April 1974).

57. On the process of routinization, see: Carl G. Gustavson, *The Institutional Drive* ([Athens]: Ohio University Press, 1966), chap. 6; and Kenneth Burke, *Attitudes toward History*, rev. ed. (Boston: Beacon Press, 1959), pp. 218, 255-56.

58. See: Dennison, "Idea of Revolution"; and his "Counsel of Record," pp. 406-8.

Chapter 8

1. As quoted in Charles Warren, *The Supreme Court in United States History*, rev. ed., 2 vols. (Boston and Toronto: Little, Brown, and Co., 1926), 2:192-93. See also the running commentary in *New York Tribune*, 22 January 1848 and subsequent issues.

2. Benjamin F. Hallett to Dorr, 11 February 1848, DC, vol. 12.

3. Ibid.

4. Nathan Clifford to Dorr, 12 February 1848, DC, vol. 12.

5. Benjamin F. Hallett to Dorr, 11 February 1848; Dorr to Nathan Clifford, 6 March 1848, DC, vol. 12. See also "Dockets of the Supreme Court," National Archives Microfilm, roll 2, vol. F, p. 2560 (1 May 1844–19 June 1849), for a note that the case would be continued.

6. See: Warren, *Supreme Court*, 2:193, alleging illness as the cause for delay; Edmund Burke to Dorr, 6 March and 22 May 1848, DC, vol. 12; and George M. Dennison, "Thomas Wilson Dorr: Counsel of Record in Luther v. Borden," *Saint Louis University Law Journal* 15, no. 3(Spring 1971):424-25. Note that the *Tribune* erred in its predictions, but C. Peter Magrath, "Optimistic Democrat: Thomas W. Dorr and the Case of Luther vs. Borden," *Rhode Island History* 29, no. 4(October 1970):109, follows the *Tribune*.

7. As quoted in Warren, *Supreme Court*, 2:192.

8. Edmund Burke to Dorr, 6 March 1848, DC, vol. 12.

9. Dorr to Estwick Evans, 12 April 1848, Thomas Wilson Dorr Papers, Miscellaneous Personal Papers, Manuscripts Division, Library of Congress.

10. Dorr to Benjamin F. Hallett, 11 May 1848, DC, vol. 12.

11. Dorr to Colonel Samuel Medary, 17 May 1848, DC, vol. 12.

12. Edmund Burke to Dorr, 22 May 1848, DC, vol. 12.

13. See: Benjamin F. Hallett to Dorr, 11 November 1848 and 8 January 1849; and Dorr to Benjamin F. Hallett, 13 December 1848, DC, vol. 12. See also Dennison, "Counsel of Record," pp. 424-26.

14. See: Joseph G. Rayback, *Free Soil: The Election of 1848* (Lexington: University Press of Kentucky, 1971); Benjamin F. Hallett to Dorr, 11 November 1848; and Edmund Burke to Dorr, 13 November 1848, DC, vol. 12.

15. Dorr to a Committee of New York Democrats, 15 July 1848, DC, vol. 12. Other letters of a similar vein are in this volume.

16. *Martin Luther v. Luther M. Borden et al.*, 7 *Howard* 34-48, 88 (1849). On the disposal of the cases, see: "Dockets of the Supreme Court," National Archives Microfilm, roll 2, vol. F, p. 2560, entries for 19 June 1849 (sustaining the Circuit Court decision in Martin Luther's case, and remanding Rachel Luther's case for trial); *Luther v. Borden*, R.I. Circuit, "Records of Circuit Court," specifically " 'Final' Records, Vol. 16, pages 87-88," on Martin Luther's case, and " 'Final' Records, Vol. 16, pages 77-87," on Rachel Luther's case.

17. This and the other Taney quotations are from *Luther v. Borden*, 7 *Howard* 41-47.

18. See: George M. Dennison, "The Dorr War and the Triumph of Institutionalism" (Paper delivered at the Organization of American Historians' Convention, Chicago, April 1973); and George M. Dennison, "An Empire of Liberty: Congressional Attitudes toward Popular Sovereignty in the Territories, 1787-1867" (Paper delivered before the Rocky Mountain Social Science Association Convention, El Paso, April 1974).

19. For the quotation, but used negatively, see Daniel Boorstin, *The Genius of American Politics* (Chicago: University of Chicago Press, 1953), pp. 74-75.

20. See G. W. F. Hegel, *The Philosophy of History*, ed. C. J. Friedrich and tr. J. Sibree (1899; reprint ed., New York: Dover Publications, 1956), pp. 85-87.

21. Michael A. Conron, "Law, Politics, and Chief Justice Taney: A Reinterpretation of the Luther v. Borden Decision," *American Journal of Legal History* 11, no. 4(October 1967):384-88, held that Taney had questioned the validity of Dorr's conviction for treason by an interested court.

22. Taney argued that if discretionary power was vested in one branch of government, the other branches could not check the exercise of that power, on which point see Story's opinion in *Martin v. Mott*, 12 *Wheaton* 19 ff. (1827), at 29-31.

23. Charles Fairman, *The Law of Martial Rule*, 2d ed. (Chicago: Callaghan & Co., 1943), p. 118, held that Taney made the ruling in an "unguarded moment." See Dennison, "Counsel of Record," pp. 424-25, for the contrary view.

24. For the Woodbury quotations, *Luther v. Borden*, 7 *Howard* 51-58. Woodbury devoted most of his opinion (pp. 58-88) to an analysis of martial law.

25. Ibid., 51, 54, 57. Compare with his earlier opinion in *Scott v. Jones*, 5 *Howard* 343 ff. (1847).

26. For Woodbury quotations on martial law, see *Luther v. Borden*, 7 *Howard* 59-60, 62, 69-70, 71-75, 82, 85(1849).

27. As quoted from Dorr's analysis printed in the *Republican Herald* and reprinted in *Providence Daily Journal*, 12 January 1849. See also Dorr to Benjamin F. Hallett, 15 January 1849, DC, vol. 12.

28. Anthony was editor of the *Providence Daily Journal;* see his editorial in the issue of 12 January 1849.

29. Ibid.

30. Aaron White, Jr., to Dorr, 1 September 1842, DC, vol. 5.

31. Aaron White, Jr., to Dorr, 3 June 1842, DC, vol. 4.

32. Aaron White, Jr., to Dorr, 17 February 1849, DC, vol. 12. For a shift in White's opinion, see Aaron White, Jr., to Dorr, 12 May 1844, DC, vol. 8.

33. See: Arthur May Mowry, *The Dorr War; or, The Constitutional Struggle in Rhode Island* (1901; reprint ed., New York: Chelsea House, 1970), pp. 235-36; Alfred H. Kelly and Winfred A. Harbison, *The American Constitution: Its Origins and Development,* 3d ed. (New York: W. W. Norton & Co., 1963), pp. 480, 982, for typically cursory mention; and Charles Gordon Post, Jr., *The Supreme Court and Political Questions,* Johns Hopkins Studies in Historical and Political Science, vol. 14, no. 4(Baltimore, 1936), pp. 104-30.

34. Conron, "Law, Politics, and Chief Justice Taney," p. 380.

35. Ibid., p. 383.

36. See William M. Wiecek, *The Republican Guarantee of the U.S. Constitution* (Ithaca, N.Y.: Cornell University Press, 1972), chaps. 3-4.

37. On the Wilsonian theory, see George M. Dennison, "American Constitutionalism and the Idea of Revolution" (Paper delivered at the Pacific Coast Branch of the American Society for Legal History Convention, Los Angeles, November 1974); Dennison, "Counsel of Record," pp. 406-8; and Dennison, "The Dorr War and the Triumph of Institutionalism." Also relevant is Dennison, "Empire of Liberty."

Epilogue

1. Aaron White, Jr., to Dorr, 10 June 1843, DC, vol. 7.

2. See: Charles Gorham, *An Historical Statement of the Elective Franchise in Rhode Island* (n.p., 1879), for a statement made before a Select U.S. Senate Committee investigating election frauds. See also Chilton Williamson, "Rhode Island Suffrage since the Dorr War," *New England Quarterly* 28, no. 3 (March 1955):34-50.

3. Aaron White, Jr., to Dorr, 3 June 1842, DC, vol. 4.

4. Arthur May Mowry, *The Dorr War; or, The Constitutional Struggle in Rhode Island* (1901; reprint ed., New York: Chelsea House, 1970), pp. 255-59.

5. For the quotation, see Noah J. Arnold, "The History of Suffrage in Rhode Island," *Narragansett Historical Register* 8, no. 4(October 1888): 327-28. See also Dorr to William Simons, 23 February 1848, DC, vol. 12.

6. See Dan King, *The Life and Times of Thomas Wilson Dorr, with Outlines of the Political History of Rhode Island* (Boston: Dan King, 1859), pp. 282-93.

7. There are no letters in DC showing an awareness of the affront to principle. See also Mowry, *Dorr War,* pp. 255-59.

8. See "Supplement," 3 *Knowles* 299-311(Rhode Island, 1854).

9. See King, *Life of Dorr,* pp. 285-93; and Charles H. Payne, "The Great Dorr War," *New England Magazine,* n.s. 2, no. 4(June 1890):400-401.

10. See George M. Dennison, "An Empire of Liberty: Congressional Attitudes toward Popular Sovereignty in the Territories, 1787-1867" (Paper delivered at the Rocky Mountain Social Science Association Convention, El Paso, April 1974).

11. Ibid.; see also George M. Dennison, "Martial Law: The Development of

a Theory of Emergency Powers, 1776-1861," *American Journal of Legal History* 18, no. 1 (January 1974):52-79; and George M. Dennison, *"The Idea of a Party System:* A Critique," *Rocky Mountain Social Science Journal* 9, no. 3 (April 1972):31-43.

12. R. W. B. Lewis, *The American Adam: Innocence, Tragedy, and Tradition in the Nineteenth Century* (Chicago: University of Chicago Press, 1955), pp. 160-61.

13. Ibid. See also George M. Dennison, "The Dorr War and the Triumph of Institutionalism" (Paper presented at the Organization of American Historians' Convention, Chicago, April 1973).

14. For discussion, see Richard Hofstadter, *The Progressive Historians: Turner, Beard, Parrington* (New York: Alfred A. Knopf, 1969), chap. 1; Lewis, *American Adam,* chaps. 2-3, 7; and Dennison, "Dorr War and the Triumph of Institutionalism." For analysis of the differing attitudes toward history and time, see J. G. A. Pocock, *Politics, Language and Time: Essays on Political Thought and History* (New York: Atheneum, 1971), chaps. 1 and 7.

15. For the quoted phrase and an analysis of its significance in terms of changing attitudes, see Pocock, *Politics, Language and Time,* pp. 141-54, esp. p. 154.

16. See Dennison, "Dorr War and the Triumph of Institutionalism," and the sources cited therein.

17. Ibid.

18. On the traditional ideology, see George M. Dennison, "American Constitutionalism and the Idea of Revolution" (Paper delivered at the Pacific Coast Branch of the American Society for Legal History Convention, Los Angeles, November 1974).

19. On the earlier view of government, see Bernard Bailyn, *The Origins of American Politics* (New York: Alfred A. Knopf, 1967), pp. 103-5; Daniel Boorstin, *The Lost World of Thomas Jefferson* (New York: Holt, 1948); and Daniel Boorstin, *The Decline of American Radicalism* (New York: Random House, 1970), chap. 4. On the change, see Carl G. Gustavson, *The Institutional Drive* ([Athens]: Ohio University Press, 1966), chap. 6.

20. For comparison, see Daniel Webster, "The Rhode Island Government," in *Works of Daniel Webster,* 5th ed. (Boston: Little, Brown & Co., 1853), 6:217-42.

21. The formulation is from Merrill D. Peterson, *The Jefferson Image in the American Mind* (New York: Oxford University Press, 1962), p. 88.

22. Loren Baritz, *City on a Hill: A History of Ideas and Myths in America* (New York, London, and Sydney: John Wiley & Sons, 1964), p. 331.

23. For a discussion of the death-rebirth paradox, see Kenneth Burke, *Attitudes toward History,* rev. ed. (Boston: Beacon Press, 1959), pp. 17, 23, 179-215, 268-70, 317-19.

24. *Dred Scott* v. *John F. A. Sandford,* 19 *Howard* 393-633 (1857).

25. For discussion, see Dennison, "Empire of Liberty."

26. This point was clearest with regard to Taney's denial that blacks could be considered citizens of the United States.

27. For pertinent discussion of the emerging social ideals, see: Eric Foner, *Free Soil, Free Labor, Free Men: The Ideology of the Republican Party before the Civil War* (London, Oxford, and New York: Oxford University Press, 1970), chap. 9; and David J. Rothman, *The Discovery of the Asylum: Social Order and Disorder in the New Republic* (Boston: Little, Brown and Co.,

1971), chaps. 2-4, 11, esp. pp. 68-69, 82-84, 265. On the changing definition of progress, see Arthur Alphonse Ekirch, Jr., *The Idea of Progress in America: 1815-1860* (1944; reprint ed., New York: AMS Press, 1969), chap. 9.

28. On ideology and its role in history, see Willard A. Mullins, "On the Concept of Ideology in Political Science," *American Political Science Review* 66, no. 2(June 1972):498-510.

29. See Dennison, "Martial Law," pp. 52-79, on the discussion that follows.

30. Institutionalization is usually associated with nominalism, on which see Roland Van Zandt, *The Metaphysical Foundation of American History* (The Hague: Mouton & Co., 1959), chap. 7.

31. On radical usage, see Jane H. Pease and William H. Pease, "Confrontation and Abolition in the 1850s," *Journal of American History* 58, no. 4 (March 1972): 923-37. On more typical usage, see Dennison, "Empire of Liberty," and Dennison, *"Idea of a Party System,"* pp. 38-41.

32. Southerners fought in defense of a way of life, but their political theory had little of the indeterminateness of peaceable revolution about it. For insight into the southern mind, see Robert Manson Myers, ed., *Children of Pride: A True Story of Georgia and the Civil War* (New Haven, Conn.: Yale University Press, 1972), pp. 625, 670, 694-95.

33. Dennison, *"Idea of a Party System,"* p. 39.

34. See John Bassett Moore, ed., *The Works of James Buchanan*, 12 vols. (1908-11; reprint ed., New York: Antiquarian Press, 1960), 12:21-26, 44.

35. See *Texas v. White et al.*, 7 *Wallace* 700 ff., esp. 725-26 (1869).

36. See R. W. Van Alstyne, *The Rising American Empire* (Chicago: Quadrangle Books, 1965), pp. 3, 196-98. See also Edward A. Shils and Henry A. Finch, eds., *Max Weber on the Methodology of the Social Sciences* (Glencoe, Ill.: Free Press, 1949), p. 57.

37. See Phillip S. Paludan, "The American Civil War Considered as a Crisis in Law and Order," *American Historical Review* 77, no. 4 (October 1972):1013-34.

38. For discussion of the use of the Rhode Island precedent, see Dennison, "Martial Law," pp. 52-79; Dennison, "Empire of Liberty"; and Dennison, "Dorr War and the Triumph of Institutionalism."

39. See Mullins, "Ideology," pp. 498-510; and Burke, *Attitudes toward History*, pp. 17, 23, 179-215, 268-70, 317-19.

40. The best discussion of this process is Gene Wise, *American Historical Explanations: A Strategy for Grounded Inquiry* (Homewood, Ill.: Dorsey Press; Georgetown, Ont.: Irwin-Dorsey, 1973), chaps. 5-6. See also Pocock, *Politics, Language and Time*, chap. 1.

41. See George M. Fredrickson, *The Inner Civil War: Northern Intellectuals and the Crisis of the Union* (New York: Harper & Row, 1965), pp. 134-35.

42. On this ideological development among peoples, see Karl Mannheim, *Ideology and Utopia: An Introduction to the Sociology of Knowledge* (1936; reprint ed., New York: Harcourt, Brace & World, 1968), pp. 20-21, 24-25, 50-53, 57, 69, 76-83, 85, 89-96, and chap. 3.

43. Aaron White, Jr., to Dorr, 1 September 1842, DC, vol. 5.

44. Fred Somkin, *Unquiet Eagle: Memory and Desire in the Idea of American Freedom, 1815-1860* (Ithaca, N.Y.: Cornell University Press, 1967), p. 5.

BIBLIOGRAPHICAL ESSAY

Debts accumulate in projects such as this one. Those familiar with the work of earlier scholars will recognize at once how much I have depended on my predecessors for guidance and insight. I have learned from every book consulted, and have profited from reading even when I disagreed. Some debts, however, are larger than others; some deserve specific mention, while others can simply be assumed as part of the legacy bestowed by those writers who have set the parameters for the field of American historical studies. Accordingly this essay mentions only those works either uncited in the notes or singularly important to me in the effort to construct an interpretive framework. A much more thorough listing of the sources consulted appears in the bibliographical section of my dissertation, "The Constitutional Issues of the Dorr War: A Study in the Evolution of American Constitutionalism, 1776-1849" (Ph.D. diss., University of Washington, Seattle, 1967).

Methodologically, five books have served as guides to historical study. Karl Mannheim, *Ideology and Utopia: An Introduction to the Sociology of Knowledge* (1936; reprint ed., New York: Harcourt, Brace & World, 1968), provided insights into the ways that ideas change under the influence of historical experience. Thomas Kuhn, *The Structure of Scientific Revolutions*, 2d ed. (Chicago: University of Chicago Press, 1970), stimulated the effort to think in terms of his analysis of paradigms. In following Kuhn, I found my thinking reinforced and clarified by Gene Wise, *American Historical Explanations: A Strategy for Grounded Inquiry* (Homewood, Ill.: Dorsey

Press; Georgetown, Ont.: Irwin-Dorsey, 1973) specifically by what Wise called "situation-strategy" analysis, and J. G. A. Pocock, *Politics, Language and Time: Essays on Political Thought and History* (New York: Atheneum, 1971). Wise and Pocock offered articulate explication of a method I developed before reading their works. Finally, Kenneth Burke, *Attitudes toward History*, rev. ed. (Boston: Beacon Press, 1959), and his other works on the topic, illuminated the process by which the prevailing symbols of authority undergo change. Kuhnian before Kuhn, Burke was one of the most sensitive writers in English on the general subject of the role of ideas in history.

These writers outline an approach to historical study and analysis stressing the role of changing ideas. The concern, as expressed by another theorist, Murray G. Murphey, in *Our Knowledge of the Historical Past* (Indianapolis, Ind.: Bobbs-Merrill Co., 1973), is to establish both a psychological and a structural, or behavioral, reality in the historical process. The former involves intentions and personal understandings, whereas the latter refers to the sequence of events as viewed externally. The scholar resorting to the methodology outlined in the books listed above seeks to discover when and how the structural reality is identical with or reflective of the psychological reality—when the discernible trends in history correlate with the conscious motives of the historical actors. Undoubtedly people have always acted on motives that have little to do with the consequences of their actions. Unintended consequences have long been of great interest to historians. I chose to employ the approach of this group of historical theorists because I thought it promised to expose the dialectical nature of the historical process and to hold in check the tendency to attribute far too much to conclusions drawn from analysis of structural reality alone.

To develop a perspective on American history, I attempted to synthesize the arguments of: Daniel Boorstin, *The Lost World of Thomas Jefferson* (New York: Holt, 1948); Arthur Alphonse Ekirch, Jr., *The Idea of Progress in America: 1815-1860* (1944;

reprint ed., New York: AMS Press, 1969); R. W. B. Lewis, *The American Adam: Innocence, Tragedy, and Tradition in the Nineteenth Century* (Chicago: University of Chicago Press, 1955); Roland Van Zandt, *The Metaphysical Foundation of American History* (The Hague: Mouton & Co., 1959); Perry Miller, *The Life of the Mind in America: From the Revolution to the Civil War* (New York: Harcourt, Brace & World, 1965), especially Part II, entitled "The Legal Mentality"; Merrill D. Peterson, *The Jefferson Image in the American Mind* (New York: Oxford University Press, 1962); Loren Baritz, *City on a Hill: A History of Ideas and Myths in America* (New York, London, and Sydney: John Wiley & Sons, 1964); George M. Fredrickson, *The Inner Civil War: Northern Intellectuals and the Crisis of the Union* (New York: Harper & Row, 1965); Carl G. Gustavson, *The Institutional Drive* ([Athens] : Ohio University Press, 1966); Fred Somkin, *Unquiet Eagle: Memory and Desire in the Idea of American Freedom, 1815-1860* (Ithaca, N.Y.: Cornell University Press, 1967); and Theodore Lowi, *The Politics of Disorder* (New York: Basic Books, 1971). I found in these works a subtle and sophisticated effort to illuminate the changing culture of nineteenth-century America—to explore the different ways that Americans themselves conceptualized America and Americans. None of these authors developed an argument stressing decay and degeneration. The point needs to be made because of a tendency to level the charge against such writers of being too enamored with the myth of an earlier and simpler age. Far from advocating a return to the founding, these scholars have sought to appreciate each of the various stages of American development in its own right. In a word, they have sought to overcome a rather persistent presentism that has distorted the writing of American history.

My purpose in this study was to bring the perspective obtained from broad reading in intellectual and cultural studies to the analysis of American legal and constitutional history. For background in the specific area of constitutional history, I drew on the standard as well as the newer work in the field. Two great early studies are Charles Grove Haines and Foster Sherwood, *The Role of the Supreme Court in American Government and Politics, 1789-1864*, 2 vols. (Berkeley and Los Angeles: University of California Press, 1944-1957), and Charles Warren, *The Supreme Court in United States History: 1789-1918*, 2 vols. (1922; reprint ed., Boston: Little, Brown & Co., 1926). Two newer studies that broaden the canvas are Donald Fleming and Bernard Bailyn, eds., *Law in American History* (Boston and Toronto: Little, Brown & Co., 1971), and Lawrence M. Friedman, *A History of American Law* (New York: Simon and Schuster, 1973). The work of a synthetic character is still far from adequate. Some seminal essays have appeared of late: particularly valuable are Kirk Thompson, "Constitution Theory and Political Action," *Journal of Politics* 31, no. 3 (August 1969):655-81 (insightful but one-sided), and Phillip S. Paludan, "The American Civil War Considered as a Crisis in Law and Order," *American Historical Review* 77, no. 4 (October 1972):1013-34 (much broader in scope than the title implies). Too much of the legal and constitutional scholarship is imbued with what can only be called a liberal bias, tending to treat American history as the inevitable unfolding of progress. As I have tried to show, this perspective first took discernible form during the "middle period" with the emergence of a new historical consciousness in the United States. One paradox of American history is that by the time the conservative school of historical jurisprudence emerged, it had liberal traditions to preserve. Much needs to be done to demonstrate the impact of this liberal historicism on the American mind and on American historiography.

Works dealing with violence in American history, and with the growth of security consciousness and the mechanisms for maintaining order, offer broad insights into the changing character of American culture and civilization. Probably the best work on the former is Hugh Davis Graham and Ted Robert Gurr, eds., *The History of Violence in America: Historical and Comparative Perspectives* (New York, Washington, and London:

Praeger, 1969), an anthology of essays contributed by scholars in various fields, including some on the European background. The article by David Grimsted, "Rioting in Its Jacksonian Setting," *American Historical Review* 77, no. 2 (April 1972):361-97, read in conjunction with Leonard L. Richards, *"Gentlemen of Property and Standing": Anti-Abolition Mobs in Jacksonian America* (London, Oxford, and New York: Oxford University Press, 1970), and my own "Martial Law: The Development of a Theory of Emergency Powers, 1776-1861," *American Journal of Legal History* 18, no. 1 (January 1974):52-79, offers a good introduction to the process whereby Americans transformed their loose and essentially voluntary system into one much more Draconian in nature. Rowland Berthoff, *An Unsettled People: Social Order and Disorder in American History* (New York, Evanston, and London: Harper & Row, 1971), and David J. Rothman, *The Discovery of the Asylum: Social Order and Disorder in the New Republic* (Boston and Toronto: Little, Brown & Co., 1971), provide useful background on the changing perceptions and the move toward institutionalization. Finally, Stanley I. Kutler, *Privilege and Creative Destruction: The Charles River Bridge Case* (Philadelphia, New York, and Toronto: J. B. Lippincott Co., 1971), offers provocative insight into the changing ideological structure in the America of the 1830s.

Other more specialized and theoretical works have been helpful in developing an interpretive approach for the book. James C. Davies, "Toward a Theory of Revolution," *American Sociological Review* 27, no. 1 (February 1962):5-19; Willard A. Mullins, "On the Concept of Ideology in Political Science," *American Political Science Review* 66, no. 2 (June 1972):498-510; Isaac Kramnick, "Reflections of Revolution: Definition and Explanation in Recent Scholarship," *History and Theory* 11, no. 1 (1972):26-63; William M. Wiecek, *The Republican Guarantee Clause of the U.S. Constitution* (Ithaca, N.Y.: Cornell University Press, 1972); and Major L. Wilson, "The Repressible Conflict: Seward's Concept of Progress and the Free-Soil Movement," *Journal of Southern History* 37, no. 4 (October 1971):533-56, all explore issues that arise in the effort to understand American political and constitutional development during the years between the Revolution and the Civil War.

The notes provide a rough guide to the important works focused on the Dorr War or Rebellion of 1842. Many valuable insights lie buried in pamphlets and in old historical magazines. Students launching new studies should consult the standard bibliographical guides before going too far on any such project. Histories and commentaries began to appear even before the summer crisis of 1842 had dissipated. One of the most intriguing of the early accounts is Mrs. F. H. (W.) Green (Mac-Dougal), *Might and Right: By a Rhode Islander*, 2d ed. (Providence, R.I.: A. H. Stillwell, 1844), first published in 1843. Mrs. Green was Dorr's confidante and wrote the book partly on the basis of information he supplied. The alternate view of the events can be found in Jacob Frieze, *A Concise History of the Efforts to Obtain an Extension of the Suffrage in Rhode Island; from the Year 1811 to 1842; and the Dorr War, 1842*, 3d ed. (Providence: Thomas S. Hammond, 1912), written by a former Suffragist (credited with having authored the charter for the Rhode Island Suffrage Association) who turned against the movement when it became an ideological crusade in early 1842. Historians since 1843 have divided into two groups, supporting the views of one of these two authors—but often without knowing it, because they had not read these early accounts. The standard work until recently was, of course, Arthur May Mowry, *The Dorr War; or, The Constitutional Struggle in Rhode Island* (1901; reprint ed., New York: Chelsea House, 1970). Much as Frieze had done, Mowry wrote from the perspective of the new American ideology that emerged in the years after 1842. While he sympathized with the Suffragists, he viewed them as irresponsible idealists who ignored the need for stability and order within any decent society. But more than that, Mowry took the Suffragists to task because they were enthusiastic visionaries who misunderstood the character of American politics and constitutional government. They had acted as if American history had no dynamic of progress insuring a better world for themselves and all mankind. In a word, Mowry imposed a "liberal" bias on his study, rejecting any other perspective. While his work provides a fairly accurate chronology and presents a mass of undigested material, he did not have access to the personal papers of the participants. Even had he uncovered such materials, it is doubtful that his interpretive perspective would have allowed him to appreciate their significance. His account reads almost like the columns of the *Providence Daily Journal*, the government mouthpiece in Rhode Island (available on microfilm from the Rhode Island Historical Society).

For sixty years Mowry's work remained standard. Arthur Schlesinger, Jr., although writing from a more definite and conscious commitment to the liberal perspective, nonetheless used Mowry as the basic source for his *Age of Jackson* (Boston: Little, Brown & Co., 1945). Only with Chilton Williamson's *American Suffrage: From Property to Democracy, 1760-1860* (Princeton, N.J.: Princeton University Press, 1960), focusing in one chapter specifically on the Suffragist attempt to modernize Rhode Island's obsolescent constitutional structure, and Peter J. Coleman's *The Transformation of Rhode Island, 1790-1860* (Providence, R.I.: Brown University Press, 1963), in some measure joining economic with political analysis to focus on modernization, did scholars begin to question the cogency of Mowry's study. Williamson differs little from Mowry, however, in that he stressed the idea that the Suffragists lost the battle but won the war; Coleman arrived at much the same conclusion although he was much more sensitive to political divisions within the smallest state.

The article literature has proliferated over the years, much of it aimed at settling points of dispute over matters of fact as well as interpretation. The most significant of the articles are: Robert L. Ciaburi, "The Dorr Rebellion in Rhode Island: The

Moderate Phase," *Rhode Island History* 26, no. 3 (July 1967):73-87; Michael A. Conron, "Law, Politics, and Chief Justice Taney: A Reconsideration of the Luther v. Borden Decision," *American Journal of Legal History* 11, no. 4 (October 1967):377-88; George M. Dennison, "Thomas Wilson Dorr: Counsel of Record in Luther v. Borden," *Saint Louis University Law Journal* 15, no. 3 (Spring 1971):398-428; Mahlon H. Hellerich, "The Luther Cases in the Lower Courts," *Rhode Island History* 11, no. 2 (April 1952):33-45; Charles O. Lerche, Jr., "The Dorr War and the Federal Constitution," *Rhode Island History* 9, no. 1 (January 1950):1-10; C. Peter Magrath, "Optimistic Democrat: Thomas W. Dorr and the Case of Luther vs. Borden," *Rhode Island History* 29, no. 4 (October 1970):94-112; John S. Schuchman, "The Political Background of the Political-Question Doctrine: The Judges and the Dorr War," *American Journal of Legal History* 16, no. 2 (April 1972):111-25; William M. Wiecek, "Popular Sovereignty in the Dorr War: Conservative Counterblast," *Rhode Island History* 32, no. 2 (May 1973):35-51; Chilton Williamson, "The Disenchantment of Thomas W. Dorr," *Rhode Island History* 17, no. 4 (October 1958): 97-108; and Chilton Williamson, "Rhode Island Suffrage since the Dorr War," *New England Quarterly* 28, no. 3 (March 1955):34-50.

The most recent contribution to the historiography of the Dorr War came to hand after this study had been revised for the last time. Marvin E. Gettleman, *The Dorr Rebellion: A Study in American Radicalism, 1833-1849* (New York: Random House, 1973), is in many ways an interesting account. Outfitted with a brief but good bibliographical essay, Gettleman's work is too present-minded to provide much insight into the Suffrage movement as a phenomenon of its own time. His overriding concern, revealing the impact of contemporary events, was to develop a "usable" past for those Americans trying to create a "decent society" today. Thus he never really deals with the Suffragists as "radicals" on their own terms, but compares them invidiously with other groups of a more modern type. While he has turned up interesting and relevant information concerning the social standing of the Suffragists caught in the government net in the summer of 1842, he erroneously assumes that this information establishes the sociological character of the movement. It should be clear that such is not the case. Many others participated who either were not caught or who were never molested. But Gettleman's data do, albeit unconsciously, say something useful about the changing character of Americans' conception of themselves and their society. The author's insensitivity to the role of ideas and ideology deprives him of the kind of insight that facilitates an appreciation for change in history. Because he does not pay sufficient attention to the process of change, he must argue that the Suffragists did not know their own history. When he said they "were not aware that the revolutionary principles of 1776 had already been ejected from the mainstream of American political conviction" (p. 189, note 50) he demonstrated aptly the consequences of a failure to attend to the differences between structural and psychological reality in historical analysis.

An understanding of the Suffragist movement requires close research in two kinds of primary sources. First, the public record for the years from 1776 to 1865 must be scrutinized. State and federal legislative debates are mines of information about the ways that people defined and understood key terms in their political language. The public press offers another entry into the mind of that period. While it can be argued that the newspaper writers often attempted to shape as well as to reflect the public mind, much can be learned from wide reading in the news accounts of the events of these years. Finally, the state and federal judiciaries have left an amazingly complete record of the ways in which key terms and phrases changed over time.

The letters, speeches, memoirs, and other papers of private persons are equally important. Wide reading here helps the student understand the language usages of the time. Among the major collections for our topic are the John Tyler Papers, on microfilm in the Manuscripts Division of the Library of

Congress; the Edmund Burke Papers, in photocopy in the same location; and the Roger Brooke Taney Papers, housed also in the Library of Congress. Published collections have also been consulted, as well as the various memoirs of prominent and less notable figures.

But most important for the purposes of this study was the collection created by Sidney S. Rider and housed in the John Hay Library, Brown University, Providence, Rhode Island. The collection consists of two parts: 1) The Dorr Correspondence: Personal and Political Letters Written to Thomas W. Dorr, with Copies of His Answers to His Correspondents Arranged in Chronological Order, covering the Years, 1820-1854; and 2) The Dorr Manuscripts. Both include manila folders of letters, speeches, newspaper clippings, memoirs, broadsides, mini-histories, and the like. Together they total forty-six volumes and/or bundles. The range is very broad. Dorr's correspondents included many of the leading figures of the time, and thus the letters contain unique glimpses into the political relationships that developed. In addition, Dorr and his close confidants in the Suffragist movement were remarkably articulate. They thought seriously about such questions as the proper principles of government, and they prided themselves on their ability to search out the truly significant from the merely contingent. A close reading of the various exchanges among the Suffragist leaders allows one to construct a frame of reference for them that is astonishingly similar to that of the earlier generation of Americans that fought the Revolution. The Suffragist leaders saw themselves as the defenders of the American faith and insisted upon loyalty to the beliefs and values of the founders. They thought and acted in terms of a "return to the founding." Because of this characteristic posture, they became severe critics of the America they knew in the 1840s. One gains a full appreciation of the Suffragists as "radicals" of an earlier vintage after reading the hundreds of letters in the Dorr collections and the issues of their newspaper, the *New Age* (titled variously, microfilm available from the Rhode Island Historical Society).

INDEX